Management for Professionals

The Springer series *Management for Professionals* comprises high-level business and management books for executives. The authors are experienced business professionals and renowned professors who combine scientific background, best practice, and entrepreneurial vision to provide powerful insights into how to achieve business excellence.

Rahul Ghatak

# People Analytics

## Data to Decisions

Springer

Rahul Ghatak
Acumetric Global Solutions
Mumbai, Maharashtra, India

ISSN 2192-8096 ISSN 2192-810X (electronic)
Management for Professionals
ISBN 978-981-19-3872-6 ISBN 978-981-19-3873-3 (eBook)
https://doi.org/10.1007/978-981-19-3873-3



This Springer imprint is published by the registered company Springer Nature Singapore Pte Ltd.
The registered company address is: 152 Beach Road, #21-01/04 Gateway East, Singapore 189721, Singapore

“HR is not just about people but now also about Tech, Data and Analytics. Upgrading numerical/analytics skills in order to have greater impact on the business, is the new wave of HR, which Rahul helps address via his own rich experience.”

—Gurprriet Siingh, *Managing Director, Russell Reynolds Associates, Mumbai, India.*

“This book would help HR & Leadership Teams find a way of discarding perceptions and uncovering truth by embracing data patterns as opposed to just continuing with incremental changes to how it has always been. This is particularly so of successful organizations.”

—Vikas Gupta, *Divisional Chief Executive Officer, Education and Stationery Products Business, ITC Limited, Gurugram, India.*

# Preface

The idea behind this book originated at a time when I took a break from my corporate career and co-founded a People Analytics start-up. This gave me the opportunity to reflect on my experiences across the organizations I had the good fortune of working in as well as with the potential clients and customers I was engaging with in my new avatar as an entrepreneur and people and talent analytics evangelist. This continuous reflection and set of experiences led me to the conclusion that businesses that're not thinking about People Analytics risk being out-competed. There are innumerable studies and research findings that cite human capital along with customer centricity as being the most important factors in maintaining competitive advantage. I have also heard proclamations from CEOs, business owners and HR heads alluding to the fact that "people are the cornerstone of our philosophy" or that "people are our most important asset". These findings and statements highlight that people are essential to the long-term success of organizations. Yet, the same rigour has not been applied to understand this critical asset. In most cases, the HR domain has had limited exposure to contemporary data science tools and predictive analytics methodologies, particularly in connecting with business drivers and performance outcomes. Generally speaking, there could be a lot more of data-driven analysis tied to measurable business outcomes. The consequence is that this can prevent HR from gaining buy-in for innovation or investment behind the people practices or HR Technology or human capital architecture, no matter how much it is needed.

So, is there anything that HR can do to rectify this situation? Is this an opportunity to actually provide insightful People Analytics that have a quantifiable impact on business performance?

Fortunately, the answer to both questions is a resounding yes. HR functions actually sit on massive repositories of people data and clearly have the opportunity to leverage it a lot more than being done currently. The answer does not lie in pursuing expensive technology solutions but in simply doing a better job of applying existing data insights to critical business and people questions. Moreover, it needs to interpret and then represent the insights in a language the business understands. CEOs want HR data to be like financial data: standardized, specific and clearly linked to outcomes.

This piece of work is an exploration of the People Analytics possibility, bringing out both theoretical frameworks and detailed practical case studies from my experience in industry and business across both sides of the table, with an understanding of data science models and social, mobile and cloud (SMAC) technologies underpinning it. It further explores and lays out a business case for why organizations need to invest behind this space and why HR functions and businesses need to embrace and adopt it.

It brings out how People Analytics makes a difference to business, stages of adoption and maturity models for effective People Analytics deployment in organizations, lays out the People Analytics maturity pyramid and explores the journey from Employee Master Data Management and Conversion to Reporting Visualizations to dash-boarding and descriptive analytics to finally predictive modelling. Each of these areas has been explored in some detail with the case examples to illustrate how some organizations have gone about deploying, embedding and leveraging People Analytics models and approaches with a view to driving business outcomes. It elaborates on the importance of a "single version of the truth" for all people data, thereby focusing on the importance of a road-map towards streamlining the data structures through extraction, transformation, loading and conversion methodologies.

The book brings out the impact of big data and social networks on HR and talent frameworks and the opportunity for HR to mine these networks with a view to culling out the predictive insights for the business.

It also describes in great detail the specific applications of people and talent analytics through the case examples on: productivity enhancement; employee engagement; sales competency forecasting; HR risk identification and mitigation; optimization in pay, performance and hiring decisions; transformation through culture building; reducing attrition and churn; organization design and spans of control and its impact on business outcomes.

It provides a perspective on how organizations could build capability in this space and integrate it into the HR delivery model, thereby institutionalizing it. It articulates the need for a whole new set of competencies that could either redefine the role of the "HR Business Partner" or create an entirely new role in the form of the "HR analyst/data scientist" on the lines of "analyst" roles in other domains, for example "credit risk analyst" or "financial planning analyst" or "consumer insight analyst". It opens up the possibility of enriching the core HR curriculum further by including data science frameworks and paradigms which hitherto don't exist. It explores briefly statistical and data science modelling tools and techniques and provides a perspective on how organizations are leveraging these to bubble up the predictive insights for the business. It brings out the importance of "storytelling" through the power of insights.

It brings out the key HR, talent and people challenges organizations confront every day and the analytics response towards meeting them. These responses are a coming together of new data science-driven mindsets and competencies on the one hand and data science frameworks, tools and architecture on the other. They demonstrate how some organizations by leveraging these responses are becoming more agile and nimble than the rest and how this agility will drive future competitive advantage.

From an organization risk mitigation perspective, it explores HR and talent risk frameworks and the leveraging of People Analytics towards risk identification; assessment; management and mitigation. The processing of large repositories of people data (both internal and external) real time enables immediate deciphering of patterns that help organizations anticipate both immediate short-term operational people and talent risks and longer-term strategic risks. This capability ensures corporate governance processes are strengthened and business operations made sustainable over the longer term.

It makes out the case for HR to be metric driven focused on business outcomes. It enumerates upon the "lead" and "lag" indicators and the need to leverage relevant measurement systems with a view to analysing "real", "large" and "big" data to drive key business deliverables. It brings out the importance of staying relevant in making the right choices in metrics/measures and focusing on the critical few that drive business outcomes as opposed to the trivial many that distract and do not link up with key organizational deliverables. The linkages and integration between people data and business data on the back of these models and technologies raise the bar on more effective and timely decision-making.

It brings out the power of "visual intelligence" and data representation that goes beyond traditional tools like Excel. The simple yet impactful representation of key insights enables faster processing of data, thereby crashing down the cycle time of high-impact people and business decisions. Let us face it; CEO's attention spans are limited; so, it is all about maximizing impact in the limited face time available. The answer lies in mastering "visual intelligence" tools and techniques that enable crisp and powerful presentation of critical insights that facilitate rapid decision-making and quick buy-in from the business.

Most importantly, it brings out the power of analytics in the HR domain towards articulating a return on investment (ROI) on "people practices and processes". As HR professionals, we all have prioritized building great teams, creating best-in-class work environments and developing our people. We all want our teams to grow, develop, make an impact and stay engaged at work. The question is: how do we resource for it? The hard reality is that resources are finite, scarce with HR managers being forced to make hard choices and trade-offs about what, where, how much and on whom to invest. The HR analytics paradigm would provide HR professionals the tools to "peel the onion" and articulate the ROI on all of the investments that should be made on people, processes and teams. Organizations would not then take too long to figure out that investing in it is peoples' practices, not only is the right thing to do, but also it is the smart thing to do.

Finally, it charts out the People Analytics industry landscape and brings out the opportunities towards leveraging this capability for competitive advantage. It brings out the need for People Analytics solutions to evolve from managed services to products, applying industry knowledge and client experiences to define industry-specialized business requirements based on algorithm repositories. It brings out the power of systems thinking and the need to ask the right questions. It clearly reflects that the People Analytics industry is a "white space" significantly underdeveloped, thereby providing a massive opportunity and headroom to innovate and impact both the domain and the larger business. The book also touches upon how technologies on the back of SMAC architecture will revolutionize the HR domain and how these could be leveraged to generate cutting-edge insights for the business.

This book is very different from other works in this domain. First, it blends theoretical frameworks and practical industrial case examples which have been built into the narrative. Second, it straddles the complete value chain from Data Management to Measurement systems to Reporting Visualizations to descriptive analytics to predictive modelling. Third, it brings out the key HR and people challenges across talent, rewards, organization design, culture and engagement and the analytics response via real-time, agile solutions. Fourth, it lays out a deployment strategy that has at its heart change management. Fifth, it explores the HR risk framework and lays out the risk mitigation and audit filters that analytics could bring to the table, thereby enabling risk mitigation both present and future. Sixth, it encompasses statistical tools and models and the technologies underpinning People Analytics deployment. Seventh, it brings out the critical competencies required to first understand and then deploy analytics in HR functions and teams. Finally, it establishes the business case and ROI for People Analytics in organizations and its transformative potential in driving home a competitive advantage.

The book is meant for those who seek to challenge the status quo by helping them ask the right questions and build new capabilities with a view towards leading the change and driving transformation both in their domain, the wider business and the larger organization. It is up to them to seize the moment like never before.

I would like to acknowledge a few individuals who have played a key role in supporting me in putting this contribution together. Premanjan Biswas who with his command over statistical methodologies helped me in putting Chap. 12 together; Chandramauli my erstwhile colleague at BIC India, who helped me with some visualizations in the operational analytics chapter; Namdeo Trimbake, my colleague at Acumetric who pulled out the unique visualizations from our CRUX platform that has gone into many of the exhibits; Sameer Pai who has burnt the midnight oil in converting the exhibits into PNG within really tight timelines; Dr. S. Pandey of CCMC, who has always encouraged and motivated me towards investing time and effort in this book; my wife Dr. Disha Nawani, Professor and Dean of School of Education, TISS, who has constantly supported and encouraged me on this journey; my mother Joyasree Mukerji who is an author herself and encouraged me to pursue this and finally my co-founding partners at Acumetric Global Solutions; our People Analytics venture, Govind Sandhu and Sarajit Mitra, who have partnered with me on our product development journey through which I have gained a great deal of clarity on the subject. Needless to add, I would also like to acknowledge the support I have received right through my career from all my peers, team members and superiors who in their own ways have contributed to my analytical orientation and competencies and helped me deploy some of these solutions towards the solving of business, talent and performance challenges.

Mumbai, India Rahul Ghatak

# Acknowledgements

I would like to take this opportunity to thank all those who encouraged and contributed towards supporting me in this endeavour.

First, I would like to thank my wife Dr. Disha Nawani who is an academic at TISS, Mumbai. It was her initial encouragement that led me to contemplate such an endeavour in the first place.

Second, I would like to thank my start-up co-founding partners Govind Sandhu and Sarajit Mitra with whose support and encouragement I took the leap into entrepreneurship of a HR Tech SaaS People Analytics venture which has opened up a world of learning opportunities for me. When I connect the dots, it becomes clear to me that without this experience of first productizing an idea; second, evangelizing and propagating possibilities of the power of People Analytics among HR practitioners and the student community and then finally commercializing the proposition for organizations around adoption and deployment; I would never have been able to experience different facets of this powerful sub-domain in Human Resources that has within it the seeds of disruption and transformation.

Third, I wish to acknowledge the contributions of my team members Namdeo Trimbake and Premanjan Biswas who in their own ways have supported me on this journey. Namdeo our product lead of our core People Analytics platform CRUX has played a key role in enabling us to take the proposition to market and has contributed with his ideas towards enhancing product capabilities basis customer feedback. These brainstorming sessions around product enhancement have further opened my eyes to new possibilities in this enriching space. Premanjan with his strong statistics credentials has provided me with a rich perspective and better understanding of how statistical tools could be leveraged for data mining and prediction.

Fourth, I wish to thank Dr. S. Pandey my erstwhile teacher at TISS, Mumbai, who taught me Research Methodology and Statistics way back in the early 1990s, who has continuously encouraged me to translate my thoughts and ideas into a book. He has also enriched me with his sharp insights in our various brainstorming sessions around productizing various ideas.

Finally, I would like to thank all my ex-HR and business colleagues, CEOs and promoters I have been fortunate to have worked with who have helped me learn and grow intellectually and professionally over the years enriching me with their perspectives and points of view.

# Contents

# About the Author

**Rahul Ghatak** is the co-founder and CEO of Acumetric Global Solutions, a recent SaaS People Analytics start-up venture with its proprietary cloud based People Analytics platform. He brings 25+ years of HR deep domain experience across MNC's and Indian conglomerates straddling diverse sectors across consumer and manufacturing, financial services and BPO/ITes. Rahul has had Human Resource Management, HR Digital Transformation and Business Partnering experience across the entire canvas in large and mid-size organizations (4000+ headcount; turnover 100 million $ to 1 billion $; Indian and MNC); key role in scaling up businesses and operations across sectors and geographies; cross-cultural exposure across India, Africa, Asia-Pacific, Middle-East, US, France and UK; and he has been an integral part of global HR leadership teams in two large MNCs. He has overseen change management and organization design and restructuring; performance management; employee relations; talent management; rewards restructuring; organization development; leadership coaching; resourcing and assessments; M&A; ERP and HR digital transformation to name some.

He has held key positions across organizations such as ITC, PepsiCo, HSBC, Capita, RPG, Welspun and BIC while leading the function over the last 10 years. Last three leadership roles he held were: Vice President Human Resources—RPG (Ceat Tyres); Director Human Resources—Capita India (subsidiary of Capita Group Plc UK;) FTSE 100 company; CHRO—BIC India (subsidiary of Societe BIC); and in these roles he partnered closely with CEO's and promoters, both Indian and expatriates across multi-cultural environments. He has been a recipient of "global best-in-class certification" in Strategic HRM from University of Michigan—Ann Arbor; recipient of Harvey-Russell Global Chairman's Award for cutting-edge work done in the Diversity and Inclusion space in PepsiCo International; recipient of the NCPEDP-SHELL Helen Keller Award. He is also a certified Occupational Testing Techniques and OPQ psychometric assessor; certified by SHL as well as a Diversity and Inclusion Practitioner, certified by DDI.

Rahul has also been involved in various professional and learning forums such as CII Training Sub-Committee, IQPC Forums on HR Technology, CIO Choice Awards, World HR Congress and has been part of several conferences in HR Technology and Great Place to Work conclaves. He has also in his spare time lectured at various Business Schools such as TISS, IIM's, ICFAI, SOIL, Great Lakes, PIBM etc. as well as contributed articles in leading publications such as

People Matters etc. Rahul holds a Bachelor's Degree in Political Science from St. Xavier's College, Kolkata; a Masters Degree in Sociology from Jawaharlal Nehru University, New Delhi and a Masters Degree in Human Resources Management from Tata Institute of Social Sciences, Mumbai.

# People Analytics—Making a Difference to Business

# 1

## 1.1 Context

We have been witnessing a massive explosion of data and data sources across all domains and spaces: physical and cloud. However, beyond just this data, it is the dynamic interpretation, underlying meaning and insights derived from this data that will present the real opportunities for HR and the business.

HR teams need to understand the scale of the data being produced as well as the speed at which it is being created and the range of data points from which that data will emerge. The scale of data being generated and produced provides a great opportunity for the Human Resource function to reinvent itself.

As global workforce demographics trends shift tectonically and as the war for talent intensifies, the need for HR to reimagine itself and provide a competitive advantage to organizations is being felt like never before. The question that arises is: How do HR functions and teams deliver such sustainable competitive advantages to organizations? How do HR practitioners and teams leverage this data explosion to cull out compelling insights that enable sharper decision-making triggering higher shareholder value? How do HR practitioners build the capability to collect, interpret and analyse relevant data for delivering critical insights to their business stakeholders towards enabling robust and agile decision-making. How will HR build a compelling case for directly impacting organizational outcomes in a digital and VUCA age?

## 1.2 People Analytics and a Single Employee View

The answer is "People Analytics"; so what is it about? In a nutshell, People Analytics is about considering your workforce, candidates and all matters "talent" and "workforce" from a data perspective. People Analytics helps organizations move beyond making decisions about hiring, exiting, promoting or around culture and



R. Ghatak, *People Analytics*, Management for Professionals,
https://doi.org/10.1007/978-981-19-3873-3_1

engagement or performance, based on gut instinct or corporate belief systems. Instead business leaders and managers can start to make evidence-based decisions basis analysis of data; something more sustainable, reliable and forward thinking than the approach typically used to make people decisions in the past. For those practitioners who swear by gut feel and intuitive understanding of human behaviour, People Analytics could be just the instrument they need to validate their decisions. The purpose of People Analytics is to help a leader make a better, more informed decision about people and talent by providing him/her with relevant data coupled with sharp insights.

People data is never found in one place; invariably, it is spread across a multitude of source repositories. For example, payroll data in payroll system, employee data in HRMS, attendance data in legacy system, training data in some learning management system, etc., thereby making it almost impossible for the leadership to view the data in a single source system. Further, the business data is invariably captured in systems that do not interact with the people data. Teams of Excel using analysts spend much of their time reconciling data across these systems trying to make sense of it, and by the time they see some light, the underlying data has already changed as the data is dynamic and changes rapidly in real time.

> Imagine if you could bring all relevant workforce-related data together in one place and further enhance it by including connected external datasets or combine it with other systems within your organization. If you could get real insight into the correlations between the data and understand what the implications would be if you specifically focused on improving employee engagement for example, or changing how you reward and recognize your people?

## 1.3 Difference to Business

It is critical to establish a clear business case for investing behind People Analytics. The predictive power of analytics for instance in analysing employee turnover trends, understanding underlying reasons, anticipating likely leavers or future trends or for that matter providing clues towards taking actions that might reduce future churn; all of it needs to be demonstrated with data and evidence to convert the typical sceptic.

People Analytics needs to find a place within the overall human capital strategy of an organization. For HR to deliver tangible business results, and improve productivity, it is important to align people data with business data and leverage it appropriately to pull out critical insights for robust decision-making.

> Analytics is to be leveraged to manage risk, enhance productivity, optimize cost, maximize revenue and manage transformation ultimately with a view to impacting growth and profitability.

Finally, it is not enough to use people data to make predictions. What needs to be done is a periodic follow-up to show which predictions came true. More importantly, HR leaders need to understand that there is a Return on Investment (ROI) for almost everything they do and they need to be able to bring that out clearly.

As the global economy continues to evolve and get interconnected, as companies expand their network and increasingly get used to managing the aspirations and complexity of a global workforce, it is all the more critical that organizations commit to understanding and analysing more deeply the most vital cog of its success—its people. The investment in People Analytics comes with it an enhanced focus on analytical thinking, data science approach and digital delivery systems based on SMAC (social, mobile, analytics, cloud) capability. It also facilitates a deeper integration between HR and the wider business allowing for greater collaboration and joint problem solving.

The question to be asked is "Why now?" The old metrics, such as FTE count, the cost of rewards, time to fill, and attrition/retention, have outlived their relevance in the context of a dynamic and fast changing business environment. These are essentially operational metrics and do not go far enough to create shareholder value and align people decisions with organizational and business outcomes. The reorientation requires leveraging data science and other methodologies around phenomena that have historically been perceived as difficult to quantify, like why people quit organizations or how happy they are in their jobs or why are some more productive than others Rather than accepting human capital cost only as an expense on the income statement, finance experts are coming to realize the power of human capital management and that it requires to be looked at with a different lens.

## 1.4 Tangible Business Impact

What links exist between People Analytics and organizations' business results? The evidence on this question falls into two (related) categories: how the use of People Analytics itself affects business results, and how various specific measures of people or human capital management are associated with business results. Evidence on the first question again comes primarily from surveys about the use of People Analytics. The sources of answers on the second question are more varied, with some coming from publicly reported results within a single company, and others coming from cross-organizational empirical studies.

Among the organizations using human capital reporting or analytics in some way, Lombardi and White found key differences in organizational performance between those that are most mature in their application of HR applications (based on timeliness of data access, accuracy of data, and ability to use data for workforce planning) and others. The most mature 20% (which they call "best-in-class") report 11% year-on-year increases in profit per employee and 6% year-on-year increases in revenue per employee (measured as full-time equivalents, or FTEs). The least mature 30% ("laggards"), on the other hand, reported a 7% year-on-year decline in profit per employee and a 1% increase in revenue per employee.

Differences are even more dramatic in comparing organizations using human capital reporting and analytics (regardless of level of maturity) versus those that are not. Organizations using human capital reporting and analytics in some way reported a 4% overall year-on-year increase in profit per FTE and a 4% overall increase in revenue per FTE. Those not using reporting and analytics reported declines in both measures (5% decline in profit per FTE, 1% decline in revenue per FTE).

Survey results from Cedar Crestone are consistent with Lombardi and White and include the finding that organizations using workforce analytics reported 18% higher sales per employee. They also find higher rates of sales growth among organizations with broader scope to their succession planning process (11.5% for those applying it to all managers, compared with 4.5% for those applying it only to top management). Organizations with talent processes and systems classified as "integrated" had two-year sales growth of 18.2%, compared with 9.6% for those with no talent management processes or systems.

Consistent findings also come from an Info HRM survey of more than 200 HR executives around the world. Roberts notes that "leading-edge" organizations (those able to "analytically identify the workforce drivers of business success; readily translate workforce analysis and findings into action; and employ an analytics Center of Excellence model with a dedicated workforce analytics team") are dramatically more likely to report that the use of analytics has influenced cost-saving decisions (63% of leading-edge organizations, compared to 32% of others) and that analytics has influenced revenue-increasing decisions (53% versus 14%).

## 1.5 People Analytics Enables Agile and Robust Decision-Making Through

- Enhancing effectiveness through interconnectedness
  Analytics-driven decisions helps in driving business results by improving the consistency of data to improve the quality of decisions. The ability to connect multiple data streams both people and business data together and look at patterns holistically also enables agile and robust decision-making.
- Speed of decision
  Analytics provides faster insights into employee data thus meeting or sometimes even exceeding the employee needs and expectations. It identifies opportunities for action without any delays and comes up with solution to problems much faster than a tedious manual process.

- Agility
  With constant changing market conditions and competitors activities, People Analytics removes dependence from the "gut feeling" decision-making to one that is more reliable and agile. New propositions can be implemented quickly without any delay.
- Decision accuracy
  - Validate all data used to minimize error
  - Make decisions faster and better
  - Create granular segmentation models to better address employee aspirations
- Decision consistency
  Analytics provides the user with centralized control over all decision points. Consistency arises out of using validated and automated data. This minimizes manual intervention in the decision-making process, thus providing consistency.

People Analytics drives the way forward in assessing talent requirements and matching that with critical skills required to fill those key roles across various business establishments.

The costs of replacing critical human assets of the company are increasing manifold every year. Hence, critical insights about the workforce let organizations decide future course of action regarding various challenges, especially higher costs.

People Analytics helps organization decipher what is required, when it is required and how will it be implemented effectively. It structures the endless amount of data to provide valuable insights on workforce planning without which effective implementation would still be a dream.

## 1.6 Transforming Mindsets

There is a critical need to transform mindsets; compartmentalized approaches with silo thinking have predominated both HRM curriculum and practice, and there is an urgent need to shatter them and explore a more holistic paradigm facilitated by new HR Technology, approaches and frameworks, at the heart of which is analytics.

> The question is: Do organizations truly understand what are the factors that enhance performance? Do we know for instance why one sales person outperforms his/her peers? Do we understand why certain leaders thrive and others burn out? Can we develop predictive models around team and individual performance attributes?

The response to most of these questions lies in the negative. The vast majority of hiring, management, promotion and rewards decisions have traditionally been made on gut feel and intuition, personal experience and corporate belief systems. It is no longer an optimal way to make decisions and yes, while mindsets are changing and data evidencing is being leveraged to a greater extent with assessments and predictive modelling emerging as key focus areas; this change needs to be accelerated.

HR has to be re-imagined and as part of this re-imagination, new cutting edge tools, analytics and visualization technologies, predictive modelling, data science; hitherto never part of traditional HR lexicon; need to be deployed to interpret the gigabytes of data being generated, to throw up patterns and predict behaviour, trends and events, thereby enabling proactive management action and faster, more agile and optimized real-time decision-making.

There is no turning back for HR professionals and teams. There is no choice. Either they need to adapt to leverage data with a view to driving business outcomes or will be left behind as there is no place for "experience and gut feeling"-based decision-making. While most disciplines and professionals in other functional areas have already made the switch many years ago, the HR domain continues to struggle to adapt to the new reality.

The conversations I keep hearing from a number of fellow peers about not "getting a seat at the table" are meaningless. In my opinion, we need to "earn the right to a seat at the table" as the requirements for leadership today are as much about visioning, commercial and business acumen and communication as they are about data-based decision-making. Without a deep understanding of people and talent analytics, HR professionals are never going to be able to master the latter.

As a result, special attention needs to be provided to this area of Human Resources with a view towards equipping HR directors with the perspective and ammunition required to enable them to more directly drive business strategy and develop a share of voice in the boardroom.

## 1.7 Real-World Case Study Examples

Leading technology companies and other evolved corporations have now adopted more sophisticated methods of analysing their employee data to enhance their competitive advantage. Successful organizations have taken the gut feel out of people management by leveraging analytics to improve their methods of attracting and retaining talent, connecting their employee data to business performance, differentiating themselves from competitors, and more. What are successful organizations doing differently?

These evolved corporations see the value of data and put data right at the centre of decision-making.

Let us look at an example of how such organizations leverage data to enhance performance and take robust talent decisions. The company started by testing the hypotheses that managers help improve performance by analysing performance scores of managers and team scores through a survey approach.

At first glance, managers were performing well; however, after splitting out the top and bottom quartile of performers, it became clear that the top performing managers had higher performing teams.

A qualitative analysis of managers was then carried out that sought answers on:

- What team members thought of their managers
- The annual performance evaluation
- Manager reviews in performance evaluations and
- Double-blind interviews of managers.

From this, the company identified certain common behaviours of good managers as well as development areas. After sharing the results across the company, a learning and development journey was initiated for managers based on the research. After a couple of years, the survey showed that manager performance started improving.

The company, apart from being able now to sharply spotting top performers, is also now better able to identify those who are struggling, support them more and zero in on those people who are not suitable for managerial roles. While it is not easy to link this to business impact across most disciplines, it is easier in business facing domains such as sales or supply chain.

Some best-in-class retail organizations can precisely compute the value of a 0.1% increase in employee engagement among store employees. At a particular such company, for example, that value is more than $100,000 in the store's annual operating income.

Many companies base their hiring and selection strategies at the outset and to begin with on academic credentials of candidates along with business school ranking—but some technology companies have established through quantitative analysis that a demonstrated ability to take initiative is a far more reliable predictor of high performance on the job.

Employee attrition and churn can be less of a problem when managers see it coming. Some organizations have been able to develop predictive models using data science and software tools to predict early attrition trends along with an early warning system that sets off red flags or trigger alerts on who may leave and why, allowing managers to then have proactive conversations with a view to retaining their critical talent.

In a few weeks from date of joining, a technology company was able to predict which top performers would exit the organization and why—this data and analysis is now driving global policy changes in retaining critical talent and has established the business case to invest behind People Analytics capabilities and technologies.

A global chemical company has enhanced its workforce planning capabilities by mining historical data on its large employee database to forecast promotion rates, internal transfers and overall talent availability. The company has been able to develop a custom modelling tool to segment the workforce and compute future headcount for each business unit. These detailed predictions can project workforce trends for the entire company. The company can now deploy "what if" scenario models, altering assumptions on internal factors such as employee career growth or external factors such as geopolitical and compliance considerations.

*Let us illustrate the impact on business through a case example of a BPO company that leveraged workforce analytics to drive up operational productivity of its first line managers, clearly measured* via *operational KPI improvements.*

**CASE 1: Workforce Analytics to improve Productivity**

**The Problem**

The BPO was under pressure to drive up operational productivity and reduce cost as its profitability was in decline. The first set of studies around productivity opportunities did not throw up anything alarming.

But then, the CEO decided to bring in a consultant, Rishi and team who came with a fresh pair of eyes and no historical baggage to analyse the productivity opportunity.

Rishi and team got to work to identify first line manager (FLM) performance enhancement opportunities through "Leveraging Workforce Analytics" which threw up significant opportunities.

**Hypotheses**

Rishi and team found that "Work and Time Utilization" trends were a key predictor of FLM operational productivity. In statistical terminology, high work and time utilization correlated positively with FLM operational productivity.

**Scope**

- To enhance first line manager operational productivity
- Phase 1: Pilot in one large account in one delivery centre
- Phase 2: Replicate across the business.

**Analytics Insight Programme Objectives**

1. Improve change and performance management competence among FLMs
2. Achieve sustainable improvements in operational performance across the above categories
3. Enhance FLM productivity levels, thereby driving up business results
4. Transfer knowledge, capability and skills to sustain the improvements
5. Enhance capacity planning accuracy.

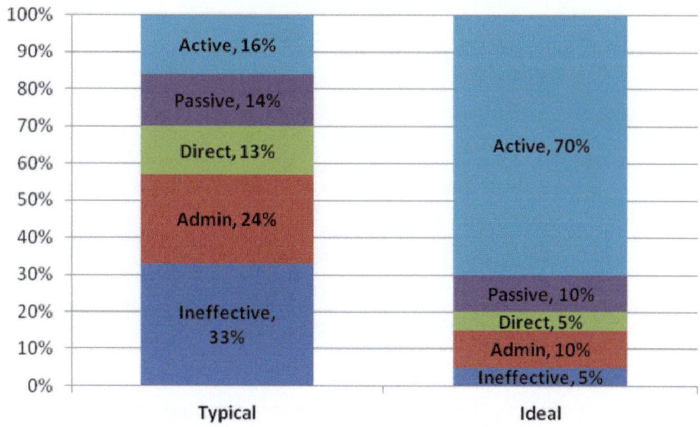


**Exhibit 1.1** Actual versus Ideal—FLM proactive management utilization trends

## 1.8 FLM Work and Time Utilization Trends Deploying Analytics

The study revealed that highly effective and high-performing FLMs allocated their time as follows (Exhibit 1.1).

Leveraging analytics towards understanding the breakdown of activities across a typical work day and categorizing them in this way demonstrated the delta from best practice while automatically exposing the extent of the improvement opportunity. It is to be noted that there is always a considerable difference between the typical and ideal work day highlighting the significant gains to be secured by changing behaviours.

The study showed that It was not unusual for FLMs to spend as little as 10–15% of their time focusing proactive management attention on team members. The propensity to become involved in less value adding pursuits is high, but this can be quickly adjusted when managers are introduced to best practice ways of thinking and behaving and coached in the use of new skills and tools. For many FLMs, the shift meant that an additional 50% of their total time now could be deployed to develop their teams: a huge gain.

## 1.9 Analytics Insight Programme Framework

The *analytics insight programme* framework developed by Rishi and team consisted of five steps that established a picture of an ideal FLM. This benchmark was then used to compare the skills and behaviours of existing FLMs. Subsequent to this, clear performance standards were established, and they were tracked and measured on a week on week basis.

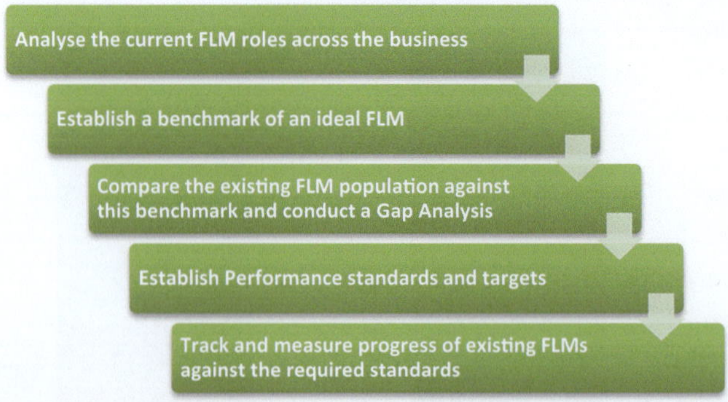


The above steps were condensed into three stages, namely

Step (1): role benchmarking and competence assessment
Step (2): gap analysis between actual and ideal competencies and behaviours
Step (3): performance tracking and measurement.

**Key Outcomes—What was in it for the Organization?**

- A proven methodology that enabled the business to realize full potential from FLMs:
  FLM utilization rate improved by 15% (BPO); opportunity to right-size and reduce headcount by 10% (100 on a base of 1000) in one large account (BPO), thereby leading to massive savings
- A toolset that established clear ownership and accountability for performance improvements among FLMs
- Measurable improvements in operational performance;
  operational metrics improved by 20% at the BPO (rework down; accuracy up)
- A coaching culture leading to a more motivated, confident and capable workforce:
  Organization health survey results improved; critical talent retention improved
- Focused investment in FLM development.

**Key Benefits**

- Delivered a productivity improvement of 20–25%
- Delivered an ROI within a year
- Equipped operational managers with the tools and time to effectively coach, mentor and build high-performance teams
- Created sustainable cost reduction, improved productivity and increased profitability.

## 1.10 Summing up

There is a change in the role HR is playing in organizations today with a demand for more tangible business impact. Role of HR is changing dramatically in organizations from of being a "transactional support function" to "a key business lever" an acknowledgement of it being something that impacts business directly. For HR to contribute and impact business directly, it is rapidly making the journey from "intangibility" to "tangibility", and PEOPLE ANALYTICS is emerging as a key enabler in that journey.

To comprehend this better, let us examine a typical interaction between four critical stakeholders as they struggle with the data conundrum and engage to figure out a way to eliminate guesswork from decision-making.

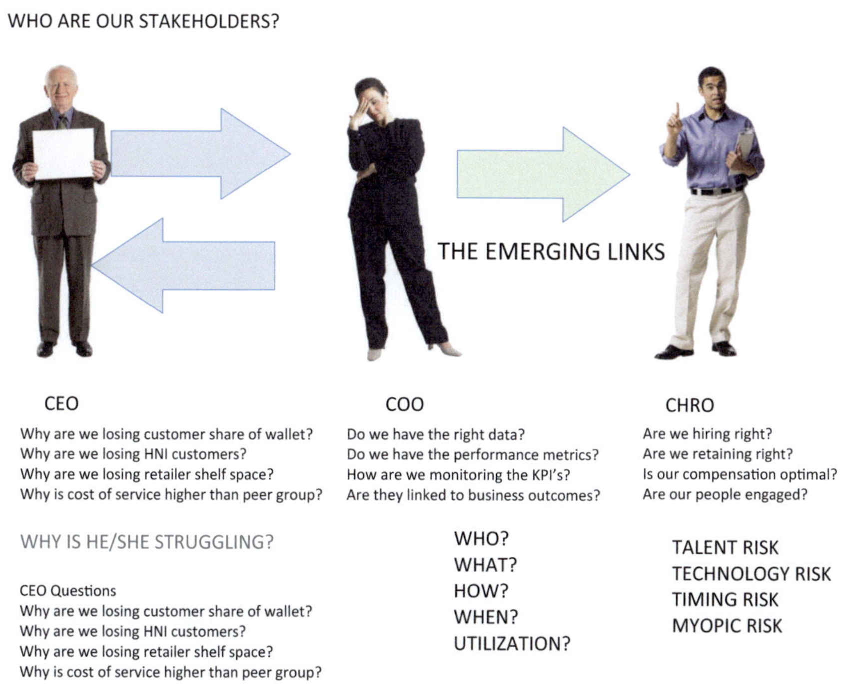

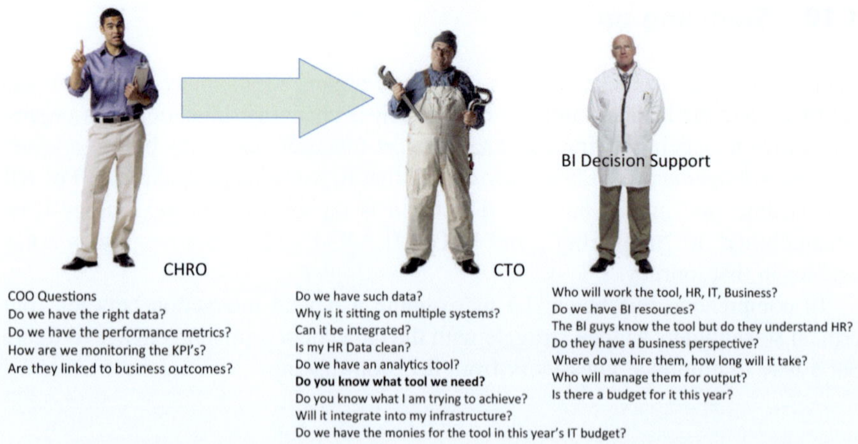

BI Decision Support
CHRO
CTO
COO Questions
Do we have the right data?
Do we have the performance metrics?
How are we monitoring the KPI's?
Are they linked to business outcomes?
Do we have such data?
Why is it sitting on multiple systems?
Can it be integrated?
Is my HR Data clean?
Do we have an analytics tool?
Do you know what tool we need?
Do you know what I am trying to achieve?
Will it integrate into my infrastructure?
Do we have the monies for the tool in this year's IT budget?
Who will work the tool, HR, IT, Business?
Do we have BI resources?
The BI guys know the tool but do they understand HR?
Do they have a business perspective?
Where do we hire them, how long will it take?
Who will manage them for output?
Is there a budget for it this year?


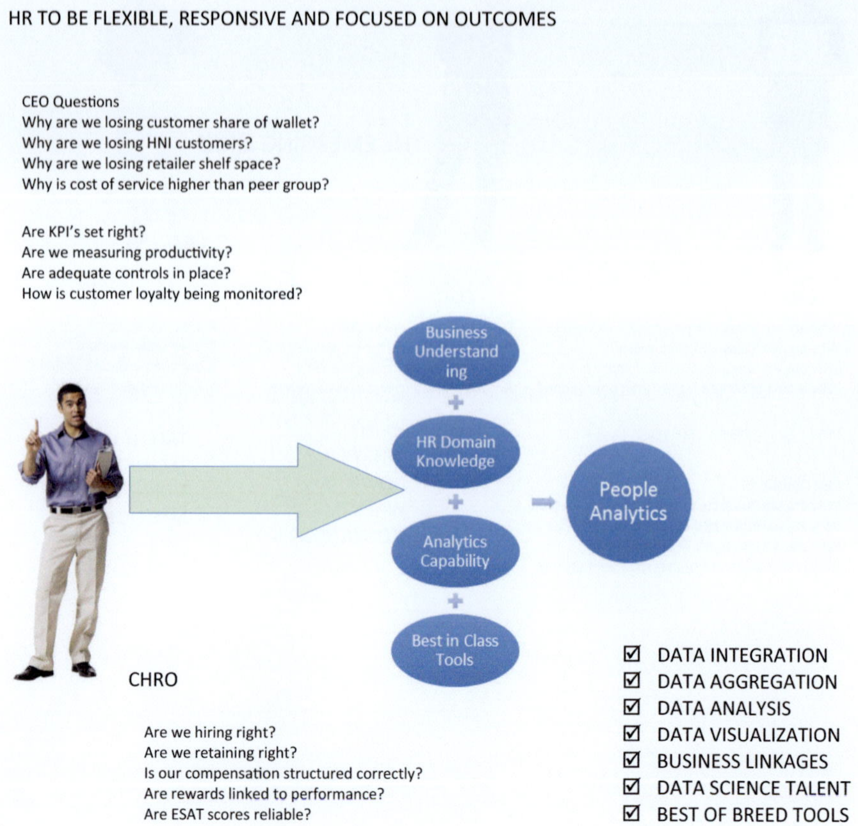

HR TO BE FLEXIBLE, RESPONSIVE AND FOCUSED ON OUTCOMES
CEO Questions
Why are we losing customer share of wallet?
Why are we losing HNI customers?
Why are we losing retailer shelf space?
Why is cost of service higher than peer group?
Are KPI's set right?
Are we measuring productivity?
Are adequate controls in place?
How is customer loyalty being monitored?
Business Understand ing
HR Domain Knowledge
Analytics Capability
Best in Class Tools
People Analytics
CHRO
Are we hiring right?
Are we retaining right?
Is our compensation structured correctly?
Are rewards linked to performance?
Are ESAT scores reliable?
☑ DATA INTEGRATION
☑ DATA AGGREGATION
☑ DATA ANALYSIS
☑ DATA VISUALIZATION
☑ BUSINESS LINKAGES
☑ DATA SCIENCE TALENT
☑ BEST OF BREED TOOLS

# Operational Analytics and Predictive Modelling

# 2

## 2.1 Context

Predictive analytics deploys a varied set of statistical, data science and software tools including artificial intelligence, cognitive machine reading and text mining that analyse large and big data to make predictions about future events. These tools help establish linkages between different sets of variables to then arrive at a set of projections of future scenarios that support more objective decision-making. Predictive modelling can be deployed in a variety of domains such as telecommunications, actuarial science, marketing, financial services, retail, travel, health care, pharmaceuticals and supply chain. Predictive modelling involves rigorous data analysis, which are widely used in business and marketing for segmentation and decision-making such as consumer insights but now are starting to get leveraged even in people management.

## 2.2 Predictive Modelling in Human Capital Management

It is critical to collaborate with client groups to develop algorithms by applying statistical methods to weigh the relationships between internal and external factors, along with critical outcomes that get reflected at a later stage, for instance process, service and performance improvement and measurement. With a view to bringing out these relationships, clients collect relevant data on which statistical methods could be applied to cull out critical insights.

The real benefits of analytics methods lie in the underlying patterns that it throws up along with a certain rationale and logic underpinning it. So it is not merely about statistics as it is critical to know when to apply what statistical tools to cull out which insights for solving specific business problems. Large organizations that are global are too complex to be able to establish meaningful



R. Ghatak, *People Analytics*, Management for Professionals,
https://doi.org/10.1007/978-981-19-3873-3_2

relationships between data points making it almost impossible to bring out any patterns or interlinkages. This is where analytics tools come in with their computing power to bring these out, enabling more robust decision-making.

There is a natural hesitation among managers to accept that their decisions based on gut and intuition or collective memory could be wrong as opposed to statistical and analytical methods. In Jac-Fitz-enz's view out of 136 studies on managerial decisions based on judgement, only eight studies showed managerial judgement to be superior to statistical methods. It is fair to draw the conclusion that it is not one or the other; it is about supplementing manager judgement with statistical methods and data science tools aided by new age technologies leveraging AI and machine learning. With the employee value proposition laid out, we can begin to save the business some money.

## 2.3 Predictive Models

Predictive modelling is a technique used to analyse current and past data to predict future outcomes, events and behaviours. The most common business application of predictive modelling is in the area of consumer insights, where they seek out hidden data patterns to throw up clues and insights around customer and consumer behaviours. Predictive models often bring out the risk/benefit ratios of buying decisions taken by a customer. Predictive modelling is now starting to get leveraged in human capital management where the study and analysis of historical patterns of behaviour, persona traits and demographics are starting to throw up predictions around talent, rewards, performance, fraud, etc., which are starting to impact business outcomes. The target here has moved from the customer and consumer to the employee.

Predictive model development and deployment typically includes

- Taking the current and historical data as an input into building the model.
- This is followed by a data cleansing and standardization exercise of the relevant data.
- The "predictive model" would then be developed and administered on an agreed sample size of employees separately for each target segment.
- Data science tools would then be deployed on the data to bring out dependencies, correlations and predictors.
- The predictive model with the scoring of employees on flight risk/business impact would then be completed for each target segment.

At the end of this transformation project, the organization would have a "predictive model/tool" to predict attrition trends; to enable taking proactive management action to reduce attrition along with a scoring tool measuring flight risk versus business impact (Exhibit 2.1).

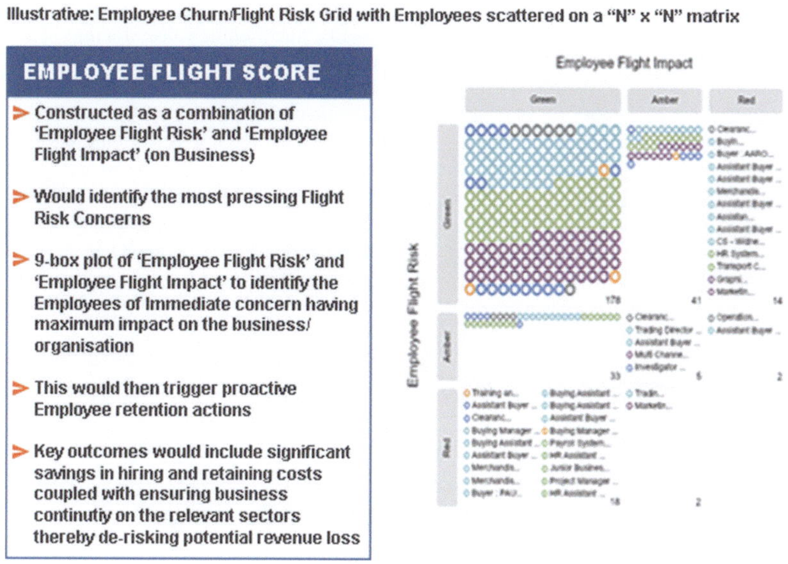




**Exhibit 2.1** Predicting flight risk and business impact

### ROI of Predictive Models: Hire More Top Performers/Avoid More Bottom Performers (Illustrative)

| | Dimensions | ROI calculator |
|---|---|---|
| 1 | Sample sales hiring scenario | • Company hires 100 sales representatives a month<br>• Of these, 26% (26 reps) currently end up as "top performers"<br>• The remaining 74% (74 reps) currently provide sub-optimal value or need to be replaced |
| 2 | Critical insight | • Detects "top performers "X% of the time" (out of sample)"<br>• Business may think (that is just a coin toss)<br>• Business needs to remember: top performers are the top quartile |
| 3 | Conservative model | • Arbitrarily reduce it to 40% true positive rate<br>• Monthly hire 40 reps likely to be "top performers"<br>• Monthly hire 60 reps likely to be "replaced"<br>• In net, 14 more good hires and 14 fewer bad hires |

| | Dimensions | ROI calculator |
|---|---|---|
| 4 | Benefits/outcomes | • Earn 14x "the lifetime value of a top performing sales rep"<br>• Earn 14x "the reduced attrition rate of a top performing sales rep"<br>• Save 14x "pay of a low-performing sales rep"<br>• Save 14x "the cost of hiring, training a new sales rep" |
| 5 | The math -additional 168 top performing sales reps a year | • Performance and attrition are dynamic, complex problems but …<br>• The goal is to deliver value, not necessarily to always be right<br>• Even a "conservative" model can pay for itself quickly |

## 2.4 Predictive Analytics—Competitive Advantage

Leveraging data to identify the likelihood of future outcomes based on historical patterns is clearly emerging as a competitive advantage for the few organizations that have built this capability. This is a paradigm shift from pure statistical methods and trend reporting which essentially describes past events or phenomena. While the use of predictive analytics is still sporadic with a select few being able to make predictions about their workforce based on analysis, most organizations use data reactively to inform critical workforce decisions.

However, as more success stories emerge, further interest in predictive analytics will undoubtedly follow. Enhancing talent retention and improving the quality of hiring are both areas in which predictive analytics will find great application and utility.

Let us take the case example of an executive search company, that helped a global market research organization, to enhance its hiring effectiveness.

Resumes in this part of the world are poorly structured, often with key details missing. Employers have then been forced to take the easy way out by just focusing their efforts on simply the best institutions believing that they would get the best candidates from these institutions only. The students from these institutions were thereby better positioned to land these opportunities. The client organization had a sense that there could be better quality candidates with the right fit from these lesser known institutions but was struggling with the problem of identifying and filtering them. They brought in this executive search firm to solve for this problem. The search company's approach in tapping into a larger candidate base to determine the "right-fit" matched the client organization's culture and specific job requirements to the individual applicant's personality and unique capabilities. An immediate impact was noticed. The number of applicants quadrupled, offer acceptances increased by a quarter, while first-year retention, a critical metric for the client organization, went up by over 20%.

Let us look at another case example of a predictive analytics study conducted by a reputed business school that brought out the linkages between age and business performance. The analytics team researched more than 400 restaurants of a popular food retail chain and found that employees who had crossed the retirement age of 60 had a significant influence on the company's overall performance. The research brought out that customer satisfaction levels were at least 20% higher in restaurants that had deployed at least one employee above 60 years. The data clearly highlighted the linkages between business enhancement and an age-diverse workforce strategy thereby building out a business case for diversity in hiring practice. For the food retail chain, it demonstrated that the deployment of retired employees enhanced customer satisfaction, and in a service business, this satisfaction drove positive business outcomes.

Data science if it has to be impactful needs to be directed at a specific business problem, with a clear understanding of the underlying elements of the problem. If we listen, the data would tell us where our preconceptions of those elements are wrong, to then enable us to build greater rigour into the model.

The evolution from hindsight to insight to foresight reflects the journey that analytics as a discipline has embarked on over the years, and the Human Resources domain clearly is in catch-up mode as it seeks to make up lost ground (Exhibit 2.2).

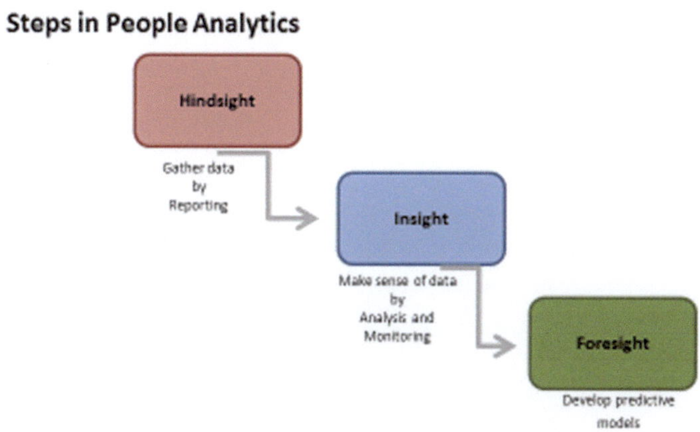


*Source: Akshay Raje "Paper on Analytics"*

**Exhibit 2.2** Steps in People Analytics

## 2.5 People Analytics Through Cost Modelling: Understanding the Business Impact

The critical objectives for business entities are to enhance the commercial value for shareholders. Finding ways to optimize costs or propel revenue growth is key to realizing these objectives. Cost models enable quantification of costs in relation to core processes such as hiring errors; mistakes in succession planning; inability to predict or manage churn and voluntary turnover, thereby enabling business leaders to get sharper in their decision-making or understanding the fallout of poorly managed people/business processes. Cost models as a result mitigate the risk of the company losing money across key activities such as hiring, exiting and promoting.

**Cost models** also create a repeatable process enabling managers to apply this model to multiple situations—i.e. if attrition goes up by 2% what will that cost the business versus if attrition goes down by 6% what will that save the business. Through such cost models, the company can develop a KPI that becomes the standard expected rate of return for various project actions (i.e. what is the expected rate of return on hiring someone).

(This can be compared to customer analytics projects calculating the expected rate of return for customers. Many customer analytics projects today calculate the expected rate of return—or even predict the lifetime value of a customer. This exact approach is applied with calculating employee value) (Exhibit 2.3).

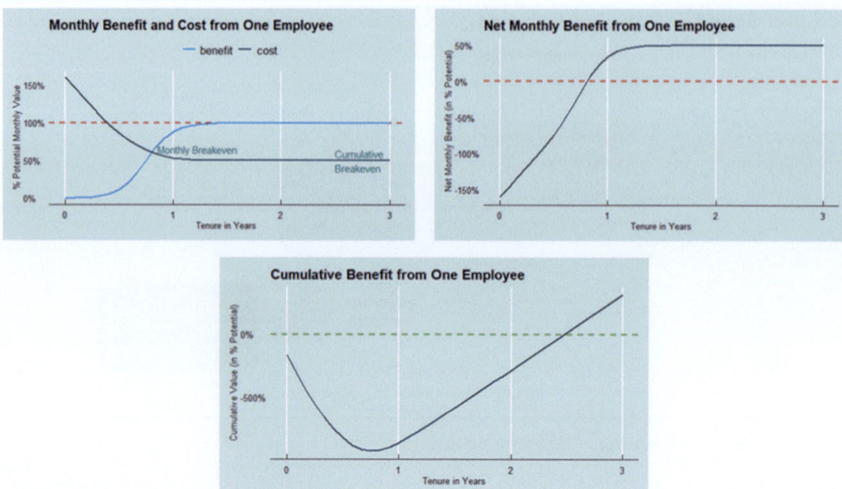




**Exhibit 2.3** Cost modelling—calculating net value (benefit—cost)

**Illustration**
The illustration reflects a cost/benefit curve for an employee over a period of three years. In the initial period, the costs are prohibitive—reflected through a recruitment process, administrative expenses, learning and development, etc., all kick in upfront. Once a year is completed however, the primary expenses incurred are around salary and overheads. The illustration suggests that to reach targeted productivity, an employee would take close to a year. The nature of the curve will depend on the type of role, but the basic nature of the curve will not change much.

If the organization seeks to intervene to bring costs down due to churn, it needs to focus on a few key actions:

- Bring down overall recruitment and on-boarding cost
- Reach levels of full/near full productivity much faster
- Make the salary versus productivity ratio more competitive
- Reduce early attrition in the phase where full productivity is yet to be reached
- Improve hiring quality to enhance the proportion of employees who are likely to be retained till the full productivity phase.

**Cost Measurement**
Not too many organizations have a fix on the costs and benefits for any given role. We see organizations focusing on lifetime customer value, but hardly any have turned their attention to lifetime employee value. It is to be noted that not all roles are directly business facing like "sales or customer service" or "factory shop-floor employees"—for instance what is the direct business contribution of roles such as "consumer insights" or "data scientist" or "HR manager".

People Analytics models and tools make it possible to evaluate employee cost vis-à-vis potential or contribution. The "eureka" moment is realized when we look at (benefit/cost) and then arrive at a break-even point as in the illustration.

As reflected, the employee contribution and value start kicking in after 10 months and break even only after 2.5 years. By deploying analytics, we can analyse the impact of all these factors. We can study the patterns and arrive at "break-even" points for each role. The trick is to apply the right predictive model to reduce the time to "break-even" or increase the likelihood of an employee to stay in a role within a specific time window.

## 2.6 Cost Modelling Project

Organizations need to take up cost modelling projects with a view to generating a sharper understanding of both costs and benefits related to people-related metrics and interventions.

The steps are as follows:

(A) Project Task: Organization identifies role and KPIs to be cost modelled.

For example:

1. Understand the costs related to; for example, 45% turnover in the sales manager role
2. Understand cost savings with reducing turnover by 5 or 10% or
3. Understand the costs associated with missed sales targets in the sales manager role
4. Understand which is costing the company more: not finding top performers or hiring too many bottom performers.
    - Define data requirements and available data
    - Define performance metrics, groups and other data variables present in organization's employee datasets.

Modelling

1. Combine cost data with KPI data

(B) Deliverables

1. Detailed summary of cost/benefits/data break-even points/cumulative break-evens
2. Which areas to focus on to reduce costs and increase benefits.

## 2.7 Optimizing Cost Through Operational Analytics—Some Examples and Tools/Visualizations

1. **Cost Per Hire**
    - Cost per hire compares sourcing channels and related costs to identify the optimal way in which to acquire fresh talent.
    - The cost per hire computation also includes the geographical challenges of employment (travel, relocation etc.) and associated time costs for talent acquisition.
    - Key decision support: The analysis enables HR to make the right calls around sourcing channel mix and processes around time to fill.
2. **Absence Factor**
    - The absence factor is used to compute and assign a weighted attendance employee score that is a crucial input into both payroll, disciplinary, well-being, productivity and workforce planning and deployment decisions.
    - The absence factor is used to analyse relative absence within and across teams and its linkages to factors of productivity and cost.
    - Key decision support: The analysis enables HR to set absence thresholds via heat maps to highlight cases for disciplinary action or formal monitoring of utilization to drive productivity.
3. **Absence Heat Map**
    - Measuring absence rates and patterns as possible predictors of engagement, performance/flight risk

- The absence heat map enables managers to deploy thresholds for various categories of absence depending on its impact on business and operations (Exhibits 2.4 and 2.5).

4. **Labour Cost**
   - The salary, bonus and related expenses incurred on payment to employees during a specific period; this is split into direct and indirect costs.

| | |
|---|---|
| No concern | 1 |
| Some concern | 22 |
| Action Required | 45 |
| Consider Disciplinary | 100 |
| Serious Disciplinary Likely | 900 |

Average Absence Days per employee

| Absence Occurences | 1 | 1.5 | 2 | 2.5 | 3 | 3.5 | 4 | 4.5 | 5 | 5.5 | 6 | 7 | 8 | 9 | 10 |
|---|---|---|---|---|---|---|---|---|---|---|---|---|---|---|---|
| 0 | 1 | 1.5 | 2 | 2.5 | 3 | 3.5 | 4 | 4.5 | 5 | 5.5 | 6 | 7 | 8 | 9 | 10 |
| 1 | 2 | 1 | 3 | 27 | 1 | 1 | 1 | 1 | 1 | 1 | 1 | 1 | 1 | 1 | 1 |
| 2 | 16 | 12 | 10 | 10 | 10 | 10 | 10 | 10 | 10 | 10 | 10 | 10 | 10 | 10 | 10 |
| 3 | 27 | 36 | 90 | 36 | 36 | 36 | 36 | 36 | 36 | 36 | 36 | 36 | 36 | 36 | 36 |
| 4 | 101 | 192 | 112 | 101 | 101 | 101 | 101 | 101 | 101 | 101 | 101 | 101 | 101 | 101 | 101 |
| 5 | 125 | 175 | 600 | 180 | 180 | 180 | 180 | 180 | 180 | 180 | 180 | 180 | 180 | 180 | 180 |
| 6 | 306 | 252 | 360 | 306 | 306 | 306 | 306 | 306 | 306 | 306 | 306 | 306 | 306 | 306 | 306 |
| 7 | 760 | 760 | 760 | 1519 | 760 | 760 | 760 | 760 | 760 | 760 | 760 | 760 | 760 | 760 | 760 |
| 8 | 1280 | 1280 | 1280 | 1280 | 1280 | 1280 | 1280 | 1280 | 1280 | 1280 | 1280 | 1280 | 1280 | 1280 | 1280 |
| 9 | 1742 | 1742 | 1742 | 1539 | 1944 | 1742 | 1742 | 1742 | 1742 | 1742 | 1742 | 1742 | 1742 | 1742 | 1742 |
| 10 | 2800 | 2800 | 2800 | 4700 | 5900 | 3400 | 2800 | 2800 | 2800 | 2800 | 2800 | 2800 | 2800 | 2800 | 2800 |
| 11 | 6171 | 6171 | 6171 | 6171 | 6171 | 6171 | 9922 | 5566 | 6171 | 6171 | 6171 | 9196 | 6171 | 6171 | 6171 |
| 12 | 9840 | 9840 | 9840 | 9840 | 9840 | 5328 | 9840 | 9840 | 7920 | 9840 | 9840 | 9840 | 9840 | 9840 | 16272 |



**Exhibit 2.4** Illustrative absence heatmap

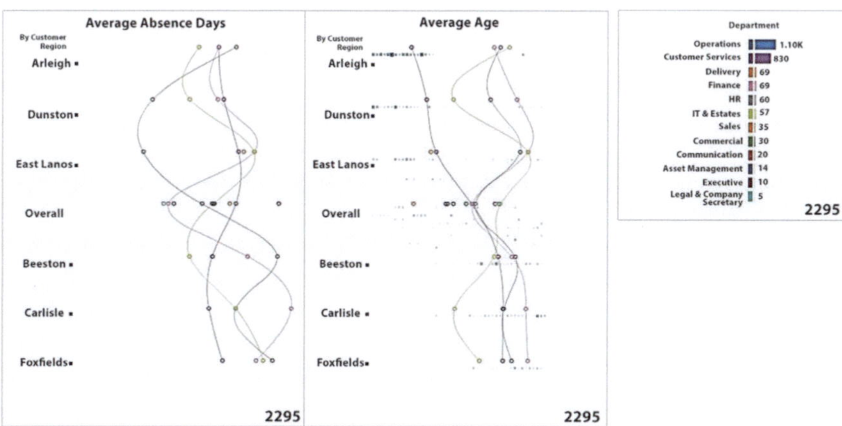




**Exhibit 2.5** Absence function wise split by age and tenure

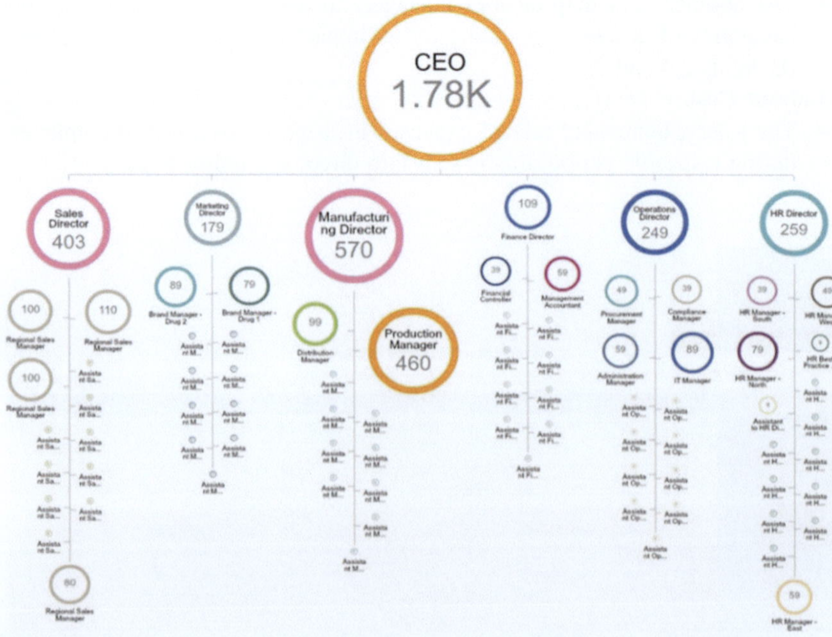




**Exhibit 2.6** Salary cost and spend roll-ups—role and function wise split by performance

- Key decision support: Analysis enables HR to monitor cost thresholds and highlight which are the business units/levels/roles, which are not in line either with market reality nor in line with internal parity (Exhibit 2.6).

5. **Cost and Impact of Attrition**
   - This analysis will allow you to determine the impact of employee turnover on the business and profitability.
   - Often the costs that are apparent such as hiring or on-boarding or training are easy enough to trace back and compute; it is often the more hidden costs that cause a problem.
   - Key decision support: Analysis enables HR/business to get a view of all hidden costs related to attrition; providing a more tangible view of cost/benefit ratios (Exhibit 2.7).

   This histogram mirrors how analytics is used to predict tenure by modelling the probability of an individual to terminate or attrite at a certain duration. The outcome of an analytics model will be a density curve, much like the histogram, showing the probability of termination for; "good fit" blue and "bad fit" brown, employees at each point of tenure (Exhibit 2.8).

**Exhibit 2.7** Probability of employee attrition histogram—histogram to predict turnover/tenure

**Exhibit 2.8** Compute your organization's cost of attrition

6. **Turnover Rate**
   - Employee turnover is the rate at which employees exit the company. A high turnover rate is reflective of instability and a rapid burn through of employees.
   - A healthy organization that requires a steady injection of new capabilities, fresh perspectives and passion requires a reasonable turnover rate to allow for the churn.
   - Key decision support: Analysis enables HR/business to arrive at an optimum turnover/retention balance. A bulge analysis of turnover across levels/roles/locations and businesses throws up imbalances that require corrective action (Exhibit 2.9).

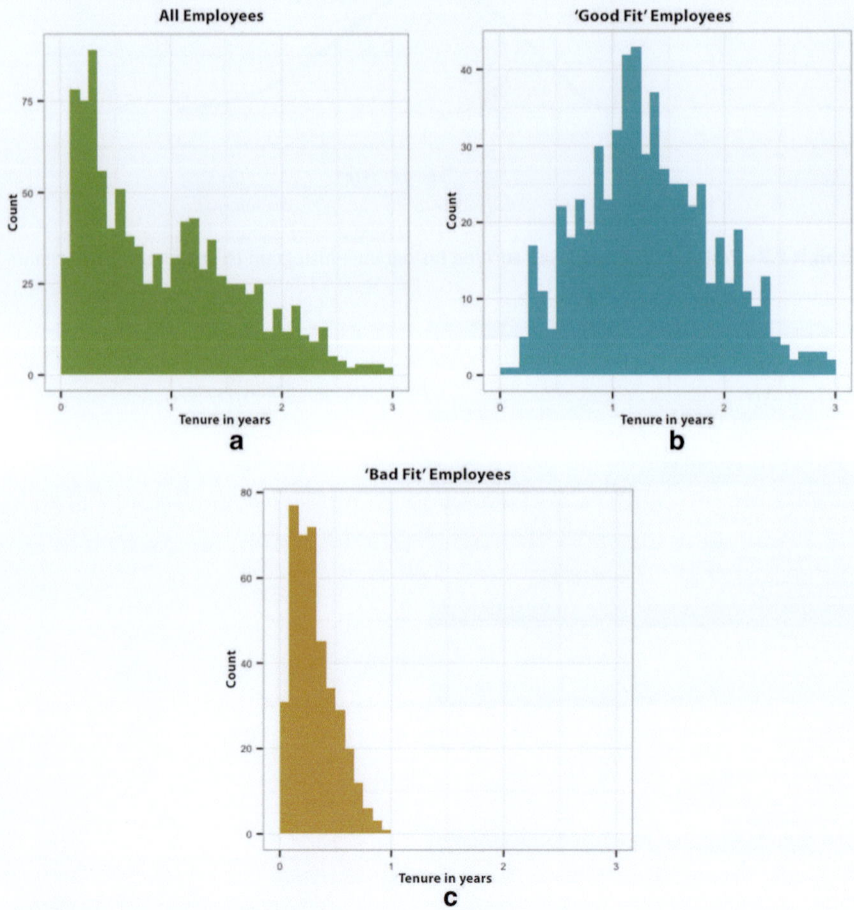




**Exhibit 2.9** Attrition histogram

The histogram allows you to analyse how employee turnover plays out and impacts organization performance. This can be developed from regular HR data with a deeper analysis being culled out from the graphic. Most managers are able to understand histograms with some coaching. In Exhibit 2.9a, the horizontal "X"-axis reflects tenure (number of years) in a given role. The "Y"-axis reflects employee headcount against the tenure. There is a spike in early exits in the first nine months, then another spike later. However, this is deceptive. The spiked pattern is actually the sum of two simpler employee clusters "good fit" individuals in Exhibit 2.9b who left the role by being promoted or being hired away and "bad fit" individuals in Exhibit 2.9c who left the role because of underperformance problems, working hours, commute time or for disliking or not fitting into the work/role (Exhibit 2.10).

7. **Performance Management**
   - It is the process of setting specific standards around objectives and goals to an individual or team with a view towards measuring their effectiveness over a designated period.
   - A performance-driven organization is one that continuously raises the bar, i.e. standards.

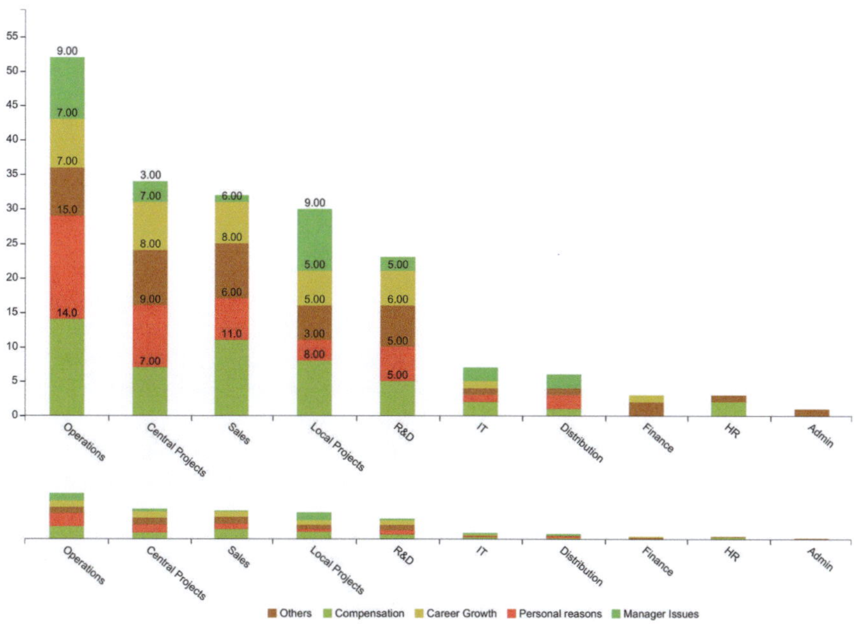




**Exhibit 2.10** Attrition analysis—key reasons

- Key decision support: Analysis enables HR/business to highlight performance gaps across role hierarchies/levels/business units/locations; to enable corrective action (Exhibits 2.11, 2.12 and 2.13).

8. **Headcount Utilization/Optimization**
   - This brings out how effectively headcount in FTEs is being utilized.
   - This metric highlights the productivity standards in an organization and whether those standards are being met or exceeded in terms of units produced or sold or services rendered.
   - This has a direct impact on both labour/people cost as well as revenue in terms of business per employee or team.
   - It is critical to track headcount evolution on a regular basis to stay on top of people planning and optimization.

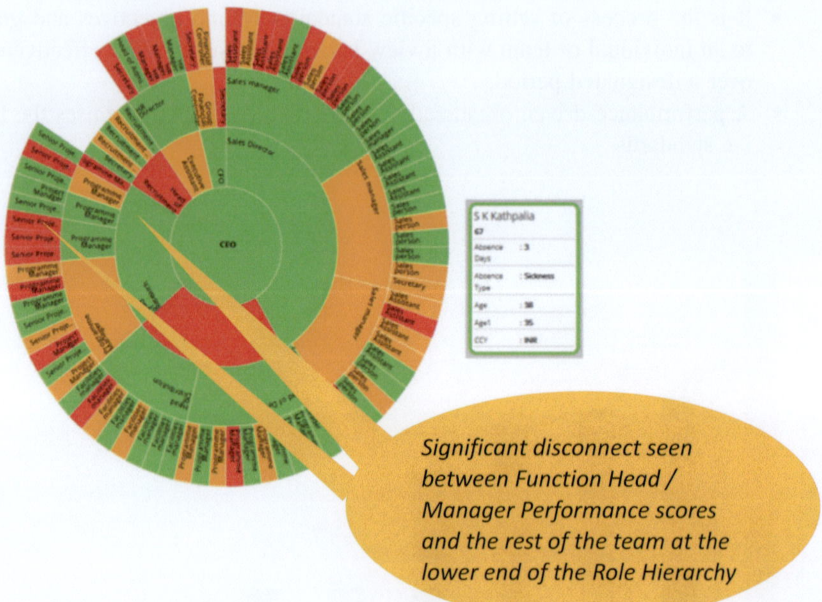




**Exhibit 2.11** Sunburst provides a holistic view of performance across the workforce. The Sunburst depicts both **span of control** as well as **the performance distribution of an organization, team with an individual drill down view**. The illustrated Visualisation has the senior most team member / role holder in the centre and each subsequent concentric circle depicts the next reporting layer. The "greens" represent Excellent performers, "ambers" good performers, "reds" poor performers and "whites" not evaluated. The sunburst view can additionally be deployed across multiple parameters to bring out key insights. The Sunburst gives a quick snapshot of where the **talent risks and challenges** lie. The performance distribution matrix across the organization can be visualised at a glance and key insights derived with **strong/weak pockets of team and individual performance highlighted or anomalies related to performance scores across hierarchy**. This may help build a case for leadership assessment and development in certain parts of the organization. Over a period of time the Sunburst would highlight quick wins for development and rationalisation

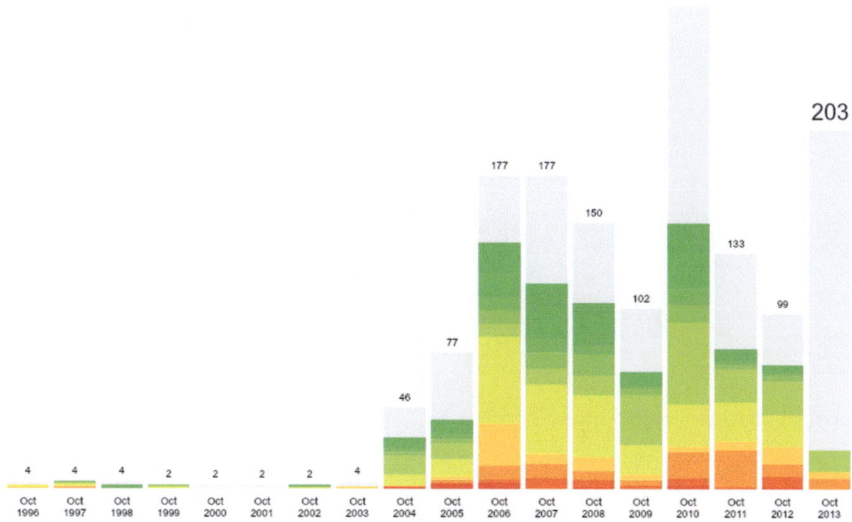




**Exhibit 2.12** Performance by year of joining—highlighting historical patterns on performance

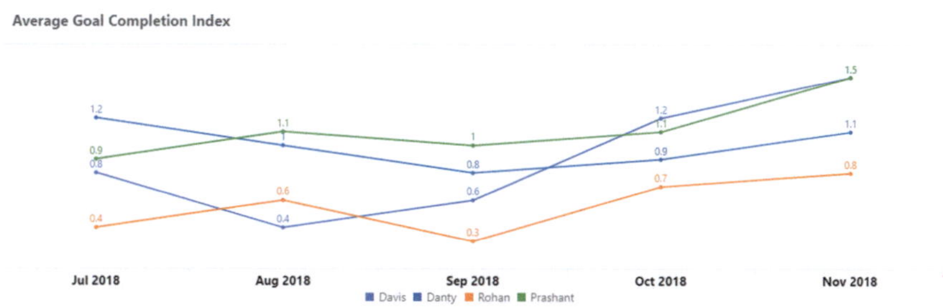




**Exhibit 2.13** Performance management—goal completion analytics

- Variance analysis in terms of actual versus budgeted headcount and cost across roles, locations, business units and functions is critical to highlight cost overruns and surplus manpower which would impact people/labour productivity standards.
- Key decision support: Analysis enables HR/business to highlight whether they have the optimum staffing model (in production, sales, services or support/ancillary areas) or do they need to restructure or redesign the organization to meet productivity standards or exceed the standards to drive profitability—"to get more with same or less"; "alter their teeth-to-tail ratios" by having more headcount deployed in customer facing roles for instance (that generate revenue) as opposed to support or production roles

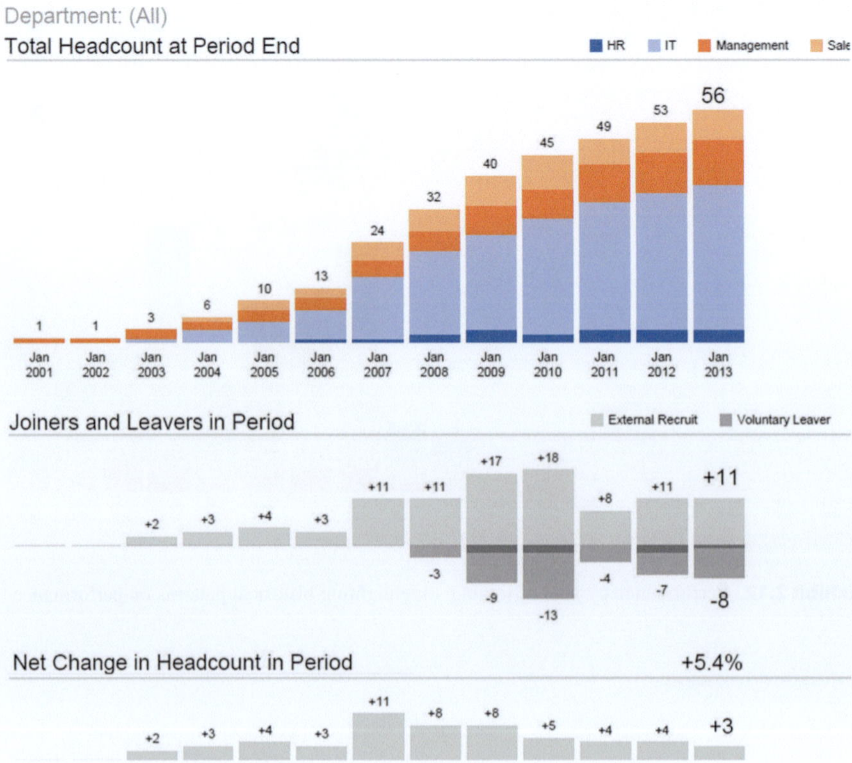




**Exhibit 2.14** Headcount management

which could be automated; ability to forecast capacity with headcount and skill requirements for the future (Exhibit 2.14).

9. **Demographics and Diversity**
   - This highlights how age, tenure, education, ethnic identities and gender diversity play out in an organization to drive sustainability and growth with profitability.
   - The interplay of demographic and diversity factors with other variables like performance, compensation, engagement, etc., provides critical insights for HR and business leaders.
   - These factors determine both the diversity quotient and the demographic mix of the organization which in turn impacts both growth and profitability by ensuring diverse set of ideas play out enabling teams to collaborate and engage more effectively to deliver key outcomes.
   - Key decision support: Analysis enables HR/business leaders to deploy the optimum demographic and diversity mix to build the right culture; enhance engagement and drive business outcomes (Exhibit 2.15).

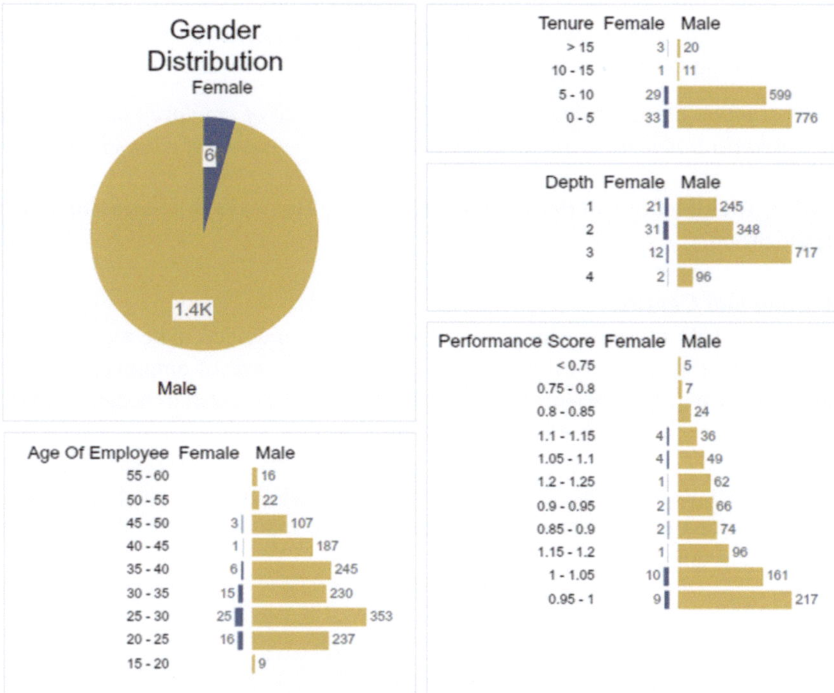




**Exhibit 2.15** Gender diversity

10. **Cost to Serve**
    - The activities that people do create the workflows in organizations. However, these activities that are typically captured in job or position descriptions are limited in nature and neither reliable or detailed enough to cover all key aspects of any given role.
    - Database that visually depicts people data quickly reflecting the organization hierarchy.
    - Unique visualizations that enable managers to dive into the insight rapidly.
    - Seamless cleansing and updating of the data.
    - Respond to questions around people and data—with a wide range of analytics, dashboards and organograms? What is the strength of the team? Who is responsible for what range of activities? Does the organization have the right fit? Is the organization bringing in the right capabilities with the right mix, in the right domains?
    - Key decision support: Analysis of process cost; time spent by each employee on each process; time and cost of customer facing and revenue

generating processes versus back-end support processes; time spent on non-value adding activities versus value adding versus time spent on decisions (Exhibit 2.16).

*Let us examine a case example of predictive modelling of employee turnover in a Sales organization of a Consumer company through leveraging of data science tools.*

## CASE 1: Identification of Predictors of Employee Turnover in a Sales Consumer Organization

### Situation and Context

Every year ~15% of employees leave XYZ company and need to be replaced with the talent pool available in the job market. The percentage of employee turnover (employees leaving, either on their own or because they got retrenched) impacts the company negatively due to the following reasons:

- Project delays, resulting in a reputation loss among consumers and partners
- An enhanced employee headcount needed to be maintained as attrition cover increasing employee costs

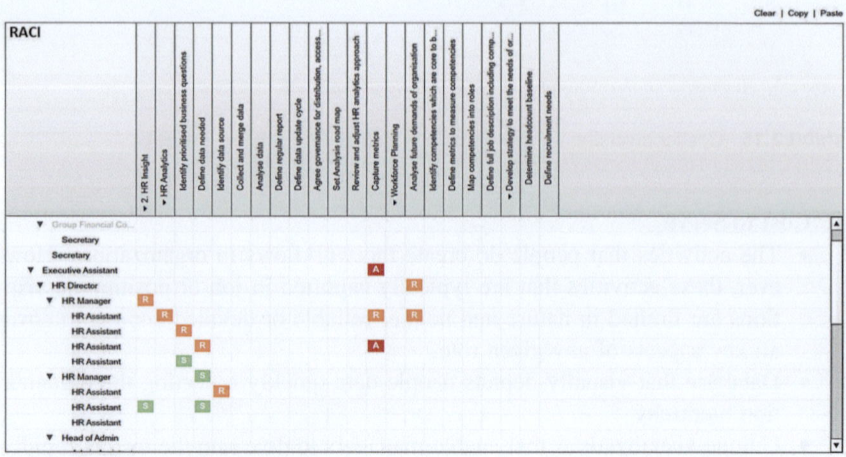




**Exhibit 2.16** Cost to serve—role analysis and process mapping—RACI MATRIX visualization and costing of processes linked with roles

- Productivity impact due to training and acclimatization of new hires before being put on the job thereby losing valuable time
- Increased salary cost as invariably new hires came at a minimum 30% higher salary
- Impacted engagement levels in the salesforce.

Given the alarming situation, a cross-functional team was quickly put together led by Ketan from the -business planning and MI team which pooled skill sets from multiple domains such as HR, business planning and MI and sales. The team was as a result able to deploy a set of tools to analyse this phenomena and pool its resources for maximum impact.

Data science and statistical modelling tools were used to analyse the data that was collected painstakingly from multiple sources. The study was carried out methodically with a governance process in place to review status.

**Analytics Objectives**

- To identify key predictors of employee turnover leveraging data science tools
- To understand what factors XYZ company should focus on to curb turnover
- In other words, what changes should be made in the workplace, in order to get majority of their employees to stay engaged and productive
- To isolate the factors that correlated highly with attrition and then deepen the understanding of those factors.

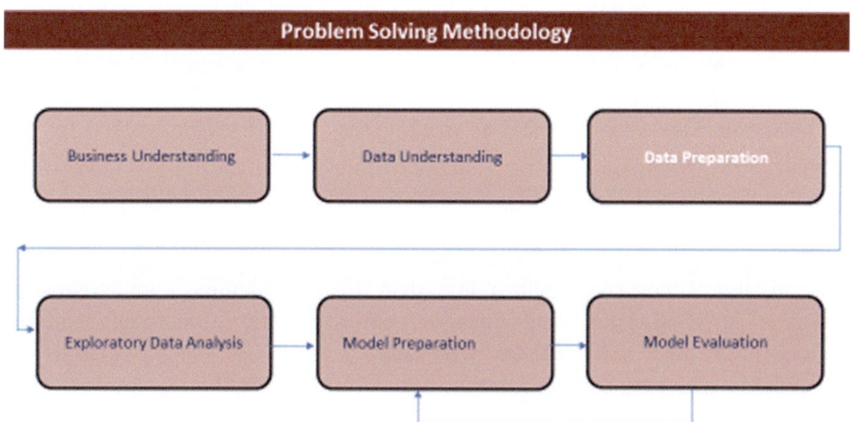

**Data Understanding**
The following datasets were collected and analysed.

- General data. It contained demographic information and other behavioural information of the employees. It had 4410 observations and 24 variables.
- Employee survey data. It contained survey data collected from the employees with 4410 observations and four variables.
- Manager survey data. Contained survey data collected from the managers with 4410 observations three variables.
- In-time data. It contained a year worth data of the employee's office in time in date time format with 4410 observations and 262 variables which contained in-time details for days 01/01/2015 through 12/31/2015.
- Out-time data. It contained out-time details for days 01/01/2015 through 12/31/2015.

Merging datasets—There was a need to merge general data, employee survey data and manager survey data along with time data by key variable employee ID to create master employee dataset.

**Data Preparation**

- In-time and out-time data converted from wide format to long format using R programming to calculate the average working hours and then eventually merge with the master employee data
- Derived a new variable called time in office based on the average working hours.

  An employee was classified as working overtime if he/she worked for more than 10 avg. hours.

  An employee was classified as working less time if he/she worked for less than 7 avg. hours.

  An employee was classified as normal if he/she worked between 7 and 10 avg. hours.
- Missing values were treated as follows:

  missing values (NA values) less than 1% in columns Num. companies worked, total working years, environmental satisfaction, job satisfaction and work–life balance were replaced with mode.
- Variable with unary data or constant values were removed.
- The variables employee count and standard hours contain a single constant value which does not help in analysis and modelling hence were removed.
- Employee ID column removed as it has no use in the modelling and analysis.
- All categorical variables converted to factors and then dummy variables before model building
- All continuous variables were scaled or normalized for the purpose of model building. (Exhibits 2.17 and 2.18).
- Attrition rate was found higher for following variables.

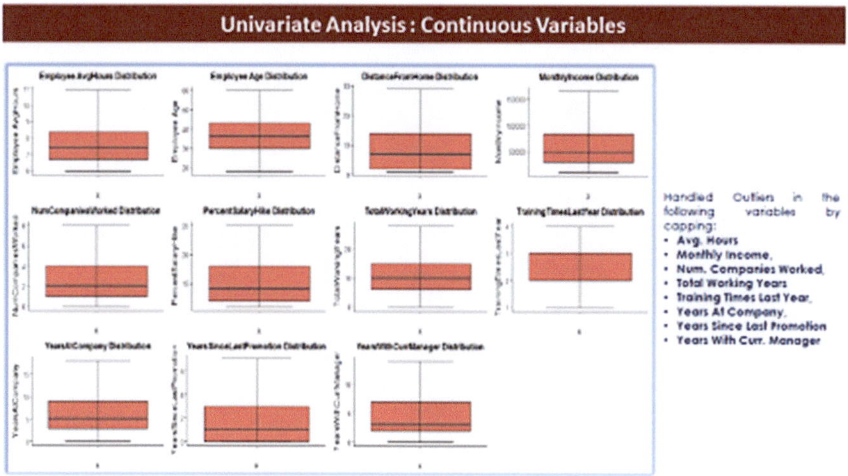




**Exhibit 2.17** Univariate analysis: continuous variables

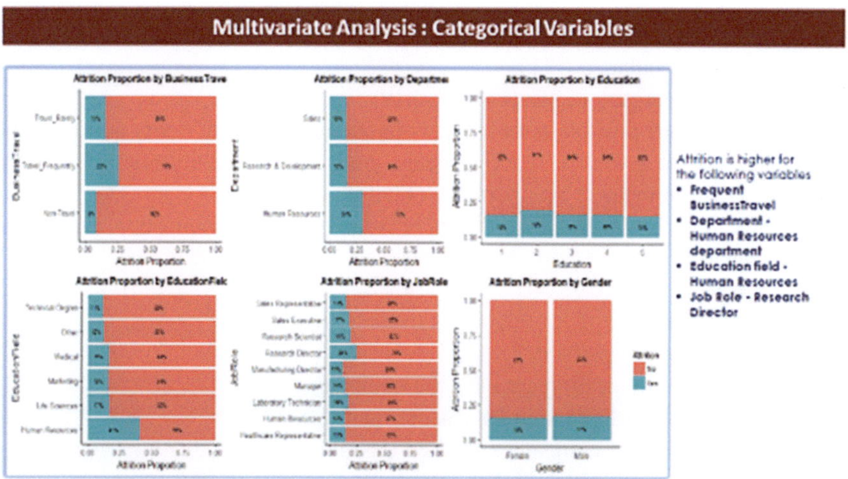




**Exhibit 2.18** Using stacked bar chart for multivariate analysis with categorical variable

- Frequent business travel—26%
- Human Resource department—30%
- Education field—Human Resource—41%
- Job role—Research director—24%—an exception
- Single marital status—20%
- Low environment satisfaction—25%

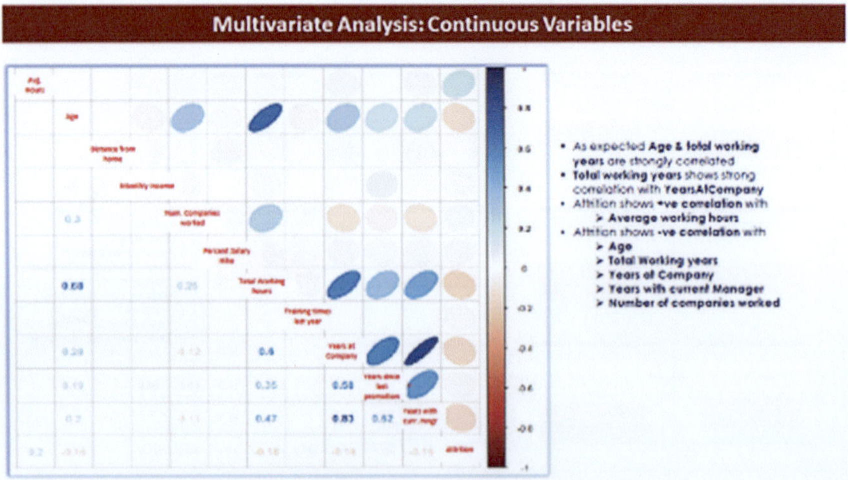




**Exhibit 2.19** Correlation plot coloured by attrition was used for multivariate analysis of continuous variable

- Low job satisfaction—23%
- Low work–life balance—31%
- Low job involvement—22% (Exhibit 2.19).
- Attrition showed positive correlation with average working hours and negative correlation with age, total working years, years at company, years with current manager and number of companies worked
- The box plot below indicates high attrition rate for employees across the following cohorts:
- Who travel frequently
- Younger in age
- With lesser work experience
- Working less number of years with the company
- With less number of years under current manager
- With less number of companies worked (Exhibit 2.20).
- Green bar below indicates higher information value and thus indicated strong association for the following variables with attrition:
- Total working years
- Average hours worked
- Years at company
- Age
- Years with current manager
- Marital status
- Time in office
- Business travel

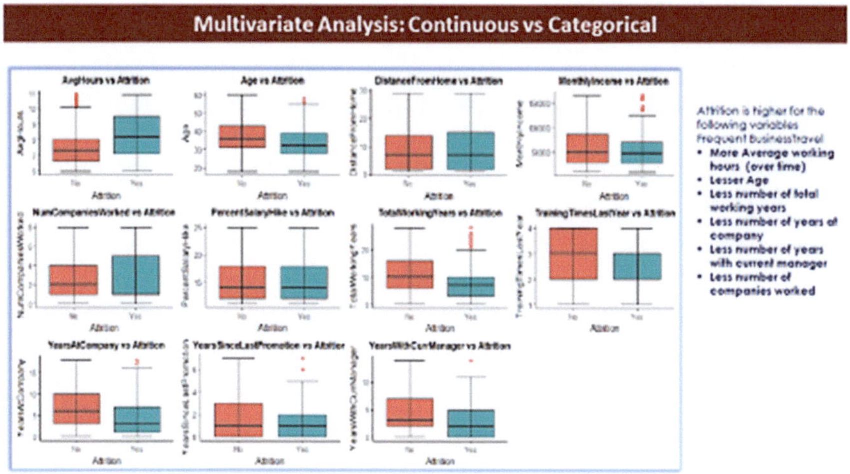




**Exhibit 2.20** Box plot of continuous variable coloured by attrition showed

- Number of companies worked
- Environmental satisfaction and job satisfaction (Exhibit 2.21).

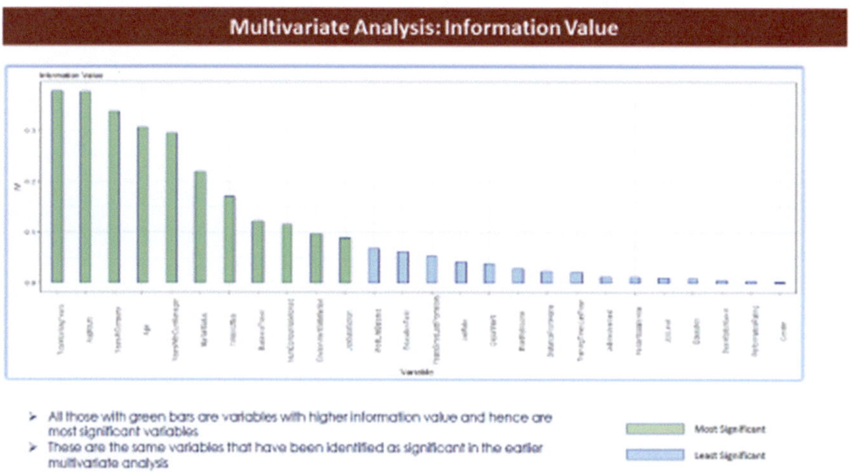




**Exhibit 2.21** Information value

## 2.8 Key Outcomes

- Key predictors of employee turnover were identified in order of ranking.
- Organization then reworked its policies in the identified areas to mitigate the risk.
- Enhanced stability in the frontline sales team with turnover brought down by @5% YOY.

# All Things Talent and Organization Networks

# 3

## 3.1 Context

The war for talent presents a fantastic opportunity for Human Resources to add tremendous value to business. Research goes to show that organizations that invest behind business and People Analytics can enhance their engagement manifold, drive up revenue and positively impact key business KPIs by enabling agile and robust decision-making.

People Analytics contributes to more reliable people and business decisions through a deeper analysis of people and business data by getting these data types to interact with one another and derive insights from these linkages. Crucial interventions around talent acquisition, retention, engagement, performance, learning, productivity and employee loyalty can now be analysed and better comprehended by leveraging statistical, data science and other tools, thereby putting data at the heart of people decisions.

As the war for talent intensifies unfolds, some organizations are starting to explore solutions:

- Understanding the persona traits of high-performing domain specialists to be able to better attract, select and eventually hire top talent.
- Identifying work-related factors along with behavioural triggers that are linked to fraudulent actions thereby making available the tools to management to mitigate loss fraud risk by highlighting underlying trends and patterns that hitherto were hidden but now made visible.
- Coming up with internal portals to enable tenured staff to locate new roles within the rganization through a match between skills and capabilities on the one hand and role descriptions on the other.
- Building predictive models that peel the onion on employee turnover so managers can recalibrate the work environment, work-related policies, processes or behaviours to keep top talent from exiting.



R. Ghatak, *People Analytics*, Management for Professionals,
https://doi.org/10.1007/978-981-19-3873-3_3

- Recalibrate rewards on the back of more robust decisions related to pay distribution between fixed and variable; incentive scheme effectiveness, customization in pay models across demographics, talent mix and skill demand and supply realities in the labour market; with a view to maximizing business performance while ensuring critical talent motivation and retention.

Interest in People Analytics is accelerating rapidly as more companies acknowledge the importance of human talent. The realization is dawning on CEO's and business leaders that in today's knowledge-driven economy human capital is turning out to be the primary and sustainable source of shareholder value. It follows then that any data-driven and evidence-based insights enabling organizations to attract the right-fit talent; retain them at high levels of contribution and enable them to learn and grow to next levels of responsibility; would be of enormous value not only to get on top of the "here and now" but also towards shaping the future business strategy with a view to gaining competitive advantage.

Organizations over the years have come to view talent retention as a key potential outcome of investment behind People Analytics. Significant efforts have gone behind putting in place early warning systems on the back of predictive models related to engagement and attrition and the predictive triggers linked to the same. Detailed deep-dive into and analysis of both structured and unstructured data on the back of data mining tools can bring out with reasonable accuracy which individuals are likely to exit along with the persona traits of likely exits and the key predictors which if addressed would reduce this trend in the short and medium term. As it is hiring and replacing top talent especially at senior levels and critical roles can be both time consuming and expensive thereby impact business outcomes. A key aspect to watch out for could be that some business leaders view the visibility and transparency that data and evidence-based insight brings as a threat with the hard evidence clearly coming in the way of their personal judgement and bias. It is when organizations derive clear business benefit from deployment of People Analytics, the resistance to data and evidence-based insight will seem to slowly dissipate. There is as a result therefore considerable degree of change management and top management commitment that is necessary to take the People Analytics movement forward.

## 3.2 Critical Challenges in Talent Management

Globalization and rapidly dynamic business realities are forcing organizations to develop new strategies and learn new ways of operating. Business leaders are most concerned about the capacity and capability of the organization to forward business strategy. Besides that, capability risks also emerge as the most concerning for business corporations, including the issues that organizations face in recruiting and retaining key talent, and developing skills and capabilities for the future. Some of these key challenges are:

1. **Low pipeline of top talent**

   Organizations are looking at a talent pool with new age skill sets to pave the way in future, but most middle and senior managers come from a generation where these skills did not exist and thus there are insufficient future leaders that could pave the way for cost-effective and efficient operations.
2. **Low internal bench strength**
   The millennial talent pool, especially in emerging markets, is not prepared to stay in the organization for longer tenures, hence individuals who could fill critical roles for the organizations shift to other organizations in search of more challenging roles that fulfil their individual aspirations or career development paths.
3. **Retention a struggle**
   Retaining talent has always been difficult, and in the present market scenario, organizations are grabbing every opportunity to attract the best talent. Hence, engaging people to stay and contribute long term in the organization is a growing challenge every organization has to face. Shaping a suitable culture that would create an environment for individuals to thrive is also a critical agenda for leadership.
4. **High cost of critical skills**
   In India, what is seen is that the cost of critical skills is becoming more and more expensive. There are people that occupy critical roles, and those skills have become quite unaffordable. Good talent is always in demand, and they are driving the cost point up, every year. Wage costs are going up YOY, and this is causing huge stress on profitability.
5. **Hiring top talent not easy**
   The millennial generation needs the vision about their level of contribution and the ability to shape the organization, which fulfils their need for challenge, learning, social contribution and leadership. Organizations that lack concern on these aspects are facing difficulties to recruit top talent across key roles. It is also about the employer brand and whether the organization has been able to communicate that effectively through both internal and external social networks. The employee experience has now become a crucial factor in determining the attractiveness of a future "employer" as far as the new talent pool is concerned.
6. **Performance management taken as a process not a business driver**
   Performance management has become more a process to drive the bell curve, rather than actually serving any real talent objective. It is therefore important to look at the entire talent supply chain and not only one aspect of talent. Valuable insights into all the aspects of talent will yield the right results.
7. **Skill gaps to meet future requirements**
   There is an urgent need to anticipate the future in terms of critical skills required and then to build those capabilities. Currently, the demand supply gap on key skills across roles is enormous and will take significant time to bridge.

## 3.3 People Analytics—Pivotal Role

People Analytics can play a pivotal role in meeting the above-mentioned challenges by enabling organizations to manage its human capital from a strategic perspective, to leverage rewards towards driving productivity gain, engaging talent pools with challenging roles and ensuring the organization meets revenue and profitability targets. The key stakeholders of the HR function are also now viewing the function more as a strategic business partner with a consultative data-driven approach as against the more traditional view of HR as an administrative function.

HR needs to evolve overtime to reach its maximum potential. It should change its role from being operationally reactive to strategically proactive and understand the linkages between workforce planning, rewards structures, functional/leadership competencies, desired behaviours, core values and other key elements to enable the organization significantly enhance its return on investing behind talent, learning, productivity, engagement and productivity. It needs to map out its role in the organization with the business strategy to have the right pool in proactively achieving the organization goals.

Holistic insights coupled with real-time feedback are crucial prerequisites towards understanding the linkages between workforce and business data. Powerful metrics, alerts, reports, insights and predictive models for managers enable them to better understand how workforce factors are affecting individual departments and businesses thereby triggering more proactive action leading to for example more timely talent retention conversations; more effective design of pay packages; sharper assessment and selection strategies and more impactful performance management.

There is a growing sentiment among organizations for HR to understand business challenges first hand thereby value adding significantly to the organization. Organizations want HR to be ready to assess impact of any changes in the economic and regulatory framework that affects the organization's talent. Business leaders require HR to provide them with insights in building organizations that are efficient and capable of growing to meet future demands.

Recently, there has been a shift from qualitative to quantitative methods of analysis. Quantitative studies base their analysis and research on data science and statistical methodologies. A particular strength of quantitative research is that statistical analysis founded on data science tools allows for a multidimensional view as against analysing factors in isolation. This process of using quantitative methods to derive actionable insights and outcomes from data is termed as analytics. Insights from the existing data help to drive operational excellence, leading to improved margins and higher return on investments (ROIs).

Fragmented and inaccurate employee insights can lead to low utilization of employee skill sets, ineffective resource allocation, poorly managed succession planning; critically missed opportunities to cross-sell and up-sell to customers because the right person with the right skills was not there at the right time to convert the sale. Put simply, a current and accurate view of employees is essential for long-term success and growth for the company and its people. The best way to get real and usable employee insights is to create a consolidated view of employees with data collected across all touchpoints, over time.

Organizations need to maximize the value of every employee throughout their whole employment with the firm, possibly even combine it with external data. So if employee data is stored in multiple systems, inaccurate or incomplete, HR teams cannot effectively identify, develop and retain star employees and those who need developing against business needs.

With an accurate, unified view of employee activity, HR teams can create personalized, one-to-one employee communications for business strategy, via the right channel and at the right time—crucial for maximizing the potential for employee engagement and customer experience.

With people and talent analytics, institutionalized HR teams start developing the ability to analyse, profile and segment employees: find out where organizations have real problems to fix; for instance:

- Identify drivers of attrition among the most valuable/critical talent; act before they leave.
- Identify all opportunities for relevant, timely rewards and get increased engagement.
- Reveal gaps in employee knowledge and skill sets.
- Stop wasting recruitment resources: Identify employees with the characteristics you want.
- Identify and act on cross-sell and up-sell opportunities: place the best most customer-centric people in front of customers.
- Activity-based process costing made easy: How much is the people cost for a given business process? Zero in to the detail rapidly.
- Reorganize/restructure/integrate or even see a dynamic organization chart sliced and diced by demographics and performance measures on the desktop; tablet or mobile device.

## 3.4 People Analytics in Talent Management—Some Frameworks

As we delve deeper into talent management, it is critical to understand the key frameworks that underpin it to arrive at analytical and predictive models:

- Talent and skill forecasting—predict resourcing, talent requirements and skill mix
- Talent acquisition—alignment of hiring with your business strategy
- Churn and attrition—predicting employee churn and attrition
- Potential—predict future leader talent; deciding on "whom to nurture, grow and invest in"

- Performance—support employees to achieve goals; predict top and bottom performers.

**Talent and Skill Forecasting—Anticipate and Predict Resourcing, Talent Requirements and Skill Mix**

| | Dimensions | Areas to investigate and analyse |
|---|---|---|
| 1 | Challenge | • Resourcing for growth: Once a white space is identified in a geography, what skill sets and how many people does a company invest in? Overinvesting with lack of growth undermines the P and L, while underinvesting with high growth leads to opportunity loss<br>• Forecasting quantity and quality of resourcing required to fund growth areas/businesses: Where do labour/skill surpluses reside? What skill sets are required?<br>• Rightsizing: At what pace should a company reduce headcount in one part of the business (low growth/geography) to fund resourcing in another part of the business/geography? |
| 2 | Opportunity | • Resourcing is still based on estimated growth numbers rather than a data science approach?<br>• Talent and skill set forecasting is still done intuitively |
| 3 | Methodology | • Talent analytics quickly and quantitatively measures a set of identified factors using the "data science" approach<br>• The factors underpinning "resourcing" and "talent/skill set mix" are then applied to a specific business growth scenario<br>• To eliminate bias, data science needs to be leveraged to first collect data samples, build, evaluate and then deploy models around talent, workforce planning and rewards |
| 4 | Benefits/outcomes | • The right resourcing and talent mix to resource for growth and business requirements |

**Talent Acquisition—Is your Talent aligned with your Business Strategy**

| | Dimensions | Areas to investigate and analyse | Business outcome |
|---|---|---|---|
| 1 | Hiring effectiveness | • What is the current hiring status—open versus closed?<br>• What is the "time to fill" status for all critical vacancies?<br>• What is the optimum channel mix that drives sourcing effectiveness?<br>• What is the channel conversion rate (consultants, direct portals, referrals, media, etc.)<br>• What is the assessment to selection ratio?<br>• What is the walk-in to on-boarded ratio?<br>• What is the offer to joining ratio?<br>• What is the quality of hire? | Operating cost<br>Growth |
| 2 | Recruitment cost | • What is the direct, indirect, total cost per hire?<br>• What is the cost per hire mix across grades, functions, locations, roles? | Operating cost |

| | Dimensions | Areas to investigate and analyse | Business outcome |
|---|---|---|---|
| 3 | Attrition and churn | • What is the voluntary, involuntary and total attrition by manager, function, location, grade, roles, business unit?<br>• Who, when, why and how of attrition? What are the key drivers of attrition across roles, functions and locations, teams?<br>• What is the flight risk of critical talent? What is estimated impact on business?<br>• What is the % early attrition within first 3 months? What are its key predictors?<br>• What is the correlation between voluntary attrition and business results? i.e. sales target achievement, customer service levels, etc. | Operating cost<br>Growth<br>Innovation<br>Brand reputation |
| 4 | Succession | • What is the succession pipeline for key roles?<br>• What are the talent gaps across role hierarchies?<br>• What would be our future talent requirements 3–5 years from now?<br>• Who among your talent pool are likely to impact, sustain and grow into leadership roles and who are likely to burn out? | Growth<br>Leadership risk |
| 5 | Retention | • What are the key drivers for "future leader" talent?<br>• What is the success ratio of talent retention programmes?<br>• What are the key drivers for critical talent retention? | Growth<br>Leadership risk |
| 6 | Career development | • What is the success ratio post promotions, role, business unit, function, location or reporting manager changes?<br>• What is the impact of redeployment, transfers and churn on the business and team?<br>• Are certain career pathways contributing to higher retention levels of critical/future leader talent? | Operating cost<br>Growth<br>Leadership risk |

## Churn and Attrition—Predict Employee Churn and Attrition

| | Dimensions | Areas to investigate and analyse | Business outcome |
|---|---|---|---|
| 1 | Challenge | • Reporting a prior year's employee attrition is at best interesting, but it says little about how to solve for "attrition"<br>• Understanding mega workforce trends is good but will not help predict who will leave or how to hire employees who perform and stay engaged<br>• Current attrition management efforts are often a stepping stone to greater insight | Operating cost<br>Growth |

| | Dimensions | Areas to investigate and analyse | Business outcome |
|---|---|---|---|
| 2 | Opportunity | • Employee attrition has moved from being a hot HR topic to being a hot CEO/CFO and analytics topic<br>• Employee attrition models (like customer attrition models) deliver direct and significant ROI to the business<br>• Who, when and why of attrition a "black box" today | Growth<br>Cost<br>Sustainability |
| 3 | Methodology | • Talent analytics tools quickly and quantitatively measure "raw talent" for the targeted set of employees using the "data science" approach<br>• The factors underpinning "raw talent" can be measured<br>• These can be applied to job families and roles. For instance, a set of persona traits may match up pretty well with a particular job family while others may not. As an example if you were to take the case of a job family related to accounts and finance, a trait such as "attention to detail" may well be a strength but can also be a weakness for a job family related to sales; service orientation could be great for a job family related to customer service or hospitality but may not be relevant for a collection agent. Different sets of persona traits are reflected in individuals across multiple job families | Operating cost<br>Growth<br>Reputation |
| 4 | Benefits/outcomes | • Reduced churn and attrition contributes to increased sales and higher customer satisfaction | Growth<br>Service level |

## Potential—Predict "Future Leader" Talent

| | Dimensions | Areas to investigate and analyse | Business outcome |
|---|---|---|---|
| 1 | Challenge | • Who are the core group of people who will lead the organization into the next phase of growth?<br>• Who are the people to invest behind?<br>• Who are the people that must be retained for the longer-term health of the business? | Sustainability<br>Growth<br>Cost |
| 2 | Opportunity | • Future leader talent identification is still a "hit and miss" exercise<br>• Predicting "who will lead in the future?" is still a perception driven and intuitive exercise<br>• Developing a leadership talent pipeline and talent pool to be based on hard data and insight | Growth<br>Reputation<br>Sustainability |
| 3 | Methodology | • Talent analytics tools quickly and quantitatively measure a set of identified factors using the "data science" approach<br>• The factors underpinning "future leadership potential" are then applied to predict the likelihood or otherwise of somebody being more likely to succeed in future leadership roles<br>• The predictive model developed can then be tested and validated | Sustainability<br>Growth<br>Reputation |

| | Dimensions | Areas to investigate and analyse | Business outcome |
|---|---|---|---|
| 4 | Benefits/outcomes | • Making the right choices about our future leaders is critical; we should care about investing behind the right people who will provide the right leadership; we should care about optimizing learning costs | Growth<br>Sustainability<br>Cost |

See Exhibit 3.1.

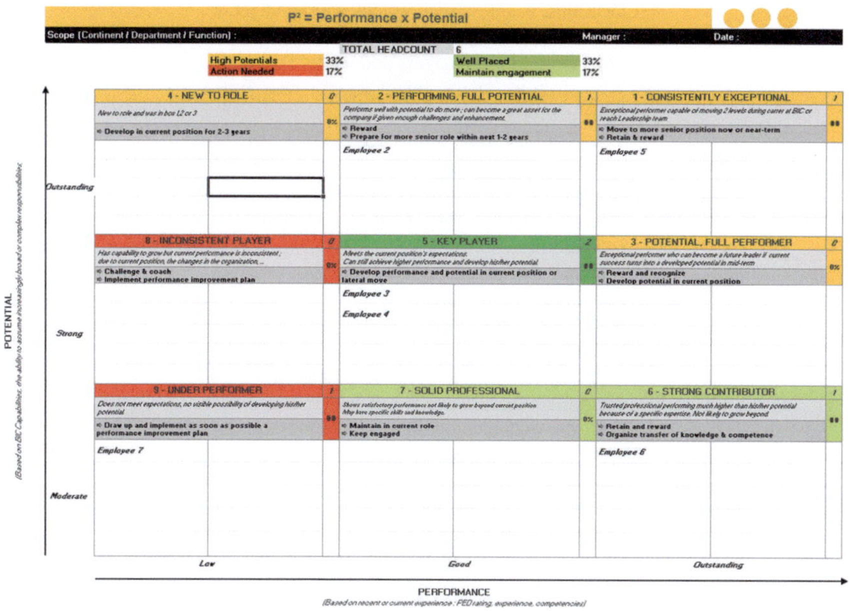




**Exhibit 3.1** Performance versus potential—9 box grid

**Performance—Support Employees to achieve their Goals; Predict Top and Bottom Performers**

| | Dimensions | Areas to investigate and analyse | Business Outcome |
|---|---|---|---|
| 1 | Challenge | • Underperforming employees dramatically hinder top line and bottom-line results<br>• Your business has a ratio where 1 bottom performer wipes out performance of "x" top performers. Do you know the ratio for your business?<br>• What is the performance distribution across teams, locations, business unit, grades and managers?<br>• Which are the high-performing and low-performing managers and teams over history?<br>• Why are some teams, functions, business units outperforming others?<br>• What is the correlation between performance and compensation; vintage in grade, qualification, engagement level, manager leadership style, span of control, tenure, role changes, retention programmes, etc.<br>• What are the key behaviours and competencies that drive high performance?<br>• Are career pathways defined for high-performing individuals?<br>• What are the factors that differentiate high performers from average and low performers?<br>• Does the organization differentiate between high-, average-, and low-performing individuals and teams and if so how?<br>• Does this "differentiation" contribute to higher retention among high-performing employees and teams or is the correlation tenuous at best? | Sustainability<br>Growth<br>Profitability |
| 2 | Opportunity | • Predictive talent analytics uses a similar, predictive cost–benefit approach used by financial institutions for making credit decisions<br>• In high volume employee situations (sales, call centres, bank tellers, engineers, service centres, data scientists, etc.), marginal improvements can result in significant business results<br>• When predictive analytics reveals that one "wrong-fit" recruit eliminates the value of x "right-fit" one, recruitment decisions immediately get impacted bringing out the value of analytics to the recruitment process | Growth<br>Sustainability<br>Profitability |

| | Dimensions | Areas to investigate and analyse | Business Outcome |
|---|---|---|---|
| 3 | Methodology | • Talent analytics tools quickly and quantitatively measure "raw talent" for the targeted set of employees<br>• This dataset proves to be extremely useful in creating high value predictive models and enhancing missing or incomplete data. In many cases, the raw talent dataset provides the independent variable needed in predictive models<br>• Existing KPI data is used. There is no requirement to implement a full HRMS solution before starting on predictive modelling | Sustainability<br>Growth<br>Profitability |
| 4 | Benefits/outcomes | • Sustainable business growth with profitability<br>• Raising the bar on performance right through the role hierarchy<br>• Embedding and reinforcing the right "behaviours" that drive business performance | Growth<br>Sustainability<br>Profitability |

Analytics models can as a result be developed across the following areas:

- Passive talent pool recruitment
- Recruiting "right"—via personality trait clues and gamification triggers
- Leadership pipeline/succession triggers
- Potential versus performance triggers
- Talent mix forecasting and mobility.

High-impact predictive projects can also be taken up in the following areas to enable organizations take proactive actions to maximize retention, engagement, performance and productivity:

- Predict top and bottom performers
- Predict employee attrition and churn
- Predict future leader talent potential.

## 3.5 Data-Driven Recruiting

Planning and decision-making around recruiting are now done basis data-driven insights acquired through HR Technology such as applicant tracking systems and recruitment marketing platforms. As in the case of business functions like sales and marketing, every stage in the talent acquisition process can be monitored and measured. The conundrum of first identifying and then hiring the "right-fit" talent has been an ongoing challenge for talent acquisition specialists and head-hunters alike. Given that "right-fit" talent is critical for a company's success, the capability to hire right is absolutely important.

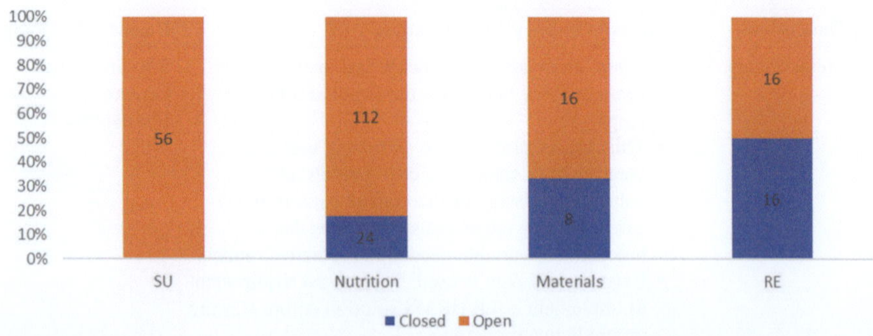




**Exhibit 3.2** Position tracking—typical position tracking would provide a view of open versus closed positions for efficient tracking of the hiring team

Lack of visibility around the talent acquisition process not being aware of the barriers to hiring "right-fit" talent or the process/method gaps may cost the company dear. This realization has led to companies focusing on leveraging both digital solutions and data-driven insights to jump-shift key metrics such as time to fill, cost per hire, quality of hire, employee experience, early engagement, quality of on-boarding and collaboration.

**Some Illustrations and Views**

See Exhibit 3.2.

Average time to fill or ageing would show time to fill for closed positions and ageing for open positions. Easy correlation can be drawn when the two are compared; for example in Nutrition BU, average time to fill is 85 days while the ageing for open positions today is only 69 days which indicates that the current performance is in line with past performance, while in materials, the performance on closed positions was better than open positions (Exhibit 3.3).

Exhibit 3.4 presents the no. of positions worked by each member of the recruitment team with a split of each BU wise positions. This can help evaluate underutilization and over-utilization recruiter wise; moreover, it can give insights regarding efficiency of the recruiter.

Exhibit 3.5 presents usage of the sources/channels of recruitment. This can help evaluate channel effectiveness recruiter wise.

Exhibit 3.6 presents the funnel of hiring flow with count at every stage; it shows that approx. three times CVs are needed to be sourced for closure of offers.

## 3.6 Applying Talent Analytics

Most HR professionals struggle to make linkages with business outcomes. A great deal of time is wasted on HR process flows, details of various programmes and

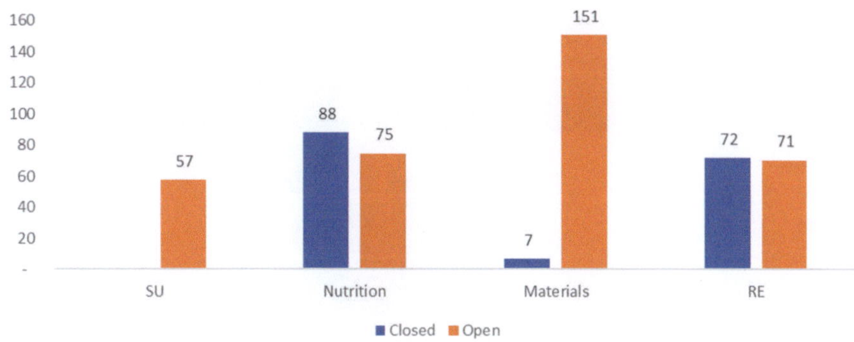




**Exhibit 3.3** Average time to fill or ageing

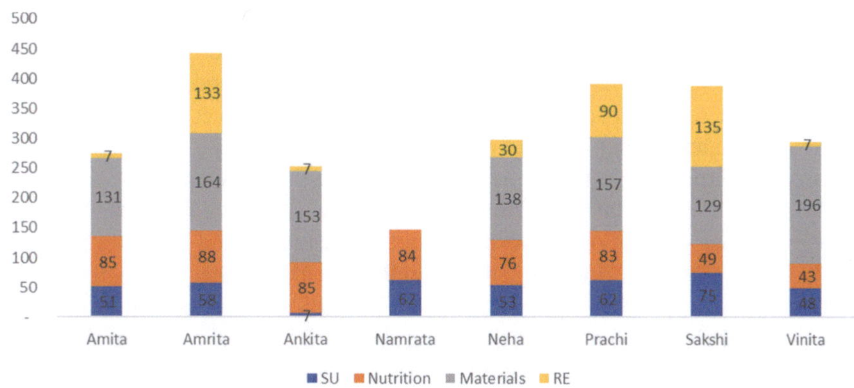




**Exhibit 3.4** Recruiter wise split

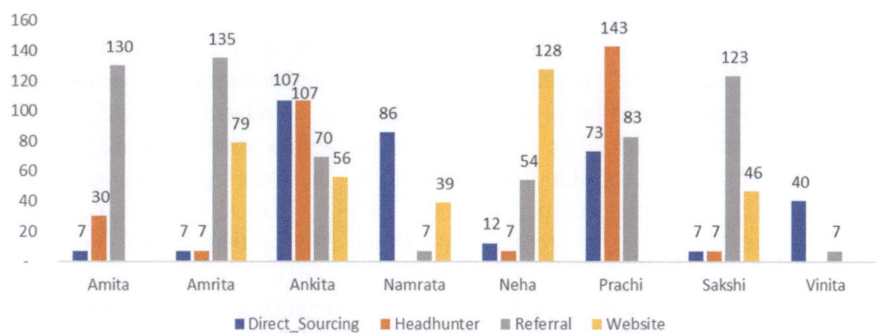




**Exhibit 3.5** Sourcing channel mix

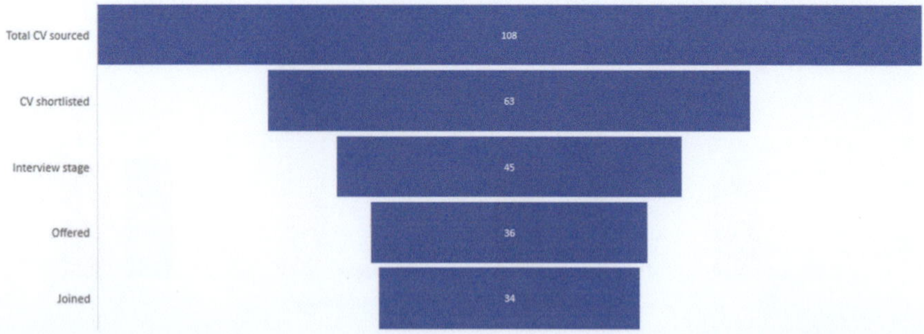


*Copyright: Acumetric Global Solutions Pvt Ltd – all rights reserved*

**Exhibit 3.6** Hiring flow funnel

their reporting instead of asking the right questions: What critical business problem requires solving? What relevant data needs to be collected and analysed for me to provide solutions and alternatives? How will data help me, and what data should I use? Which roles impact key business drivers the most, i.e. revenue, growth, market share and profitability and how do I hire significantly more "right-fit" as opposed to "wrong-fit" in these roles? Or how do I enhance retention of key talent in these roles? Which talent drivers for instance will enhance customer loyalty? Is there a strong correlation between employee engagement and customer loyalty? While this is a nascent domain, it is a rapidly developing one, with a few organizations showing the way by leveraging the body of research as well as running bold experiments like what Google did with Project Oxygen. Companies that have leveraged People Analytics successfully have clearly brought out the business case through the connections they were able to establish between different threads of data across multiple domains and data types—both structured and unstructured.

Organization health—Analysts in a reputed aviation company developed a metric—the "crew-member net promoter score"—that monitors employee engagement and predicts financial performance.

Hot spot identification—Managers at **a famous aircraft manufacturing company** used an automated system to collect timely performance review data and identify areas needing improvement. The company correlated knowledge management and training data with performance data with a view to identifying top talent while also trying to establish which learning and development programmes were contributing to enhanced performance. These insights allowed the company to devise learning strategies around content and delivery that directly impacted performance.

Retention rate improvement—A food services organization was able to bring out on the back of analysis and evidence-based insights a correlation between employee empowerment levels on the one hand and engagement and retention on the other. This was a eureka moment for the company which then replicated its employee first actions that enabled empowerment of its delivery associates (customer facing staff) resulting in significant enhancement of their retention levels by 20% points, thereby saving massive spends around hiring and training.

Maximize productivity—A manufacturing company that is known for innovative practices leverages analytics to demonstrate linkages between rewards, hiring and talent practices on the one hand and workforce productivity on the other. The analysis revealed that business units with higher engagement levels emerged more productive and profitable in the medium term.

## 3.7 Organizational Networks—Uncovering "Hidden and Passive Internal Talent Pools"

Organizational network analysis is a mechanism (using passive and active analysis) to **uncover how employees interact with each other** to get the job done. There are tools available today to lay the ground for agile networks that enable better collaboration, knowledge sharing and talent risk mitigation. This is a process that allows you to analyse informal networks and relationships within the organization to provide deeper insights into informal structures and teams that shape organizational outcomes. With much of the communication within and outside organizations going digital, an analysis of this digital footprint via data mining of communication networks is thus made possible. This enables organizations to analyse at a deeper level, the communication network which hitherto was not possible.

**Passive and Active ONA**

Modern organizations that are large and complex are driven by work, knowledge and collaboration. They sit on massive repositories of communication data that is hardly ever analysed or utilized. How can we slice through this complexity to truly understand modern organizations and use that knowledge to drive performance. Networks are everywhere. For example, think about the people that you know well and which of them know each other. That is a network. But, most importantly, modern organizations are a collection of networks—both inside and outside of the organization. ONA allows you to collect information on these networks, to analyse them, to truly understand them and, in doing so, to drive change and improvements. Think about all the sources of network data available—e-mail communication, instant messenger conversations, 360° performance reviews, enterprise social networks like Yammer, social networks like Twitter and so on. With ONA, you can interact with it, visualize it and analyse it.

Organizational network analysis has two sides to it—passive ONA and active ONA. Passive ONA is about analysis of communication data, for instance e-mail or messenger logs to analyse how people and teams are connected within an organization. Active ONA is about using a series of survey questions regarding relationships among employees and across teams—Who do you go to for problem solving in your network? Who do you approach for coaching on the job? Who do you reach out to for guidance and advice? Who do you work with often?

**ONA Technology**

Today, there are cloud-based technologies that enable organizations to analyse these informal structures and networks and derive critical insights, impacting business outcomes.

**Key Features—Upload, Analyse and Collaborate on any Set of Network Data**

- 100% web based
- Fine-grained user permissions for collaboration
- Upload networks using Excel or in more advanced formats
- Export to Excel, PNG, SVG or more advanced formats
- Create, save and share multiple views
- Multiple network metrics
- Multiple layout algorithms
- API access.

**Key Uses of ONA**

ONA is used to identify **key stakeholders** in the network such as Influencers, key players, knowledge brokers, change catalysts as well as blockers through an **analysis of social and work networks** in organizations. It is used to figure out how high/low-performing teams function; position employees where they can deliver the most impact; identify people to serve as catalysts of change during transformation; demonstrate where work begins, stutters and halts; analyse the impact of DandI interventions; develop insights into knowledge exchange and collaboration across teams and hierarchies. This enables companies to holistically analyse social networks to enhance collaboration across the organization.

The major benefits of organization network analysis includes

- Identifying individuals who are either key risks or key talent
- Identifying hidden operating process issues
- Optimizing functional relationships to improve: cross-sell; client services
- Mobile workforce optimization
- Collaboration within and between teams, groups, etc.

**Key Metrics—Some Examples**

1. **Identify influencers**: This is about leveraging network analysis to identify key influencers who are common points of contact for multiple networks and teams.
2. **Collaboration matrices**: This is about understanding the nature of networks to understand collaboration levels within and across teams.

*Identify Influencers*
A key functionality of ONA is about the ability to identify key influencers or knowledge brokers who are connected to the maximum number of individuals in the network. This group of influencers may be leveraged as catalysts for change or may be used as a bridge between the leadership and other levels within the organization from a communication and degree of collaboration perspective.

*Collaboration*
ONA also summarizes the interactions between different groups in the network. It brings out levels of communication and collaboration within and between teams—for instance sales and credit risk or customer services and shared service support; while some teams, such as RandD, are more compartmentalized. The analysis around team working and support across location, hierarchy, functions, gender and ethnic groups also bring out the "Diversity and Inclusion" quotient of the teams and networking within the organization.

## 3.8 Organization Networks—Impacting Talent Outcomes

ONA enables organizations to both enhance operational effectiveness and drive change in a cohesive and smarter way leveraging network data via communication platforms both internal and external to the organization.

**Enhance Operational Efficiency**
Formal organograms and structures largely are not reflective of the flow of people who get the job done. ONA insights could be used to redesign organizations and formal structures, thereby positioning the right people in the right roles for creating maximum impact.

**Organization Transformation**
In most cases, individuals featuring at apex levels on organization charts are rarely the people who are approached regularly for advice or guidance on a day-to-day basis. ONA goes beyond job titles and increases the probability of identifying those real leaders and influencers who in reality take ground level decisions and get the work executed to drive real and sustainable change.

**Use Talent Efficiently**
Actual work cannot be fully represented by designations or job descriptions. ONA brings out the level and degree of interaction and collaboration between roles, teams and units.

- **Role clarity**: ONA reveals the true worth of the role or job by going beyond the formal job description thereby providing the true picture around resourcing costs and role fitments—are we trying to fit a square peg in a round hole or vice versa?

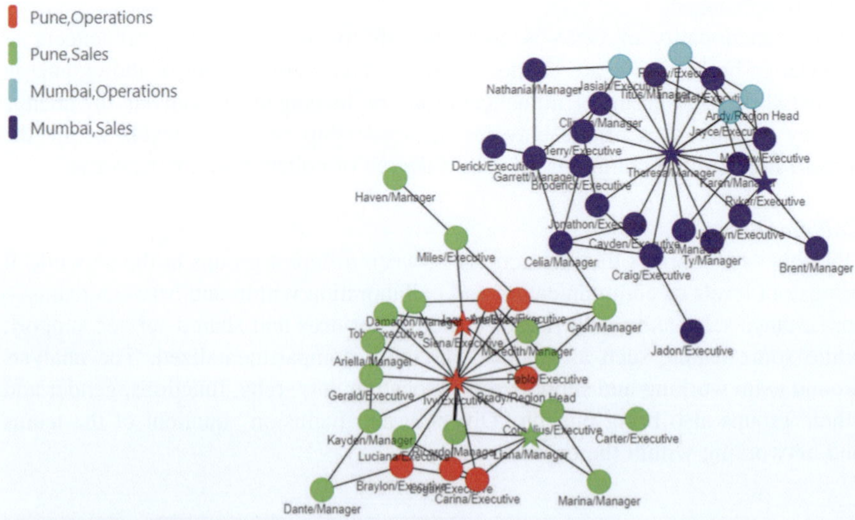




**Exhibit 3.7** Organization network analysis—illustrative network map

- **Role description**: ONA reveals how work ebbs and flows through an organization. This can throw up unique insights into matters of governance and reveal how decisions are made and by whom and their impact on work. Through these insights, management is provided with the right inputs towards integrating the right individuals into the decision-making flows. A classic case is that of an MandA situation when job titles of incumbents in the target company are not what they seem. Role redundancies in teams or networks which may not be easily visible on the outside get bubbled up through an ONA diagnostic, thereby identifying productivity or value addition opportunities (Exhibit 3.7).

## 3.9 Illustration: Employee Churn, Prediction and Retention

Employee churn may be a significant problem for several firms these lately. "Great talent is scarce, hard to keep and in high demand". It leads to disruptions, client's dissatisfaction and time and efforts lost in finding and training replacement. Retaining valuable employees is always less expensive as compared to hiring new ones. As a result, it is critical to understand the key triggers and predictors of employee disengagement where analytics could be leveraged. Reliable predictive models for employee churn could be useful in devising employee retention plans. Using built predictive models, we can design better employee retention plans and improve employee satisfaction.

**Objective**
Minimize the cost to company by identifying critical talent at churn and retaining them.

**Employee Churn**
Employee churn if not managed optimally can impact organizations negatively more so in BPO/Ites and service/retail sectors.

Negative or regrettable churn is a problem due to the following reasons:

1. Finding "right-fit" backfills for employees with relevant experience and special skills
2. Cost of hires—allocating resources (time and money) to hire more people
3. Disruption of ongoing projects and services, which impacts relationships with clients and key stakeholders
4. Ramp-up time taken for new hires to get to full productivity and matching levels of expertise
5. Employee churn impacts business continuity and stability of an enterprise. Churn rates can be 15–20% annually in consumer businesses and could go up to 30–40% in service and outsourced businesses.

The reasons why employees churn could be many. The positives may include career growth, better pay and benefits, work environment, role change or location, etc., while negatives could include work-related conflicts with team or reporting manager, dissatisfaction with current role profile, working conditions, pay, etc.

Exit interviews at most provide only a glimpse into surface level reasons for leaving. It is important then to validate the stated reasons through other analysis of the individual's service history, work relationships within and across teams and levels as well as with reporting manager, performance, perceived recognition, levels of engagement, commitment and so on.

Understanding root causes for employee churn is critical with a view to drawing up retention strategies, workforce planning and enhancing engagement levels. Predictive models help in peeling the onion and bringing out the real reasons for churn thereby enabling management to take proactive action to pre-empt such instances going forward.

It is important to distinguish between the predictors and the target variable. Whether a particular employee will churn or not is indicated by the target variable. The predictors contain information that could be potentially related to our target variable. In this case, employee churn is target variable, and it will depend upon the predictors like age, marital status, salaries, grade, qualifications, promotions and job rotations, department, performance ratings, training, previous company, join date, leave date, engagement survey information like job satisfaction score, likelihood to recommend company to others score, work pressure score, ability to do the job score, brand perception score, etc.

An impactful talent retention strategy has two critical elements:

1. Identify the critical talent employees those at risk of leaving.
2. Identify the responsible factors causing employee churn.

Businesses tend to respond to employee attrition on a reactive basis, acting only after the employee has initiated the process to switch the job. At this stage, the chance of changing the employee's decision is almost impossible. Predictive analytics can help us predict this behaviour, so that the company can take the appropriate preventive actions to retain the individual. The statistical methods and tools like logistic regression, artificial neural networks and decision trees will help us resolve the underlying problems. Even leveraging attitudinal data available from employee engagement surveys, we can calculate the employee loyalty score which can be taken into account to observe the churn.

A predictive framework would typically seek to begin with first identifying the independent variables and then procuring data around them for statistical and other analysis.

**Employee Churn**

- Has unique dynamics compared to other problems
- Predicting who, when and why employees leave
- Translating employment processes into tractable data mining problems.

*An illustrative example on how a call centre was able to deploy predictive tools to reduce early attrition among its customer service representatives would throw more light on how to operationalize predictive modelling techniques towards driving business results.*

**CASE 1: Predictive Model to Reduce Early Churn and Enhance Faster Deployment of CSRs**

Bringing down early attrition/churn and enhancing process exam pass rate and faster deployment of customer service representatives (CSRs) in a financial services call centre.

**Situation and Context**

- Thousands of call centre agents were hired and deployed every month
- 12 weeks of training on phones a prerequisite for deployment on floor
- Critical path: requirement to pass a key process exam before deployment
- High training and retraining costs resulting from high early attrition.

Preeti, the operations manager in this critical call centre, part of the retail customer service arm of a large BPO, was frustrated to the core. Given that there was considerable churn in this business, it was critical to keep the sourcing pipeline lubricated all the time. However, while the recruiters were hiring the required numbers, the problem was that a significant number of them were failing the test which led to either their deployment on the call centre floor getting delayed (impacting

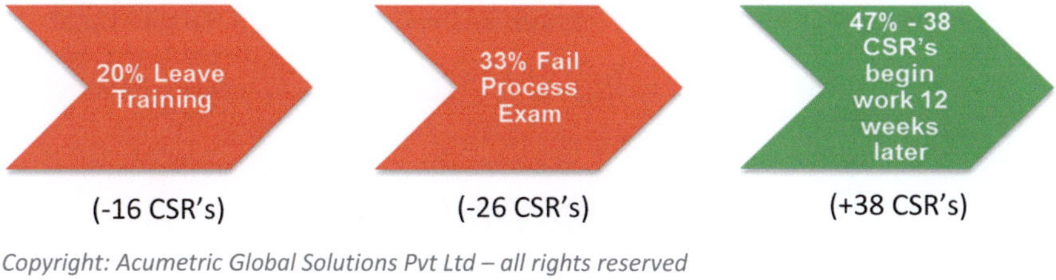


**Exhibit 3.8** Problem: early churn—illustrative (1 batch of 80 new hires)

both revenue and productivity) or rehiring having to be done, thereby increasing cost of training and hiring. She took her concerns to HR who did try to initially address the problem by sourcing through a new channel partner; refining the hiring specifications, etc. Neither of these solutions worked.

The BPO was under severe pressure as this particular line of business was due for a rebid, and clearly if the situation did not turn around the end, client may transfer the business to a competitor. Preeti then decided to escalate the matter to the CEO (Exhibit 3.8).

The situation was getting out of hand with operating costs rising rapidly and customer complaints also going up. The CEO needed to take quick action as the current churn rates impacted both revenues and the bottom line.

A cross-functional task force from a mix of Bi, planning and HR was quickly put together and tasked with finding a solution. Ravi, the task force leader believed that they had to approach the problem from a very different paradigm. They reached out and consulted Devika, a behavioural scientist who suggested that to solve the problem in a sustainable manner, they needed to take the following steps:

- Develop a "persona traits" instrument basis the presumption that certain personas passed the exam more often than other personas. Those persona traits had to be identified first.
- With the "persona traits" identified, a raw talent trait instrument had to be designed which had to be tested and validated on existing "persona groups" that had passed the exam with flying colours in the past.
- On successful testing and validation, this new "persona traits" instrument was used to hire fresh CSRs (Exhibit 3.9).

**Predictive Model Results: Over 8–10 Months**
**Key Benefits**

- Those predicted to pass exam (that did pass)—increased; true positive increased—47 to 59%
- Those predicted to pass exam (that failed)—decreased; false positive decreased—49 to 35%

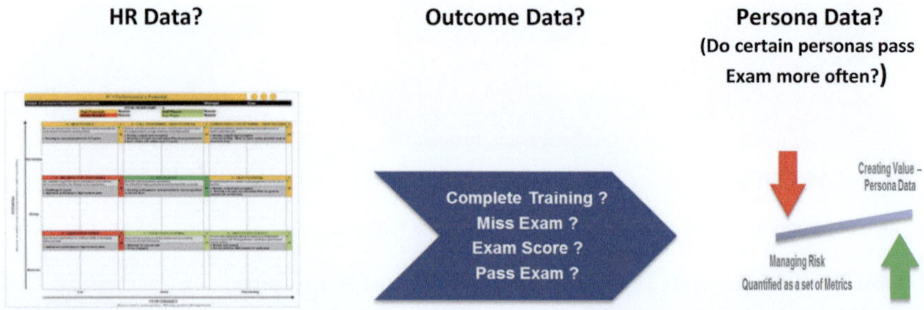


**Exhibit 3.9** Predictive model development: What data yields the maximum predictive power?

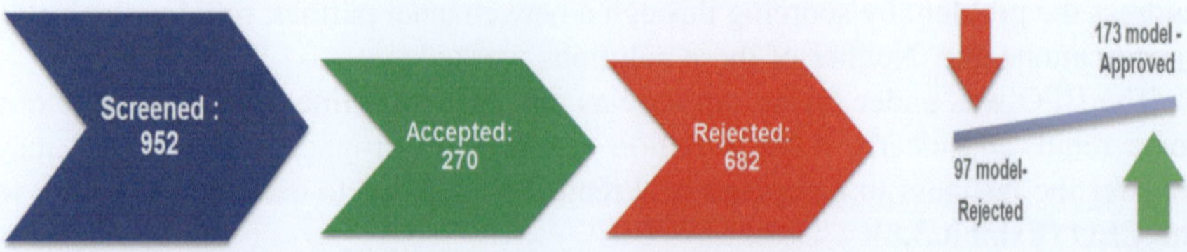




**Exhibit 3.10** Predictive model results: Over 8–10 months

ROI: 11% more pass exam; 14% less not passing examination; significant savings in hiring and training cost apart from enhanced productivity resulting from faster deployment.

**CASE 2: An illustrative example of how a BPO company developed a "predictive model" around "EMPLOYEE RETENTION"**

**Situation and Context**

A large BPO was facing massive attrition and set out to have a predictive model developed around "RETENTION" with a view towards hiring candidates who would stay and perform as opposed to getting trained and leaving early thereby impacting both profitability and customer service.

See Exhibits 3.10 and 3.11.

- The overall annual retention rate was 27%—i.e. for every 100 new hires, only 27 remained after 365 days in the dataset of 1177 employees
- After doing the clustering,two clusters identified—2 and 3, where the average retention after 1 year is 40% and 43%, respectively
- Raw talent "personas" were then developed of employees who were part of clusters 2 and 3
- By hiring candidates with "personas" as mentioned in clusters 2 and 3, the average per annum retention enhanced to>40% over a period of time.

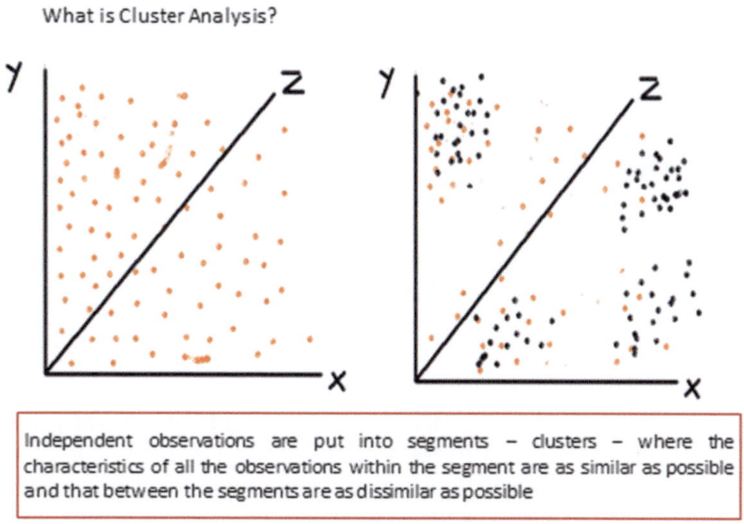




**Exhibit 3.11** A cluster analysis was done wherein "retention clusters" were identified

| Cluster Nos | Age | Last Drawn Salary | Total Exp# | BPO Exp# | Salary Monthly Avg | Row Labels | <365 days | >= 365 days | Total | % |
|---|---|---|---|---|---|---|---|---|---|---|
| Cluster 1 | 31 | 25663 | 50.6 | 38 | 27954 | 1 | 92 | 12 | 104 | 12% |
| | | | | | | | | | | |
| Cluster 2 | 24 | 12529 | 21.0 | 9 | 15167 | 2 | 241 | 163 | 404 | 40% |
| Cluster 3 | 22.5 | 6432 | 8.9 | 6 | 12564 | 3 | 73 | 55 | 128 | 43% |
| Cluster 4 | 26 | 18882 | 41 | 22 | 18955 | 4 | 458 | 83 | 541 | 15% |
| | | | | | | **Grand Total** | **864** | **313** | **1177** | **27%*** |



**Exhibit 3.12** Cluster analysis—profile mix

## Key Benefits

- Faster ramp-up to productivity
- Significantly reduced retraining cost
- Reduced staffing costs
- Higher revenue growth.

*Let us explore through another case example below how by leveraging talent analytics an organization could craft out a business focused talent acquisition strategy. The case brings out the underlying insights that can completely turn around perceived gut feeling and belief systems held for years just on the back of data patterns and analytics.*

### CASE 3: Talent Acquisition—Hiring the Best Sales Representatives in a Financial Services Company

#### The Problem

Flat sales performance coupled with a rise in employee turnover over the last couple of years leading to a decline in profitability and destabilizing business continuity.

#### Hypotheses

A large enterprise in the financial services sector operates on a belief system perpetuated over years that good performing employees essentially come with top notch educational and academic credentials from the top colleges in the country. The company therefore placed an undue weightage on academic drivers at the time of selection and hiring of fresh candidates from campuses as well as lateral hires. The overriding hypotheses held and perpetuated by the business head and the head talent acquisition was that: high academic performance was the key predictor of sales performance. Converted into statistical terminology, they held the view that: there was a significantly high correlation between high academic performance and on the job sales performance—a Pearson's correlation coefficient of 0.8 or above.

The fact remained that this "hypothesis" was held and perpetuated purely on the back of an intuitive judgement rather than any statistical validation or testing.

However, sales performance continued to remain flat with employee turnover rising sharply.

Until a year ago when the CEO decided to augment the talent management team with People Analytics by hiring Sonia, a bright young analyst who then put a small team together. She immediately got to work, coming up with a statistical analysis of sales productivity and employee turnover. She analysed a relative new joiner's sales deliverables and sought to establish linkages between individual performance and retention patterns and trends against certain other factors such as demographics, diversity, persona traits and competencies.

#### Findings

What were the factors that correlated with successful sales performance? What were the factors that drove or were key predictors of sales performance in order of priority or significance?

1. An accurate, grammatically correct resume
2. Having gone through some education at least in one's life
3. Successful sales stints across high ticket size products
4. Success or prior promotions achieved in previous roles or companies
5. Comfortable with ambiguity and thrive in unstructured work environments

6. Ability to succeed with vague instructions or minimum supervision.

What was irrelevant?

1. The candidate's academic background and credentials
2. The college or institution the candidate studied in
3. Reference quality.

**Result and Benefit: Data told a very different story despite a deeply embedded belief system**

1. The traditional belief system/hypotheses held were proven wrong with data.
2. Within six months of implementing, a new screening process revenues increased significantly.

*A case example of talent mix and sales competency forecasting to build Organized Trade selling capability at a global FMCG company to take advantage of the massive retail/modern trade opportunity in India.*

**CASE 4: Sales Competency Forecasting and Restructuring Sales Organization for Organized Trade**

**Situation and Context**

In the early 2000s in India, consumer companies were exploring alternate channels beyond the general trade kirana ecosystem and evaluating the large format retail channel which was starting to boom. However, the challenges were immense as the organization structure was not geared for Organized Trade; moreover, the sales teams did not possess the set of competencies required to sell in a very different channel and format.

The CEO then decided to pilot a new organization structure for Organized Trade in the city of Mumbai and put together a cross-functional task force consisting of members from HR, sales and planning to come up with a solution. This would have to be cost neutral with no additional cost on headcount/salaries.

The task force then got to work along two streams:

1. Stream 1 focused on role benchmarking and competency assessment with a view to first identifying the "To-Be" new competencies required for Organized Trade selling, i.e. negotiation skills; commercial acumen on ROI; merchandizing, etc.; and then putting existing sales team members through an internal assessment to see who came close to matching the new requirements. Those closest to a match were identified as individuals who could take on the new role and be part of the Organized Trade Sales team.
2. Stream 2 focused on diagnosing the existing Sales organization structure with a view to identifying opportunities to squeeze out headcount to fund the new

Organized Trade Sales organization. This was done through analysing spans of control and optimizing reporting layers.

**Key Challenges**

- Growing Organized Trade
- High-cost structures
- People quality and competencies
- CandFA handling
- High number of SKUs.

**Key Objectives**

- Process design for order-based go-to-market
- Sales organization structure redesign
- Sales competencies redesign for Organized Trade
- Resourcing strategy: cost optimization.

**Leveraging Analytics**

- Study of organization structure and roles across FMCGs
- Benchmarking on essential competencies of Organized Trade across industry
- Sales competencies redesign basis findings
- Process mapping to drive manpower cost optimization
- Role and accountability matrix redesigned.

**Key Outcomes**

- New set of roles for Organized Trade: innovation; activation; execution; delivery; merchandizing
- New set of sales competencies: category management; commercial acumen; managing cross-functional teams; negotiation skills; managing in-store execution; shopper insights; revenue management
- Revenue and market share impact
- Tighter and more effective team management.

**Key Tools Leveraged**

1. **Role Benchmarking and Competency Assessment**

The ability to pinpoint what made the difference between the excellent achievements of one sales first line manager and the much lower level of performance of another was the driver behind role benchmarking and competence assessment. When someone consistently achieves excellence, it is often said "they are a natural". Modelling allowed the team to examine in detail exactly what someone does and the thinking strategies and behaviours behind what they do apart from other tangible and demographic factors.

A model of excellence was formed from data collection from both structured and unstructured sources: structured: performance data, development/assessment centre data, project delivery data, 360 degree data as well as unstructured: interviews and the observations of individuals currently performing the role(s) as well as their key stakeholders, dealers, customers, etc., in order to identify the knowledge, skills, values, beliefs, motivation drivers, and working patterns that make them behave and perform in the way they do. A RAC/SI matrix was used to arrive at task-specific ownership.

2. **Span of Control Analyser—SOC analysed to identify risks and opportunities**
   - Underutilization—26 managers who have only 1–2 employees reporting in to them
   - Sweet spot—47 managers who have between 6 and 10 employees reporting in to them
   - Twilight zone—48 Managers who have between 11 and 19 employees reporting in to them
   - Overstretched—31 managers who have between 20 and 30 employees reporting in to them (Exhibits 3.12, 3.13 and 3.14).
   - 34% employees in Level 1 with 45% employees in level 4/5 revealing a top heavy organization bulging in the middle layers of the Sales organization.

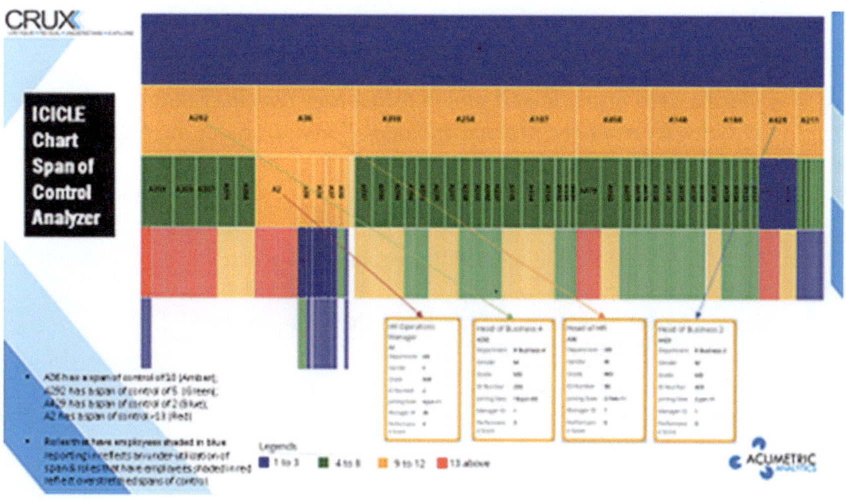




**Exhibit 3.13** Span of control icicle chart

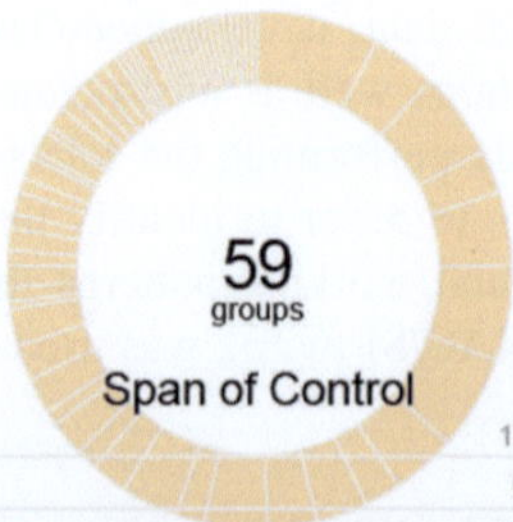


| | | |
|---|---|---|
| 1 | 17 | 0.3 % |
| 2 | 9 | 0.1 % |
| 3 | 12 | 0.2 % |
| 4 | 6 | 0.1 % |
| 5 | 10 | 0.2 % |
| 6 | 13 | 0.2 % |
| 7 | 13 | 0.2 % |
| 8 | 9 | 0.1 % |
| 9 | 5 | 0.1 % |
| 10 | 7 | 0.1 % |
| 11 | 7 | 0.1 % |
| 12 | 9 | 0.1 % |
| 13 | 4 | 0.1 % |
| 14 | 8 | 0.1 % |
| 15 | 5 | 0.1 % |
| 16 | 3 | 0.0 % |
| 17 | 5 | 0.1 % |
| 18 | 2 | 0.0 % |
| 19 | 5 | 0.1 % |
| 20 | 5 | 0.1 % |
| 21 | 5 | 0.1 % |
| 22 | 1 | 0.0 % |
| 23 | 2 | 0.0 % |
| 24 | 3 | 0.0 % |
| 25 | 2 | 0.0 % |
| 26 | 3 | 0.0 % |
| 27 | 2 | 0.0 % |
| 28 | 3 | 0.0 % |
| 29 | 2 | 0.0 % |
| 30 | 3 | 0.0 % |



**Exhibit 3.14** Span of control analysis

- This enabled the leadership to restructure the organization with optimized spans of control leading to both suitable stretch for sales managers as well as enabling better supervision, performance management and control.
- This had a spin-off on engagement levels as well with engagement levels going up in the sales teams, leading to reduced churn and attrition.

*Let us explore a case example of a global technology company that used advanced People Analytics leveraging "predictive models" and artificial intelligence to hire from passive talent pools.*

## CASE 5—Passive Talent Pool Recruiting

Organization X wanted to line up a list of probables for its "head of research and development" role.

Traditional (As-Is) approach did not bring the right results.

- Open search (job portals, walk-ins, consultants, print adverts)
- Manual scouting for talent
- Manually checking interest/fitment
- If yes: interview/assess/select/offer.

New To-Be approach leveraging predictive models applied. This involved

- Daily refresh from existing paid databases (portals)
- How? Algorithm that could scan/scoop match job/role requirements to CVs

- Prepare job descriptions/key words in specified templates
- Apply algorithm on paid databases
- Once "match" was identified, started to track their online footprint (deployed cookies/other ways)
- Invited them to join some database/community.

A team was put together to develop the algorithm.

1. Format for capturing all the key words
2. Assign weightage to each key word or cluster of key words
3. Qualifications/weightages
4. All of the above led to the algorithm having been developed.

**Output**

- Match sheet: key dimensions of the role (Point x weightage = score)
- Position 1: Cluster 1/C2/C3/C4
  Why of rating? Weightage score per dimension/backed by online footprint (courses, blogs, employers, school, alumni, batchmates, referral network, tweets, cibil score, searches)
- Intelligently analysed
- Final algorithm developed.

**Final Output**

Page 1: Context map
Page 2: Filtered relevant online tyre marks
Page 3: Subjective analysis
Page 4: Match positive—new ways found on engaging actively.

**Key Benefits**

- Time to fill cycle time dramatically reduced by more than 50%
- Cost to hire reduced by @75% as consultant /vendor costs were saved
- Reduced managerial time on hiring process thereby allowing them to focus on business
- Enhanced "match" to roles—ensuring better "role fit" leading to enhanced performance.

# 4 Deploy and Embed Analytics—Employee Lifecycle

## 4.1 Context

In most organizations, taking a rigorous, fact-based approach to decision-making about the people side of the business will represent a new way of doing things. Some managers and executives will understand quickly and embrace it. Others will come along more slowly. Therefore, a follow through strategy is necessary, including periodically touching base with stakeholders to see how they are using the findings and insights, and what can be done to help them make more effective use of the analysis. Finding ways to celebrate the success of "early adopters" can help to get the word out to the rest of the organization, so they can better understand the potential benefits they might realize with the use of People Analytics. Ultimately, People Analytics should be embedded in business processes and an organization's performance management system. When an organization has arrived at a point where People Analytics is being used to guide major investment and strategic choices, it will be able to have a significant, positive, and ongoing impact on the organization.

## 4.2 Staged Approach

Depending on its appetite and evolution in terms of data access, availability, integrity as well as leadership's vision relating to analytics and its deployment in determining business outcomes, organizations can choose their entry point on this journey. The fact remains that the bulk of organizations is still struggling at the bottom of the pyramid, trying to get their basic data sorted out: still trying to arrive at the single version of the truth. However, we do see a number of organizations that have scaled up the pyramid to explore both descriptive and predictive models.



R. Ghatak, *People Analytics*, Management for Professionals,
https://doi.org/10.1007/978-981-19-3873-3_4

The vast majority of organizations are still struggling to come to terms with the scale and complexity of data to manage. This is made all the more difficult as organizations become global with each geography/region having its own reporting structures, systems and frequency of updates. This mass of non-standard data prevents any real analysis and insight generation as the data itself is so fragmented and restrictive.

While this has led to large-scale HCM project implementations to ensure uniform, standard data workflows and reporting structures, it has still not addressed the question of insight generation for enabling effective people and business decisions. As a result, the more mature organizations from an HR analytics deployment perspective have started focusing their efforts on the following:

1. Visual intelligence
2. Descriptive modelling
3. Predictive analytics.

These efforts have started bearing fruit as the ROI from these interventions has already started paying back several times over.

The **People Analytics maturity pyramid** provides a broad framework for organizations to decide on the stage and nature of their journey as they seek to deploy and embed HR analytics.

A 2013 Deloitte report categorized 480 organizations into four clusters based on the maturity of People Analytics deployment. The research revealed that those companies that had reached an advanced level were few and far between with the majority still working to put together a data ecosystem. The study concluded that a massive 86% of the organizations surveyed were focused largely on reporting with a merely 10% of organizations having moved forward into advanced analytics—helping business leaders solve their talent challenges through statistical analyses and data science frameworks. Again, a miniscule 4% organizations were using predictive analytics to predict future talent outcomes (Bersin by Deloitte) (Exhibit 4.1).

Taking a broader approach to People Analytics in an integrated manner could be a starting point for HR. The following are some of the factors necessary for the successful and meaningful implementation of HR analytics:

- **Start from the top**—The commitment to an analytics-driven approach requires to be driven from the top leadership who support and put their trust behind an empirical evidence-based framework. The changes in culture, mindsets, competencies and processes that adoption of People Analytics would entail for the HR function and the wider business requires to be understood and supported by them.

  HR professionals must possess an understanding of basic statistical methods along with basic problem-solving approaches coupled with some comfort around data-driven and evidence-based frameworks. They need to back their gut-, convention-and intuitive-driven instincts with fact and data.

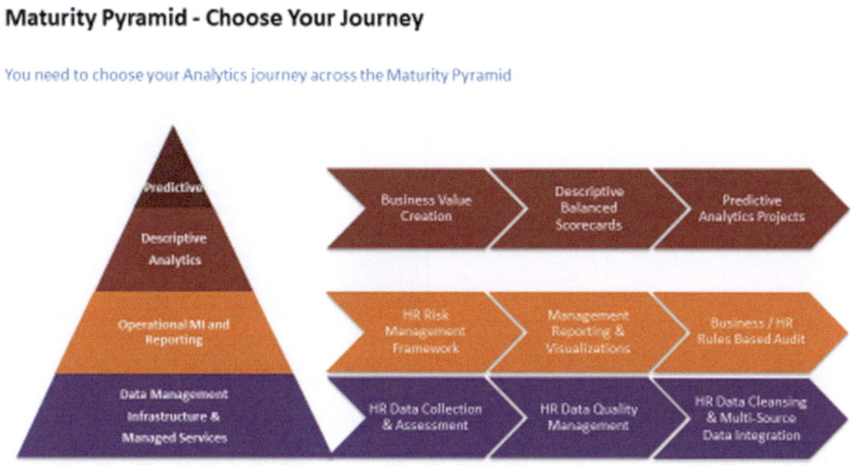




**Exhibit 4.1** People Analytics maturity pyramid

- **One platform—one team**—The data management, digital and analytics ecosystem require an integrated platform with shared tolls and technologies. This will ensure a "single source of truth", provide data visibility within and across teams and will mitigate risks related to inconsistent reporting standards, techniques, formats and definitions.

  Recruit talent who come with high-quality numeric and analytical competencies can simplify complex phenomena and can engage proactively with those who make decisions. Analytics and problem-solving competencies would need to be developed among existing team members. They need to be made aware of the data ecosystem and methods of analysis along with the latest tools and technologies, and they must learn to recognize common patterns and insights that these analyses throw up.
- **Linkage to outcomes**—Channel resources into analytics initiatives that most directly serve the company's strategy. Companies need to focus analytics into activities such as improving customer loyalty, employee productivity and employee engagement. HR must measure, test and evaluate quantitative evidence. Leaders should then gauge and reward performance the same way—applying metrics to compensation and rewards.
- **Drive technology**—Organizations need to be prepared to spend significant resources on technology such as enterprise resource planning (ERP) systems. Standard formats, integrated platforms and secure data warehouses are critical for success (Exhibit 4.2).

Companies using analytics for people management can create tangible value as long as following are addressed:

**Exhibit 4.2** Stages of analytics

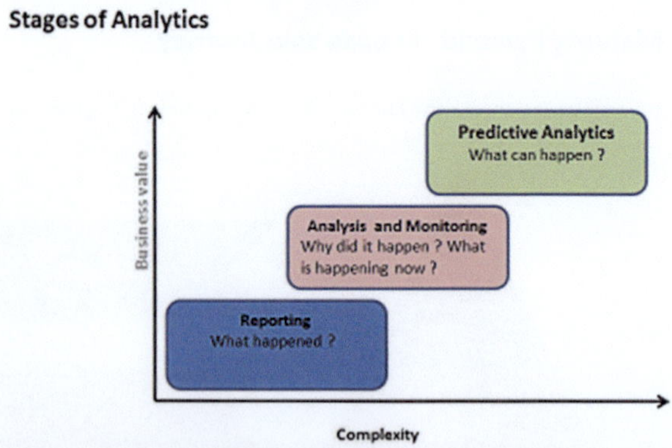


*Source: Akshay Raje "Paper on Analytics"*

- People Analytics addresses the changes in organizational goals and priorities
- Using a common platform across all levels of employees—it would be futile to utilize analytics for decision-making only for junior or mid-level employees but not for senior management.
- Narrow line of sight—Avoid over reliance on certain metrics for decision-making
- Make a beginning—Seeking perfection in collection of data before applying analytics may result in never-ending decision-making
- Tag qualitative inputs into meaningful information—It is important to capture qualitative metrics and translate that into quantitative measures.

## 4.3 Employee Lifecycle Management

The journey of the employee in an organization can be divided into various stages. Employee lifecycle management is the essence of People Analytics. HR can intervene at every stage to drive efficiencies and garner the benefits of analytics.

Different phases in the employee lifecycle are:

- Attract
- Plan
- Enable and engage
- Grow
- Retain.

Analytics which can be done under each of the five stages is:

- **Attract Phase:**
  - Recruitment Analytics: It is analytics employed at the stage of recruiting employees, e.g. what are the characteristics which HR/hiring manager should look for while recruiting.

  - Early Leavers: Predict the candidates who are likely to attrite within the first three months of joining.
  - Hiring Channel Optimization: Analyse which recruitment channel is most cost-effective
  - Demand Forecasting: Analyse skill gaps and requirements for current and future
  - Diversity Management: Analyse opportunity and impact for diversity and inclusion.
- **Plan Phase:**
  - Building Bench Strength: Plan the succession bench for the organization
  - People Placement: Analyse role fit for people and match people to roles
  - Resource Utilization Prediction: Analyse optimal use of resources.
- **Enable and Engage:**
  - Capabilities: Assess the impact of training to determine training effectiveness
  - Rewards: Analyse the rewards and recognition programmes and asses their impact on employee performance and retention.
- **Grow:**
  - Careers: Analyse the key drivers of success and/or performance
  - Job/Role: Assess the impact of job rotation on success/satisfaction of candidates
  - Potential: Assess potential vs performance to bet on critical talent.
- **Retain:**
  - Attrition and Churn: Predict the likelihood of an employee to attrite
  - Early Warning: Develop an early warning system for attrition
  - Retention programmes: Analyse the effectiveness/impact of retention programmes.

The way is to integrate data from HR systems or data repositories with data from other domains such as finance, sales, CRMs, production and bring out the inter-linkages by transforming the multiple data streams into an integrated output that throws up powerful visualizations leading to rich insight into how seemingly disparate factors impact people and business outcomes.

- **Benefits of Employee Lifecycle Management:**

  1. **Improved Speed and Accuracy**
     SLA-driven turnaround for HR queries, reduced errors, creation of a complete employee database
  2. **Reduced Operational cost**
     It is flexible resourcing, lower and virtualized cost, process automation. Improving overall profitability through more effective workforce cost control, thereby increasing the ROIs of different activities
  3. **Improved business insights**
     The focus is not to just get reports but insights into the data, e.g. providing managers insight into better manage workforce performance and capabilities,

giving visibility into top or bottom-performing employees to better develop and retain key talents, proactively identifying employees who are likely to attrite and developing strategies around retention to prevent the high performing employees from exiting, enabling managers to correlate workforce data with operating metrics to comprehend more deeply the impact of people investment on business results.

- **Organizational Success Measurement**
  Establish definition of success, measure improvements in metrics and drive initiatives to improving metrics

***The twin forces of big data and analytics to gain the desired results***
Changing business environment has been forcing HR professionals to graduate to more advanced and forward-looking analytics techniques. This could be the beginning of a shift in the way the role of HR is changing to collect, connect, analyse, visualize and disseminate intelligence and insight that will influence the decisions about the future direction of their organizations.

## 4.4 Capabilities and Skill Sets for People Analytics Deployment

Though software tools and data drive analysis and decision-making, they are clearly not as critical as the people behind them: one never comes across an analytically oriented organization without analytically oriented people. Hiring, developing, deploying and retaining analysts—the people who make up the vital cogs of an organizations wheel—is critical to long-term success.

It can also be observed that effective analysts need to be proficient not only with data, but also with people, incorporating all of the following skill sets:

- Quantitative inclusive of statistical tools and modelling
- Analytics technology
- Business knowledge and design
- Relationship and consulting
- Coaching and staff development.

Four types of analytical people exist within an organization:

- Analytics champions—decision-makers in managerial roles who depend heavily on data analyses to make business decisions and who lead major digital and/or analytics projects.
- Analytics professionals—proficient and knowledgeable analysts across the range of statistical, quantitative skills and data science frameworks and tools.

- Analytics executers—apply the models and frameworks developed by professionals on behalf of the business functions.
- Analytics amateurs/enthusiasts—those whose primary role is not analytics, but who need some understanding of the domain to successfully do their jobs.

Having the right type of analytics talent, with the right types of quantitative, business, relationship, consulting and coaching skills is absolutely necessary—but is not sufficient in and of itself. Analytics needs to be embedded in business processes and built into an organization's culture. Whenever one visits an organization that is well versed in analytics, it is usually apparent that an analytical mindset is deeply embedded into its culture and DNA. The principles of an analytical culture transcend the actual attitudes of individual decision-makers, and they are rarely communicated as structured checklists of things to do—they are largely concepts and ways of doing things that these gifted individuals just know.

These are no doubt, challenging asks for HR practitioners just getting started on People Analytics or for those who are part of organizations that are unstructured and which do not give data and analysis the respect they deserve. For those generalist HR practitioners who are keen to chart out a career in People Analytics, they need to start building a repository of skills and acquire a set of competencies that would enable them to make that transition in a relatively seamless manner.

## 4.5 Critical Competencies

To summarize, the critical competencies for People Analytics practitioners would be as encapsulated below:

| Competency Descriptors |
|---|
| Ability to determine what should be measured to assess if the organization is delivering on its goals—lead and lag KPIs |
| Ability to embed systems thinking to find interconnected factors within complex organizational problems |
| Design a plan for gathering data and implementing operational and strategic HR Analytics |
| Leveraging data science towards forecasting, scenario modelling and prediction to drive business outcomes |
| Deploying strategy maps to understand how vision links into operational goals and performance |
| Understand advanced statistical modelling tools and techniques to establish relationships across variables—segmentation, multidimensional analysis to understand cause and delivery of actionable solutions |
| Understand end to end organization design, people–process mapping and workforce planning using HR and talent analytics |
| Ability to identify key HR risks—present and future and build out a mitigation plan leveraging analytics |

| Competency Descriptors |
| --- |
| Understand HR data structures and deploying the optimal technology architecture to solve for business problems/drive business outcomes |
| Ability to cost model people metrics impacting business outcomes using analytics models |
| Project management skills in terms of both managing and leading project teams to deliver key outcomes |

The four essential skills that are increasingly being required for HR business partners who seek to deploy and embed People Analytics are:

- Connecting HR decisions to business outcomes
- Data-based reasoning and innovation
- Social intelligence
- Creative problem-solving.

## 4.6 Where Do Companies Begin?

Organizations have now started to realize the importance of building in-house People Analytics capabilities. By and large, two approaches have been followed: the first approach is to create a small team within the HR function and train this team to explore the domain through various inputs around statistical techniques, open-source platform training such as R and Python, storytelling techniques using data and so on. The purpose is not only to create a small island of expertise within the function but also to get this team to spread and share their skills with other teams within the HR domain in order that they sensitize the business leadership about the business impact of leveraging people data effectively. The second approach is to create a cross-functional team with members from HR, IT, business, etc., thereby ensuring a diversity of perspective where different mindsets and skills interact and engage with each other to create insights around workforce management. Studies have demonstrated that the second approach is more sustainable, creates greater impact and brings in the buy-in from business leaders far quicker. Ideally, a mix of individuals from engineering, talent specialists from HR, business intelligence or business planning and/or organization psychologist as well as from sales or business analytics would bring in a diverse set of capabilities that would enable such a team to hit the ground running much quicker. What is critical here is sponsorship from the very top as people from other functions should not be made to feel that they are being sidelined into HR; this therefore needs to be positioned well as a catalyst for change within the organization; in some instances. It could also be a rotational move for some where those from other functions spend a few years and then go back to their parent function.

What about the HR professional? Would not they need to reinvent themselves by doing the following things: first, asking the right business questions; second, becoming familiar with the tools and language; third, becoming a sharp and smart consumer of data and fourth; becoming a strategic business partner. But where is this new age HR professional going to come from? Universities and professional associations need to respond to this growing need and reinvent their curriculum to include workforce analytics.

While some organizations have set up their own teams, some others have seemingly preferred an outsourced option using consulting and data science specialists. Even in such a scenario, however, HR team members still need to develop competencies around asking the right business questions and then hone their skills to understand the analytics output and their impact on the business. The HR function would need a reinvention of sorts to ensure greater relevance in a world that is transforming rapidly and convince business leaders and shareholders that it is capable of delivering compelling talent, performance, engagement and productivity-centred insights that will have a significant impact on Organizational performance.

## 4.7 A Case Well Documented is Around—How a Large Technology Company Developed Its Renowned Workforce Analytics Team

By the middle of the last decade, this organization employed a headcount of @10,000 and was growing at a rapid pace, increasing in size every year. Even though it was perceived to be an exciting and innovative workplace, the company's selection process was laborious. It was a highly time-consuming process taking weeks to complete before the selected candidates eventually joined. The lengthy process frustrated candidates on the one hand, and on the other hand, precious time was wasted of company managers running these interviews, time that could have been more optimally spent on their core activities.

The company deployed an analytics approach to streamline this process. An internal study revealed that in an ideal state the maximum number of candidate interviews was four in number. Early research, for example, demonstrated that the optimum number of candidate interviews was four. Any interview beyond this would lead to the cost of having managers away from their roles, outweighing whatever benefits were accrued from these additional interviews. However, before the team got to the analytics stage, work had to be done towards ensuring suitable data was collected, sorted and cleansed over a set of variables ranging from job applicant details to interviewers to scores to headcount numbers across staff categories to churn and other data points over history. With this massive data repository, it gradually dawned on the company that it was sitting on a gold mine of data that could be mined, analysed and leveraged as part of its People Analytics agenda and scope.

The team then explored other areas, such as relationship between pay and rewards, nudging individuals towards demonstrating desired behaviours, core values and well-being (from nutrition to financial planning) and providing useful guidance to clients around business growth. Keeping pace with the rapid changes taking place both internally and externally, the team expanded its scope of work to focus on behavioural and social science research, which could become the bedrock for future workforce and business decisions and practices. The team got down to dealing with phenomena and areas that the business did not necessarily bubble up to solve in the immediate term but were issues that the company wanted to comprehend better taking a long-term view of things, requiring more time and depth of analysis. The team soon came to be seen as a research hub for cutting-edge work that would propel the practice forward and create a name for itself both within the company and outside. Supported by their relationships with researchers and university academics, the team started to run various experiments and projects to test out their ideas and hypotheses.

## 4.8 People Analytics: Integrated into HR Service Delivery Model

The HR department itself is an excellent place to get started in this transition, by starting to hire, develop and reward analytical people. It is always important to remember, however, that People Analytics, "is not just an HR exercise—it requires the collaboration of IT, HR and the business to bring together the tools and information with the expertise to use that information in meaningful ways". More importantly, People Analytics needs to be integrated into the HR service delivery model and structure.

## 4.9 Pitfalls to Avoid

There are numerous hazards along the path to successfully using and embedding People Analytics in an organization. The following represent some of the more common or dangerous traps, along with various authors' perspectives on why they should be avoided:

*Measuring the easy stuff rather than what is critical*

HR teams often focus on tactical operational metrics that improve the efficiency of their own function rather than staying focused on the business imperatives and getting more strategic with their approach.

*Thinking that Benchmarking is Analytics*

Benchmarking is merely a comparator tool to drive comparisons across similar phenomena to understand where one stands versus competition. It does not generate by itself any actionable insights that would impact individual or organizational performance.

*Assuming that one solution fits all situations and contexts*

Drawing conclusions on the back of generalizations without researching the current situation or context is a common pitfall. A simple example is employee engagement: the drivers could be dramatically different even though the companies concerned may be in the same sector or location.

*Getting caught in the ROI conundrum*

The ROI approach is a myopic one, is constraining and does not do justice to the complete possibilities that People Analytics and decision science can uncover. People Analytics is not about here and now business benefits; it is about anticipating the future on the back of decision support tools and predictive insights, the monetary value of which cannot be computed accurately upfront, but which has the potential to transform business models and drive strategic shifts in thinking.

*Striving for perfection rather than getting started first*

There could be occasions when you may not have all the relevant data to run the analysis which often is used as an excuse not to get started. The other pitfall is to strive for that perfect statistical model or correlation that would prove or disprove a particular hypothesis. This approach does not help the business; it is critical to get started and work with data that is available; also deploy the models which bring out the key insights that can be actioned upon rather than the perfect correlation.

*Claiming People Analytics for HR and HR only*

Data science and People Analytics is a cross-functional domain and requires people with multiple backgrounds and competencies to collaborate and work together; it cannot be deployed in a silo, compartmentalized approach.

*Other Common Mistakes*

- Holding on to a metric even when it has ceased to be relevant
- Banking on only a few metrics to evaluate performance which exposes you to risk
- Insisting on perfection and total accuracy of data before even starting an analysis
- Restricting oneself to simple measures to predict success, such as test scores or qualifications
- Deploying analytics only for mass hiring at lower levels rather than niche hiring at senior levels where the cost of mistakes could even lead to the company shutting down
- Focusing on HR efficiency metrics only instead of HR and talent management on business performance.

Some other barriers could be:

**Cultural**—Workforce analytics will be implemented by individuals in organizations. As a result, it could happen that personal biases and feelings, which are natural aspects of the human condition, will have its effect here too. These factors may impact the pace of the data juggernaut, but will be powerless to contain it. There are still many leaders who base their decisions on gut, intuition and wisdom of experience. However, evidence-based insights from rigorous data mining can quickly expose gaps and loopholes in such decisions, thus potentially undermining those who solely relied on them. Does this therefore make leaders insecure? This fear is, however, completely unfounded. Evidence-based insight using analytics should be viewed as an enabler, not a one or the other. The responsibility of making decisions will continue to rest on the manager: that is certainly not going away. The only change that has come in is that the data ecosystem with its tools and methods are available to managers to enhance the probability of them taking the right and optimal decisions for the business and acting proactively on the back of hard evidence and insights.

**Ethical**—Big data brings with it critical issues of ethics, data privacy and data security, the various aspects of which are still in the process of being understood by organizations and society as a whole. Companies now have the tools to peek into and collect all kinds of personal information related to their employees as well as prospective hires and candidates but can they legally do so? To what extent should an organization go in collecting personal data of employees or candidates and who decides the acceptable limits or data thresholds? Further, how will companies respond to the conclusions of their own analytics evidence? Will it lead them to, for instance, passing on or avoiding hiring those candidates that as per the data analysed are more likely to churn relatively early?

To overcome these pitfalls and obstacles, organizations need to focus on the following:

Enhance critical analytics related competencies within HR teams; ensure high-quality and standardized data, thereby getting it analytics ready; run those projects that are key to solving business problems; be rigorous in analysis; strike a balance between accuracy and pattern development. Go for small wins, the big ones will follow shortly. Go with the cross-functional approach around data collection and integration and analysis. Engage with your people and provide them the comfort that analytics deployment is meant to support decision-making and enhance their capabilities and not seek to make them redundant. Understand the legal and ethical complexities of employee monitoring. organizations will need to be open about their sources of data; why a particular set of data is being collected and for what purpose? They need to explain how all this data collection and analysis will benefit the employee and the organization in times to come.

People Analytics brings together people and talent, roles, processes, competencies and goals to build an integrated view of the organization. It is this view understood and analysed holistically that enables fact and data-based decision-making, thereby contributing to enhanced business performance on a sustainable basis (Exhibits 4.3 and 4.4).

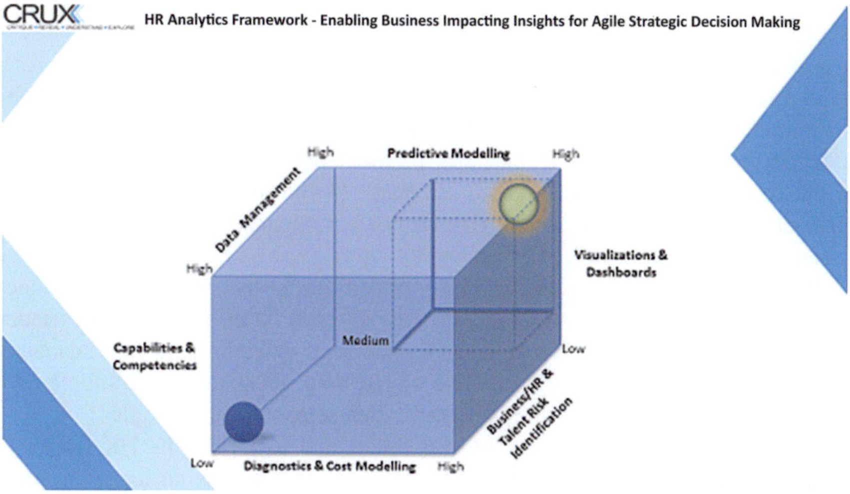




**Exhibit 4.3** People Analytics framework

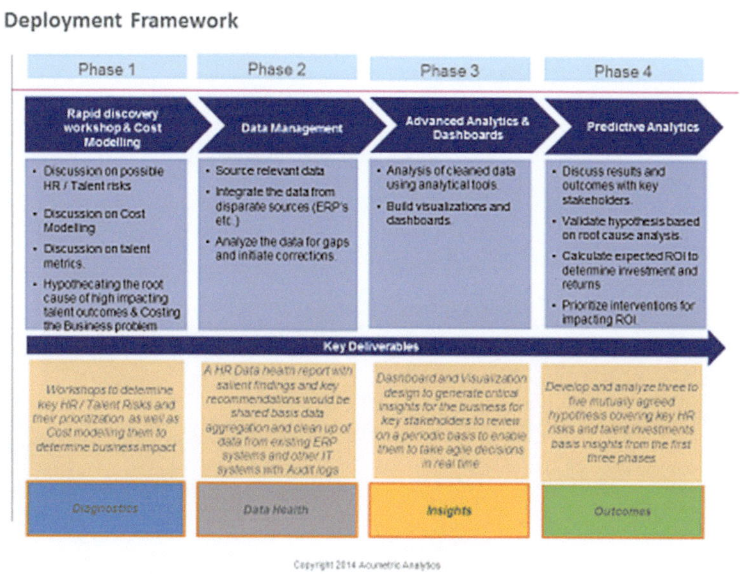




**Exhibit 4.4** Deployment road-map

## 4.10 Summing-up

It is an absolute imperative for organizations to build capability in the People Analytics space and integrate it into the HR delivery model in organizations, thereby institutionalizing it. There is a whole new set of competencies that could either redefine the role of the "HR business partner" or create an entirely new role in the form of the "HR analyst/data scientist" on the lines of "analyst" roles in other domains for example "credit risk analyst" or "financial planning analyst" or "consumer insight analyst".

The core HR curriculum needs to be enriched further by including data science frameworks and paradigms which hitherto do not exist. Statistical and data science modelling frameworks, tools and technologies need to be brought into academia with a view towards building a pipeline of HR data scientists who combine core HR domain understanding with quantitative data science methodologies.

There is a severe gap in this skill set today, and it is time the HR fraternity in partnership with academia do something about it. There is an urgent need to revisit both the curricula and the core competencies required for HR professionals to succeed in leading change by driving business outcomes at both tactical and strategic levels. The future of HR depends on it.

# 5 Data and Social, Mobile, Analytics, Cloud (SMAC)

## 5.1 Context

A key question that large organizations globally are struggling with is the critical need for standardization and uniformity around data, formats, templates, business rules and reporting metrics: with a view towards arriving at a single version of the truth and in turn the ability to take timely and effective global workforce decisions.

The datafication trends that we see in HR, herein, provides the opportunity to turn HR into a competitive advantage. The sheer volume, variety, velocity we see in people data today requires both a mindset and technology shift of significant proportion involving change management of a very different kinds.

## 5.2 The Future of People Management Will Be Grounded in Data

Data analytics is changing the way the world works. The organizations which apply analysis and evidence-based insight to how they manage their workforce today, and plan for the future, will get ahead of the game. In a world where talent is both hard to find and retain, where the total cost of employment is one of the biggest costs to an organization, and where in regulated industries working out how to ensure your people actively manage their conduct risk—are all becoming issues not just relevant to the HR function but across the whole board—can you afford to be operating blind?

Organizations that want to leverage People Analytics need to have access to high-quality data and organize the same across the enterprise, support analytical leaders, choose realistic targets for analysis and hire people with relevant skill sets. Which organizations are taking on these challenges, why have they prioritized this and are they equipped towards meeting these challenges? Much of the data about this currently comes from a variety of surveys in which organizations self-report



R. Ghatak, *People Analytics*, Management for Professionals,
https://doi.org/10.1007/978-981-19-3873-3_5

their success in this domain. What specific factors are driving organizations to turn to People Analytics? Analysing 2009 survey results from 233 companies in which more than two-thirds use reporting or analytics, or are currently building those capabilities, Lombardi and White found that the two factors most prominently driving the use of analytics were an organization's need to adapt to the dynamic external environment and factors around optimization forcing more rigour around people management decisions.

Based on a survey of over 400 North American HR professionals, IBM/Cognos found that there was significant consensus on the major benefits of People Analytics, with 76% citing improvements in workforce management, 69% citing improved levels of workforce productivity and 67% highlighting greater return on investments in talent management.

The IBM/Cognos survey found that 33% of respondents with a formal People Analytics application or system in place also reported that they were more effective in five different areas than those without an analytics system: (a) developing training strategies, (b) determining strategies for reduction in force, redeployment and retraining, (c) understanding collaboration and knowledge sharing, (d) retaining valued talent within the organization and (e) evaluating workforce performance. Research studies have highlighted that companies leveraging People Analytics and data science tools and methodologies are largely using them for purposes of identifying critical patterns and trends. A miniscule set of evolved organizations have started using analytics for deriving crucial insights as well as creating predictive and futuristic models and projections. While 36% of the organizations using workforce analytics identify historical patterns and trends in evaluating workforce performance, only 8% develop scenarios and predict future outcomes in the area of workforce performance. Similarly, 30% track historical trends in retaining valued talent, but only 9% predict future outcomes. The authors conclude that the application of further advanced analytics tools and frameworks to analyse workforce dynamics and capabilities are still very much at an initial stage.

Data from IBM/Cognos help to shed some light on broad ways to bridge the gap between the analytics knowledge residing within the HR function and how it can be applied by managers elsewhere in the organization. Their survey found that in organizations where the use of People Analytics "proactively contributes to strategy", 48% of non-HR senior managers use workforce analytics data (when available), compared with only 29% of non-HR senior executives in other organizations.

Similarly, Whiteley assessed the results of a survey of over 100 business and HR leaders and found only 12% of respondents reported that they could identify returns on human capital investments. However, among respondents reporting HR plays a "strategic" role in the organization, 50% describe themselves as being able to identify returns on human capital investment (compared with just 2% in organizations that view the HR function as being largely administrative). The survey also found a significant gap between "actual" and "desired" level of HR's

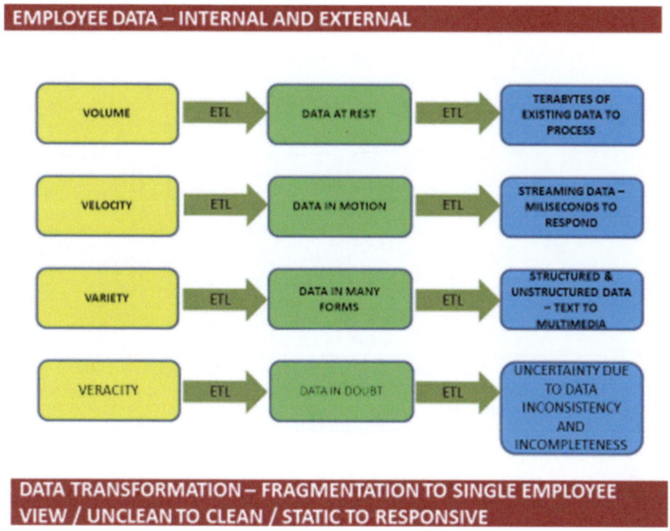




**Exhibit 5.1** Datafication—the HR data challenge/herein the opportunity

HCM capability and the function's effectiveness in contributing to strategic objectives, such as linking people with performance, talent planning and informing the organization's business strategy.

Gates also finds the most frequently used measures of human capital are not the ones most respondents believe best predict outcomes (i.e. "leading" metrics). Of the five measures that respondents are most likely to believe are leading metrics (employee engagement, leadership, employee commitment, readiness level and voluntary turnover), only two are among the metrics that are most frequently tracked (employee engagement and voluntary turnover). The other three most frequently tracked items (diversity, average age, employee satisfaction) are not among those believed to be most predictive (Exhibit 5.1).

## 5.3 People Data and Business KPI Data Integration

The opportunity does not lie alone in integrating people data across HR verticals: C&B; performance management; learning and development; resourcing and talent, etc. The scale of the opportunity enhances manifold when organizations have the opportunity of integrating this and other people data with the business KPI data, thereby throwing up real business insights for quick and effective decisions. The turnaround time taken to arrive at crucial business/people decisions has the potential of being reduced substantially.

This would involve significant change management as organizations have traditionally been used to looking at and interpreting data in a silo and not holistically.

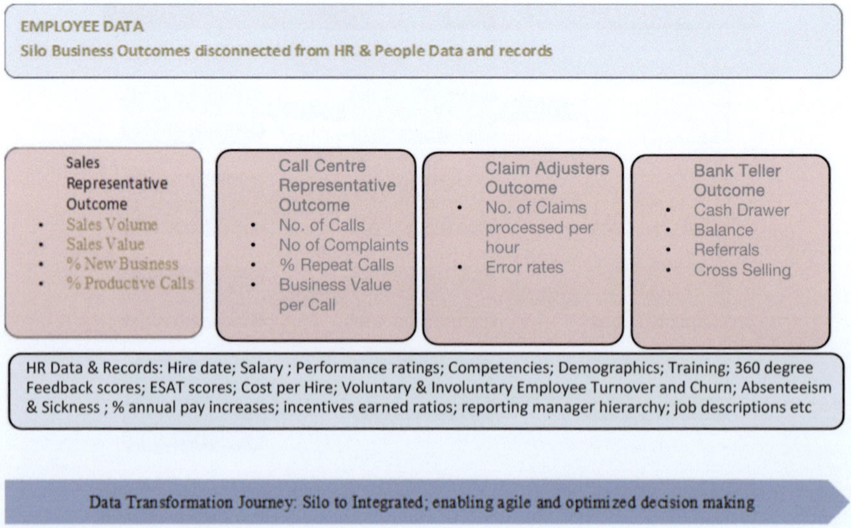


**Exhibit 5.2** Integrate "business outcomes KPI data" to "HR/people data"

The power of looking at and interpreting business KPI/HR data in an integrated manner would radically change the way HR teams are structured or managed and their mode of interaction with business leaders and teams. The critical need for timely and effective decision-making to stay ahead of competition would trigger the shift in HR organization structures and ways of working with business (Exhibit 5.2).

The data transformation continuum from data integration and reporting to insight is a journey organizations are starting to develop the appetite to embark on. This has been made all the more possible by the nature of the data itself and technologies available:

- Mostly structured
- Easy to access
- Control environment
- High value
- Evolved technologies.

Along with high-quality change management, an intelligent application of cloud technologies is also critical to make the transition. With the entry of cloud-based technologies, this question can now be addressed without incurring very much capital expenditure. The ability to mine this proliferation of people data within and outside organizations and then get it to interact with business KPI data is now eminently doable. Organizations can now get a rolled up view from a business unit to a country to a cluster to a region to a global view.

## 5.4 Challenges and Opportunities for Data Flow Management

Organizations need to be mindful of the challenges posed by the data explosion while at the same time act quickly to reap the benefits that evolved technologies and new age capabilities have to offer:

| Challenges | Opportunities |
|---|---|
| Optimising cost –time-resourcing for data extraction, transformation and loading. | 'Single accountable' outsourced services, with agreed cost per record (CPR) pricing.<br>Zero Capital Expenditure |
| International data integration from legacy systems; legislation; variations, current and archived | Global standardisation. Agile convergence. |
| Creating the 'One Source' for HR management analytics | Data-warehouse for analytics-on cloud; HRIS / ERP Agnostic |
| Data Governance | Identify country data source owners and updation; global data-warehouse gatekeeper; access and extraction rights |
| Data Protection Policies and Security | Sensitive Compensation data and personal details linked to Employee ID through unidentifiable serial number. Documented role based access controls, Masking etc. Data-warehouses certified to ISO standards. |

## 5.5 Evolved HR Technologies: SMAC—Social, Mobile, Analytics, Cloud

We are currently witnessing an explosion in the HR technology space with the digital stack once viewed as niche now pretty much mainstream. The primary reason for this explosion which has been driven by high adoption levels is SMAC. In the post-COVID-19 pandemic world, the cultural acceptance of "Work from anywhere, anytime" supplements the "Bring Your Own Device" (BYOD) trend, thereby propelling the usage of SMAC technologies across organizations big or small. It serves the mobility requirement of an individual across home and work with no need to switch devices. Further, with the sheer volume of data to be stored—cloud is gaining preference. HR is having to play a lead role in this digital transformation.

With the rapid proliferation of mobile devices and its increased use, the mobile is increasingly becoming the preferred delivery platform for HR. The challenge for enterprise applications is to make the first move to a mobile platform and then replicate the user experience and level of comfort. This has provided the opportunity to HR teams to digitize the workflows from hire to exit along with reporting and analytics in real time. This not only enhances productivity but also lays the ground for a connected workforce. HR also needs to ensure that all that investment behind HR technology and digital/data is being suitably deployed. HR needs to be aware of what tools to leverage for the outcomes it seeks to deliver, such as tools for collaboration and knowledge sharing such as Intranet portal, Yammer, GPS and location ring-fencing, voice notes and organization Network Analysis to enhance collaboration and connect within and across teams, units and locations. These tools enable organizations to fast-track their employees into digitally native mode which is a key imperative in post-COVID times.

Although business intelligence has been historically leveraging data for decision support in areas such as market research, consumer insights, financial planning, sales channel optimization, etc., Companies are starting to explore People Analytics to establish relationships and build predictive models around phenomena such a performance and pay; risk and rewards, skills and redundancies, collaboration, learning and growth, attrition and engagement, productivity and structure and so on.

The massive data and digital footprint from multiple sources manual or otherwise, i.e. HRM systems and social networks, can now be analysed. These analyses can bring out powerful correlations and linkages between people and business metrics, enabling organizations to understand how workforce dynamics are impacting business performance. SMAC provides the opportunity to throw out these analyses in the form of visualizations and dashboards in real time on multiple devices from desktops to tablets to mobile to enable managers to take decisions on the move.

With cloud-based options becoming a reality, organizations can deploy solutions and network infrastructure without incurring much capital expenditure. There are also flexible pay per use or pay-as-you-go options that are subscription based, which make them ideal and affordable for small and mid-size companies.

HR leverages SMAC to deploy analytics in an agile manner that sharpens our understanding of people and teams. SMAC sits at the heart of the new age HR toolkit that provides understanding and deep insight into areas hitherto unexplored such as social interactions, degree of collaboration, state of engagement and morale on an ongoing basis (as opposed to one or two survey dipsticks a year), knowledge sharing concerns as well as talent decisions through predictive modelling. This unique facilitation significantly enables HR to partner the business more strategically, thereby placing them at the centre of employee advocacy, culture shift and change management initiatives.

## 5.6 Leverage the Cloud

Another emerging concept is the Internet of Things (IoT) which brings out the linkages between a multiplicity of tools and devices that we use and the collective intelligence that gets generated. However, in its nascency, HR will certainly stand to again from the next wave of technology advancement.

SMAC or “**The Third Platform**” as International Data Corporation (IDC) calls it—needs to be smartly leveraged to transform the way core processes around workforce planning, rewards, performance, engagement and talent management are organized and deployed. Smart and insightful decisions can be shared with managers anytime, anywhere and on any device in real time. This is not about a black box shooting out decisions; people and managers will still make those decisions but through SMAC HR can provide managers a key menu with analysed options thereby significantly reducing the risk of making wrong talent and people decisions that could hurt the business in the medium to long term. This datafication of HR provides the function the opportunity to reinvent itself as HR could well be riding this trend as we move into the next new wave of technologies.

Let us explore a sample SMAC tool and see how it reinvents people management:

## 5.7 SMAC Tool—ORGSENS

### 5.7.1 Why ORGSENS?

It is my belief that annualized performance appraisals are an inaccurate and inefficient way to monitor, manage and reward performance. Performance management in organizations has become a chore, and the average employee satisfaction related to the annual performance management process in organizations has never been lower. The annualized performance appraisal process is a drain on organizations money and management time and more often than not leaves employees dissatisfied rather than motivating them.

ORGSENS has been designed to change that. To make appraisals data driven, make them 360° in nature and finally embed them subliminally into the organizations day-to-day operating environment and make a cultural shift in organizations towards performance management.

ORGSENS is a real-time 360 performance management mobile application. It is designed for measuring employee experience, performance and behaviour through their journey with an organization.

So how does it achieve its goals, it does so by being a non-intrusive and targeted competency and behaviour data collection and monitoring application; collecting and providing deep culture insights to organizations with minimal effort with a view to enabling organizations to shift their corporate culture.

It is a digital enabler that allows you to help organizations measure and monitor three key aspects:

- Employee experience and journey with the organization
- Employee cultural alignment to organizational behaviours
- Employee performance with a 360° view in real time.

Now let me show you how to set up a new organization in the system and use it for each one of the objectives and outcomes I stated earlier.

Let us start with employee experience through his/her journey with the organization. We all know that an employee's first 90 days are critical and determine his/her longevity and cultural alignment with the organization. Therefore, you can use ORGSENS to manage that proactively.

Next, let me show you how you can define and measure alignment to organizational behaviours. Performance is an outcome of the right behaviours so it is very important to understand the behaviours being defined and demonstrated for the various roles in the organization. A senior sales leader is supposed to demonstrate strategic skills, while a sales person is on the ground is successful if he/she can demonstrate persistence; the roles require different behaviours for success. ORGSENS allows us to measure these in real-time behaviours are also often indicators and symptomatic for future HR and talent predictions.

Last but not the least: performance management; like I said, today's annual retrospective appraisal process for performance management is sub-optimal due its lack of data; not only is it sub-optimal for measuring performance, it is also a drain on financial resources and management bandwidth. ORGSENS changes that by allowing you to define tangible goals and collecting real-time data about performance against those goals, including collecting data with a 360° view. Now when its time for appraisal, you have a person's behaviour indicators and 500+ data points on his/her performance through the year, and these data points are not retrospective making them much more real than a dated data collection which is filtered and curated.

## 5.8 Future of Work—Post-COVID-19

Work from Home! Remote Working! Virtual Team Meetings & Reviews! Remote vendor meetings! Webinar fatigue! Mental well-being challenges! Drying up of social interactions! How are individuals and teams coping with this **NEW NORMAL**! Are they staying engaged and continuing to maintain pre-lockdown levels of productivity or are they struggling to cope with the paradigm shift in ways of working? How are you keeping your finger on the pulse of your workforce ever since the COVID-19 pandemic has wreaked havoc on the world, a classic VUCA event? Can you afford to be operating blind? There is a way: **The ORGSENS WAY**:

ORGSENS—**employee engagement**! A mobile application that can be downloaded from your android or IOS play store enabling you to collect data around values, behaviours and attitudes in real time from your people and teams in byte-size chunks on the back of automated bot-driven triggers; to gauge engagement levels across a remote working and distributed workforce. The data thus collected can then be crunched into rapid analytics that can provide you with real-time actionable insights around engagement and productivity of your remote working workforce; and all of it on your mobile device in real time, enabling an agile and proactive response to red flags and other risks.

ORGSENS—**shifting your corporate culture**! The key to building a robust culture is about finding ways to embed and reinforce role-based behaviours that are reflected in core competencies. This entails the capability to collect a multitude of data points around these behaviours all in real time via automated triggers across multiple touchpoints. This data is first collected in a non-intrusive manner via byte-size chunks and then rapidly mined to produce the analytics that contribute to culture transforming decisions.

ORGSENS—**retaining critical talent**! Which employees are showing up as disengaged or seemingly as flight risks? These cases also need to be red-flagged, enabling managements to have proactive retention conversations towards ensuring you are not faced with employee attrition challenges as you seek to rapidly return to normal post the lockdown.

ORGSENS—**reinforcing employee experience from on-boarding to exit**! Business will not stop. Organizations will continue to need fresh talent and will continue to hire. However, the days of physical mass on-boarding, especially of a distributed workforce given the travel restrictions and avoidance of large gatherings, are likely to be a thing of the past. Similarly, every touchpoint in the employee lifecycle from promotion to transfer to role change to relocation needs to be converted into a delightful experience.

ORGSENS—**manage performance**! How do you monitor and track performance in real time around KPIs and core competencies, especially in a remote working environment? How do you ensure employees get real-time feedback from their peers, reporting managers and teams on an ongoing basis across a range of core competencies and KPIs, enabling them to improve and enhance performance by leveraging their strengths and bridging competency gaps.

ORGSENS—**whistleblowing**! Remote working across large distributed teams means that employees and teams will be subject to significantly less direct supervision at the work place. This increases the risk of fraud or subversive work practices leading to short cuts. Employees have the opportunity to send in anonymous feedback or whistle blow where they see or feel that a fraud is being committed or subversive practices are being resorted to. Its anonymous feedback functionality allows employees to vent and share their feelings and frustrations at the work place.

**ORGSENS** takes your people management to a whole new level. That is the power of **SMAC** (Exhibit 5.3).

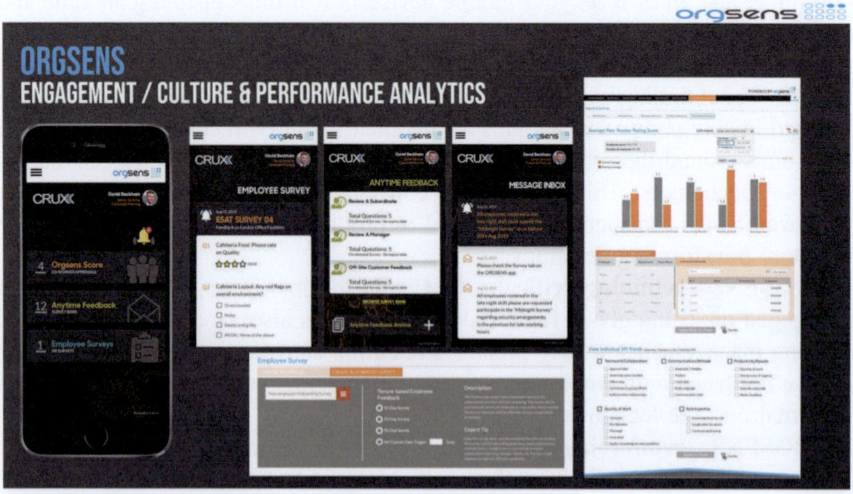




**Exhibit 5.3** ORGSENS illustrative SMAC analytics

## 5.9 Social, Mobile, Analytics, Cloud (SMAC)

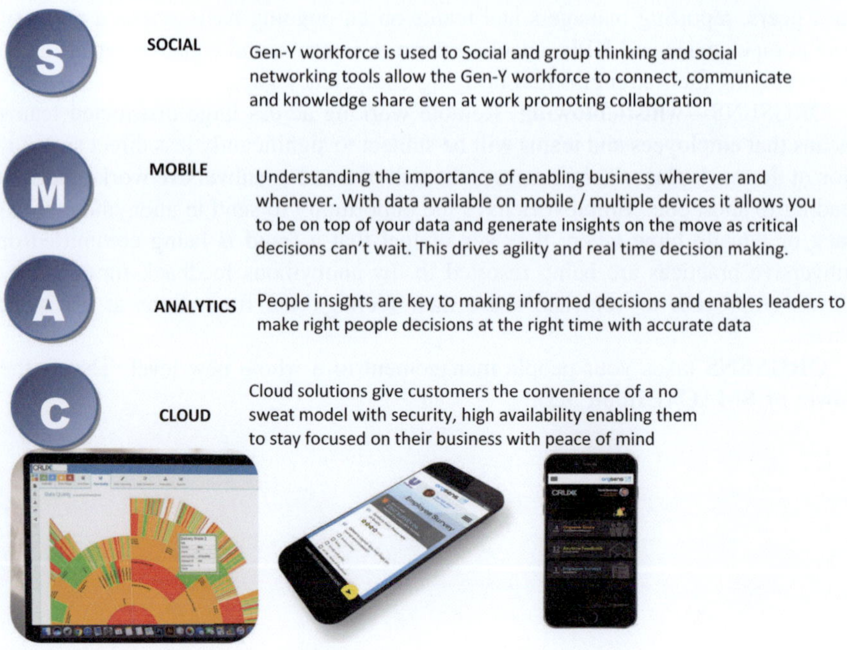

## 5.10 Data Quality

Are you struggling in a sea of data? Are the data points fragmented and residing in multiple files or source systems? Can you pull these data points together to reveal valuable insights? Convert flat dataset into hierarchical formats seamlessly? Procure both a team view and drill down individual view?

**Smart Data Management**: Fragmented "people data points" across multiple source systems need to be integrated into a single platform/repository or "data cube", thereby providing the organization with a single source repository of data which can then be cleaned and standardized.

Web forms need to be used to collect missing data electronically and then update the same in the "data cube", thereby ensuring the data is updated and made ready for analytics at all times. This also enables a running of dipsticks and pulse surveys on an ongoing basis to stay on top of employee sentiment at all times.

Once the "data cube" is constructed, an analytics layer could be built on the back of algorithms that answer "people questions". Finally, a visualization layer could be developed that bubbles up brilliant visualizations that enable business and HR heads to dive straight into the insight.

However, a data health check is absolutely critical to get done towards ensuring that the data is made usable for People Analytics or else "garbage in is garbage out". A data management ecosystem needs to be developed and embedded to make sure this becomes a sustainable process (Exhibits 5.4 and 5.5).

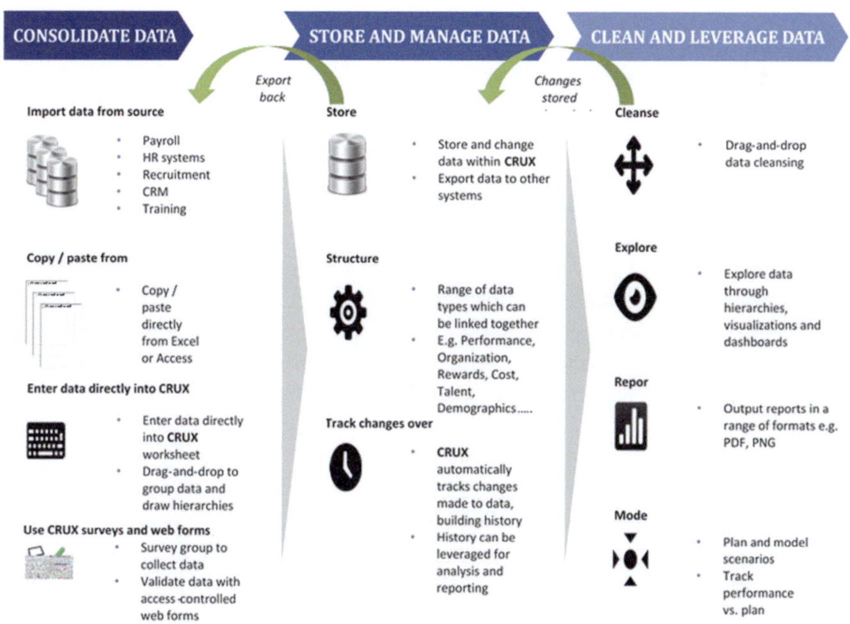


**Exhibit 5.4** Data consolidation; store and management; collection and transformation

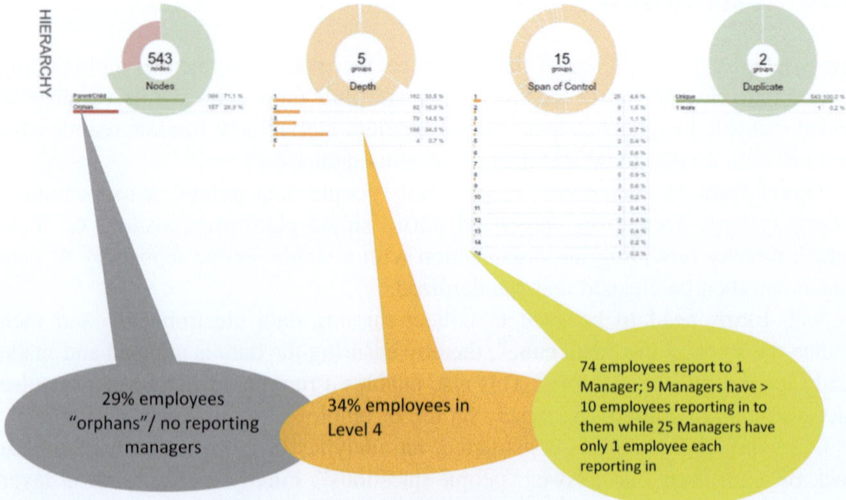


**Exhibit 5.5** Data diagnostics and quality—illustrative dashboard

Let us take this illustration of a large pharmaceutical company that leveraged SMAC technologies to enhance its salesforce performance.

**CASE 5.1: Leveraging SMAC to enhance Salesforce Performance**

## 5.11 Situation and Context

Real-time salesforce management in a large distributed environment proved to be a huge challenge for this organization. In particular, driving productivity is all about effective salesforce market working, making productive calls, having access to real-time information on incentive programmes, marketing and brand communication, etc. The company felt the need to put this infrastructure in place with a view to enhancing salesforce productivity and engagement. The company evaluated various options and then settled for investing behind SMAC technology which was both real time, agile and cost-efficient.

**Sales Tab Deployment: Integrated intelligent mobile based salesforce analytics toolbox.**

Sales tab is a next-generation product platform and specifically aimed to increase the efficiency of the sales force. The entire platform is built over cloud and delivered via native interfaces and plays in the SMAC space (Social + Mobile + Analytics + Cloud). The platform is built to be independent and to also talk with any existing enterprise system including SAP and Oracle (Exhibit 5.6).

The features of sales tab can be divided into two sets:

*Source – General Data*

**Exhibit 5.6** Sales tab interface—home page

- Commodity: Commodities are features that are standard and quintessential in any sales force system be it computerized or not
- Innovation: The features under the innovation column are the game-changers that sales tab provides

## 5.12 Key Benefits and Outcomes

1. Management could now set targets for medical representatives (MRs) by regions/customers
2. Products
3. MRs could now set their daily tour plans, monthly tour plans, schedule appointments and submit them for approval
4. E-detailing: MRs could now present product marketing materials and new research to customers and cross-sell/up-sell
5. MRs could now book orders instantly
6. MRs could now capture primary and secondary sales data (availability, RCPA, competitor data, booked orders, record closing stock
7. Brand management team could now change the branding materials on the go and update it across all or selected MR's thereby saving (and completely eliminating) paper printing costs

*Source – General Data*

**Exhibit 5.7** Sales tab MR monthly tour planner

8. MRs could now schedule a call with the product team in real time if the customer asks a question and he or she is unable to respond to it.
9. MRs could now access training and reference material for learning and research (Exhibit 5.7).

## 5.13 Key Benefits and Outcomes: Innovation Features

1. Management could now track if the MR visited the location, get a live feed of where the MRs are present (geo-location + geo-tagging)—this has a direct impact on salesforce productivity, i.e. sharper real-time data, on total calls/productive calls/value per call at the retail outlet. In this instance, the total calls per salesperson went up from an average of 15–30 and productive calls (bill cut) per salesperson from 9 to 20
2. SMAC reduced the massive training costs due to the high level of attrition in this industry. A new MR could hit the ground running from the same conversation level and data knowledge that the old MR had
3. SMAC eliminated the need of MRs to fill in their daily worksheets. The MR did not need to fill in any status reports for his/her management; they are automatically captured as he works, saving 20% of his/her time

4. It allowed the MR to capture the sentiment of the Customers (doctors) as a response to the product presentation, thus allowing the branding and product management team to understand the response of their materials and reframe their pitch strategy
5. It enabled the MR to capture the market sentiment of competitive products via interactions with pharmacists and stockists, thereby providing valuable customer insight to the category teams
6. It allowed the management to run analysis on MR performance call data, in-clinic performance data, trade data and run customized analyses for specific insights
7. It provided the opportunity to management to take real-time actions on the variables presented by the interactive dashboard, thus eliminating 30% of time in interaction with middle management (Exhibit 5.8).

**CASE 5.2: Digital HR Transformation of a Global Consumer Company—Leveraging Rapid and Reliable Data Transformation across multiple Countries—Asia/Africa/India**

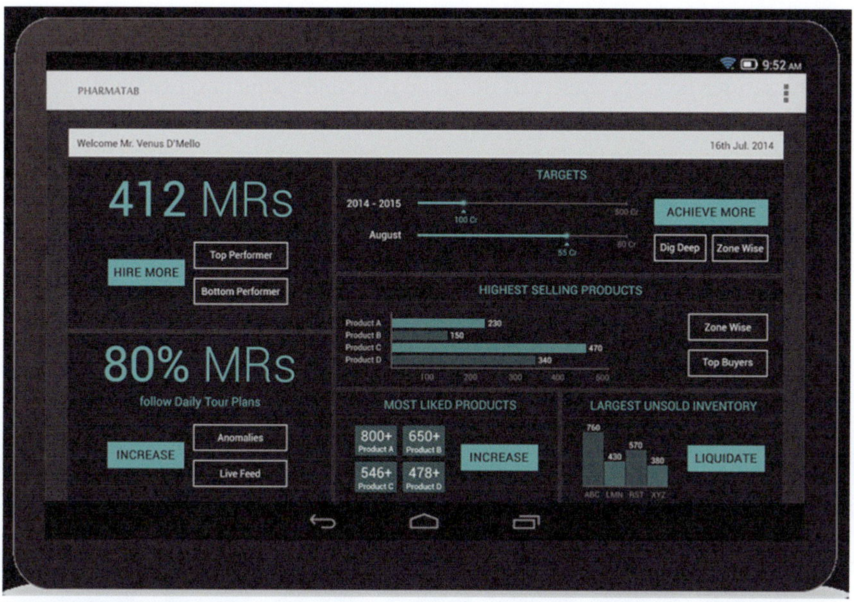


*Source – General Data*

**Exhibit 5.8** Sales tab—key metrics (MR)

## 5.14 Situation and Context

The company was going through a global HCM implementation. However, the people data was sitting in multiple legacy systems in non-standard formats resulting in the lack of a single-employee view. Further, the data was riddled with inaccuracies and far from being updated. This had to be the necessary first step before deploying HR & talent analytics globally. The organization realized that they needed third-party support to help them: standardize data templates; transform non-standard data through first collection and then cleansing and finally migrate/load the cleaned and transformed data into their global HCM solution.

## 5.15 Analytics Objectives

- Fit-gap analysis of data structures
- Data conversion and transformation as per prescribed data rule sets
- Data cleansing and standardization of formats and values
- Data quality report
- Data migration to global HCM (Exhibit 5.9).

The company defined a service delivery cycle, which was followed for every country. The service delivery cycle was designed to define a structured and well-defined

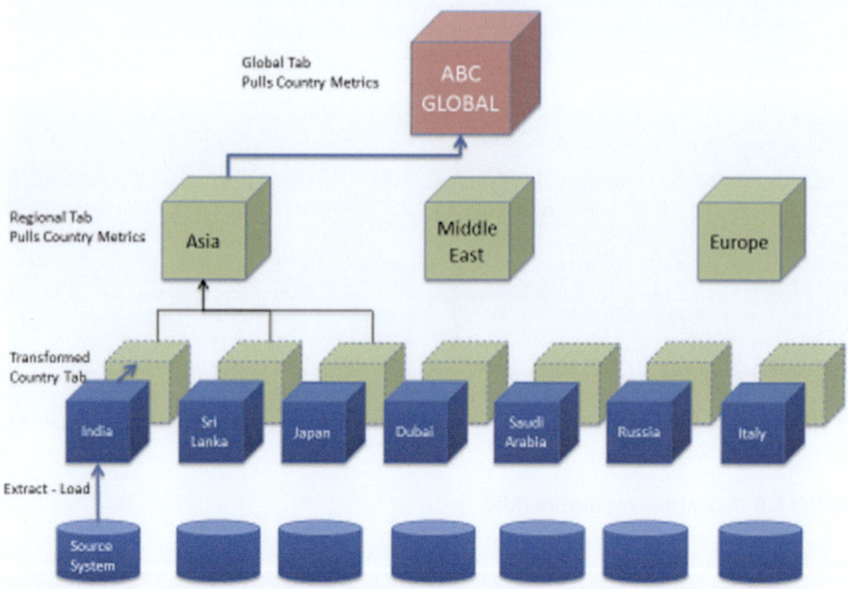




**Exhibit 5.9** Global HR data transformation—extract, transform and load (global rolled-up view)

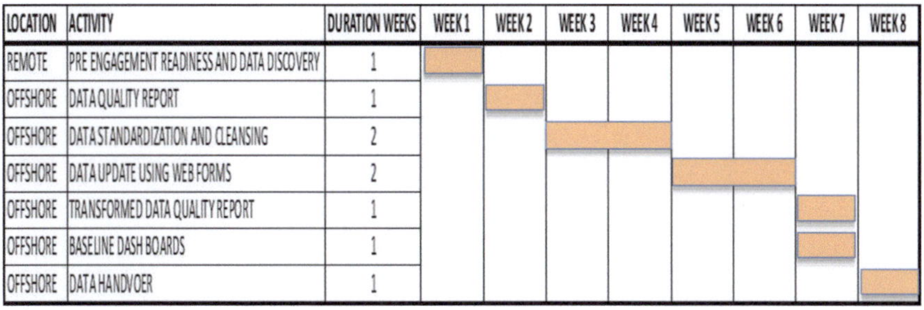


**Exhibit 5.10** Overall Gantt chart

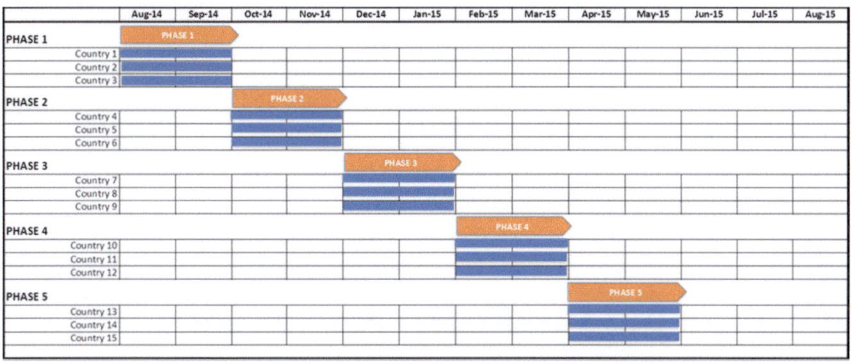


**Exhibit 5.11** Detailed project Gantt chart—illustrative

process for data transformation. It aimed to clearly define the various activities, handover points, roles and responsibilities and outputs for every critical activity till the transformed data was loaded on to the new HCM platform. The figure below captures a service delivery cycle as it was run for every geography (Exhibit 5.10).

Having defined the service delivery cycle the company decided to run three countries at a time through the cycle. This allowed them to complete 15 countries in a period of 10 months as shown in the **GANT chart** below. The three-country approach allowed it to maintain the pace while still providing the opportunity to fine-tune and optimize delivery at every new stage (Exhibit 5.11).

A data conversion SWAT team was deployed to deliver on the schedule (Exhibit 5.12).

## 5.16 Key Outcomes

- Global HCM implementation as per timelines
- Single consolidated employee view—from multiple country specific legacy systems for global HR to get a central rolled up view

**Exhibit 5.12** Project delivery team structure

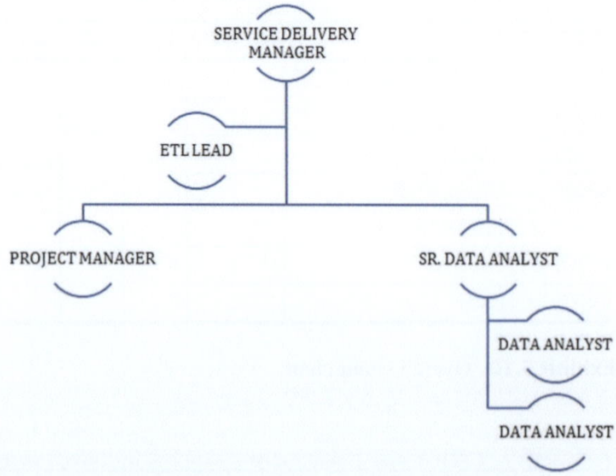


- Transformed, standardized datasets reducing region and global data reconciliation time and effort
- People data made ready for HR and talent analytics deployment
- Sharp and data-driven people decision-making.

## 5.17 Master Data Management—People Directory with a Single Version of the Truth

Managing the HR data ecosystem across multiple locations, functions and legal entities is not easy. Ensuring the veracity of this data in real time is even harder with the implication being that most organizations find it exceedingly difficult to fulfil even the very basic of requirements—tracking individuals by role or competencies or certifications or performance score or pay or learning hours completed. It is almost impossible to get a single-employee view of all people data in one place.

**Analytics Response**

- **Seamless data collection** from multiple sources—irrespective of consistency
- **Create search options**—to sift through efficiently and identify people by role, team or competencies
- **Create audit trails and track changes** to monitor and control your data feeds
- **Use smart and powerful visualization tools** to present the data and analyses in a way that enables the end-user or consumer of the report to cull out the insight rapidly.
- **Authenticate and protect the data** that you oversee and ensure only those authorized by you get to see the data, no-one else; ensure data security protocols are in place.

- **Ensure ongoing correction and update mechanism** via simple tools of storage and queuing of requests.
- **Enable the report to be exported** for sending to recipients who would want to consume it offline.

**CASE 5.3: Let us examine the case example of an Insurance company that sought to transform its Master Data Management system on the back of Data Diagnostics and Data Quality tools**

## 5.18 Situation and Context

The employee master which consisted of @ 14,000 headcount/employee records was riddled with unclean and dated data. This posed both serious compliance risk and communication challenges. Further, there was no automated/seamless mode of extracting data, cleaning the same and integrating the transformed data into their larger HCM platform. As a result, the employee master data was never accurate and required periodic manual intervention to capture, clean, update and integrate into the larger system. This was a manual, cumbersome, inefficient process and prone to error. The company incurred cost in three ways:

- Loss of business due to poor data quality as any non-conformance would lead to client/customer penalties
- Compliance risk leading to loss of reputation and brand image
- High staffing cost due to additional staff deployed to manually collect, clean and audit the data.

## 5.19 Analytics Objectives

- Multiple dataset extraction from different sources and merging into a master dataset in a single repository
- Data diagnostics with data health and quality checks to identify data gaps—Hierarchy/Dimensions/Measures
- Missing data collection through web form broadcasts and updates
- Data quality dashboards
- Data cleansing and transformation—getting its people data analytics ready.

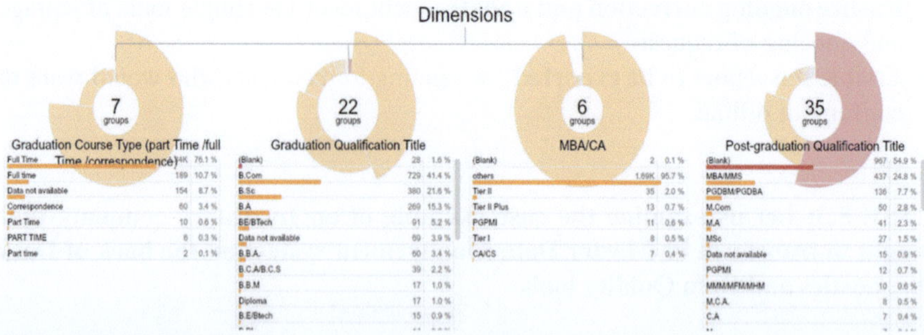




**Exhibit 5.13** Data quality dashboard

## 5.20 Key Outcomes

- Cleansing of @ 14,000 employee master dataset with over 50 fields per unique record over 72 h instead of a normal of 6 weeks via a manual process
- Data quality moving to 100% accuracy from a low 40%
- ETL process embedded without manual intervention thereby eliminating data inaccuracies
- Data collection automated via web forms, thereby ensuring data is updated online real time
- Reducing manpower cost annually by moving from manual to automated ETL process leveraging analytics and visualization tools through reduction of superfluous headcount of HR analysts doing essentially manual and repetitive work (Exhibit 5.13).

- Checking for inaccurate/incomplete data
- Checking for incomplete/irrelevant data
- Checking for duplicate data
- Ensuring quality data sources method for future
- Ensuring an audit trail through a change log.

## 5.21 Conclusion

In summary, SMAC provides a great opportunity for the current and future generation of HR professions to reinvent themselves. They need to first keep themselves abreast of the latest technological advancements taking place in this area; second, familiarize themselves with these tools and get more data savvy; third, apply these tools to provide data- and analysis-driven options to business leaders so they make the right people and business decisions. With the increased pace of change HR leaders need to stay ahead of the curve and start to anticipate the future. Only then will they be able to enable their organizations to stay ahead of the game and remain competitive and sustainable.

# 6 HR Risk Analytics—Identification, Management and Mitigation

## 6.1 Context

It is clear that people pose both the greatest risks and the greatest rewards for organizations, especially during periods of change and transition, or in uncertain times. Risk management needs to be incorporated into all stages of the talent and performance management life cycle, particularly when executing M&As, corporate reorganization, leadership changes or succession plans. It is also important to recognize that some risk aspects are more complex than others, requiring specialized expertise, proven toolsets and well-defined processes.

People Analytics could be deployed through various filters to develop an audit framework that would proactively scan and "red-flag" key risks. Effective HR analytics, workforce planning and organization design informs "risks of the strategy and risks to the strategy" (Ristuccia, Deloitte 2013), to dramatically increase the efficiency and effectiveness of HR and business processes.

HR teams need to be able to visualize their organization through a robust risk framework and then build internal audit capability by leveraging analytics tools and models.

Building capabilities around measuring organizational risk is a key prerequisite towards managing it effectively. People Analytics has a crucial role to play in this regard (Exhibit 6.1).

People Analytics enables organizations to effectively measure and monitor internal policy compliance and regulatory requirements. This invariably entails a set of critical deep-dive questions be asked across each risk categorization: operational/reputational and talent.

The **table** below attempts to do just that. HR teams need to ask themselves these questions and find answers sooner rather than later (Exhibit 6.2).



R. Ghatak, *People Analytics*, Management for Professionals,
https://doi.org/10.1007/978-981-19-3873-3_6

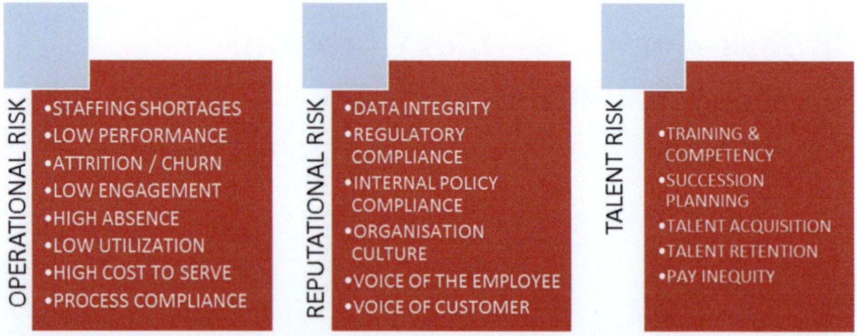




**Exhibit 6.1** Human capital risk assessment framework

The HR risk framework categorizes the "Risk" on a "Relative Strategic Value" continuum from "Somewhat Low" to "Very High" on a ten-point scale. The organization needs to categorize the level of "Risk" and its "Relative Strategic Value or Impact".

## 6.2 Human Capital Risk Matrix—Operational/Reputational/Talent

| Level—org to decide | Human capital risk area | Relative strategic value—org to decide | Key risks to be accounted for and mitigated | Related data points |
|---|---|---|---|---|
| | Standard, routine background checking—**operational/reputational** | | Criminal record, other court case involvements, credit issues, driving violations, fraudulent transactions/behaviour | One major industry player was recently fined heavily for failing to verify background check information; and the regulators also came down on another vendor recently for providing information without taking steps to ensure the information was accurate. Routine checks also do not account for other fundamental due diligence aspects |

| Level—org to decide | Human capital risk area | Relative strategic value—org to decide | Key risks to be accounted for and mitigated | Related data points |
|---|---|---|---|---|
| | Defensible, value add and/or custom background checking—**operational/reputational** | | Generally, the same information in the scope above, but is verified; and more customized; programmes are available when needed | Services are not unduly reliant on technology (exclusively) to deliver information to customers; and unlike above, the model is *not* all about high-volume transaction processing at the lowest cost |
| | HR-related compliance (cost avoidance)—**Reputational** | | Sexual harassment, equal pay, OSHA, SOX, ISO, customer standards | Non-compliance can result in multimillion dollar fines, or in some cases, government/customer contracts going away that could put businesses "out of business". |
| | Operational execution risk management—**operational/talent** | | Sourcing talent ahead of demand, addressing competency gaps, optimizing staff resource deployment, etc. | The intersection of business continuity, operating efficiencies related to staff costs and usage, and ensuring the workforce has what it takes to succeed |
| | Strategic, predictive human capital due diligence (ongoing)—**talent** | | Are key successes/achievements or competencies being exaggerated while failures are being hidden? Is there a "culture fit"? Is the commitment level there? | An example is the executive who claims he or she grew a business from $5 to $50 M, but others are making the same exact claim—or that he or she was not even there during that period of growth. Further, after a business restructuring, are key employees committed to the new organization structure? |
| | Strategic, predictive human capital due diligence (critical business scenarios)—**Talent** | | Same as above in the context of M&As, business restructurings, rightsizings, other transformational initiatives, etc. | The cultural fit and/or commitment level of key executives and other high-value resources can undermine critical business undertakings; and validating their competencies is also essential |

| Level—org to decide | Human capital risk area | Relative strategic value—org to decide | Key risks to be accounted for and mitigated | Related data points |
|---|---|---|---|---|
| | HR-M&A macro issue:<br>HR data, process and technology infrastructure—**operational/reputational** | | Redundant, incompatible and/or non-integrated infrastructure assets and processes must be sorted out | The millions spent on the key elements of one company's HR delivery infrastructure should perhaps not be the primary concern, but rather what delivery infrastructure best enables the new (combined) organization's business strategy |
| | HR-M&A macro issue:<br>Comp and benefits integration, staff consolidation and related compliance risks—**reputational** | | Compensation and benefits plans of the acquired company must be compliant (or they will invalidate the acquiring company's plans), and the total cost of offering and integrating those plans must be accounted for | Two examples that are not foreign to industry consolidators: Are pension plans in the acquired company underfunded or collateralized on illiquid assets? Further, control change provisions in employment contracts also need to be factored in. Additionally, staff consolidations must be done in a robust and transparent manner or risk litigation |
| | HR-M&A macro issue:<br>Overestimation of cultural compatibility or other business synergies—**talent** | | Realistically evaluating cultural compatibility and synergies that were factored into decisions relating to deal closure, while in addition evaluating integration costs | As alluded to earlier, cultural compatibility of the two organizations in an M&A has been known to crater many deals valued at billions of dollars. Overestimation of synergies related to both business, ways of working and people/leadership has also been factors seen in failed deals |

| Level—org to decide | Human capital risk area | Relative strategic value—org to decide | Key risks to be accounted for and mitigated | Related data points |
|---|---|---|---|---|
| | Managing leadership risk—**talent** | | Proactively anticipating and planning for gaps in mission-critical roles, by taking proactive actions (and embedding tools and systems/processes) to mitigate | Ideally, leadership-level succession planning should include a view of all viable talent options (within and outside the organization) side by side, with readiness timing, and benchmarked using the same success criteria. Leadership continuity impacts business continuity and overall performance |

## 6.3 HR Audit Capabilities

Applying data analytics as a pre-audit process can fundamentally enhance the effectiveness and efficiency of the audit process.

**EFFECTIVENESS**

- Replacing the sampling approach with universal set analysis for identifying gaps in compliance in a more holistic manner

**EFFICIENCY**

- Data audit findings to identify investigation opportunities for making the process efficient
- Using audit/risk analytics tools to make mitigation process more efficient.

## 6.4 HR Risk/Audit Analytics Framework

The data could be integrated from multiple sources into a data cube rules engine and then after an initial data health check be passed through structured data filters:

| | CHALLENGE / RISK | DEEP DIVE QUESTIONS | ACTIONS AND BENEFITS |
|---|---|---|---|
| 1 | Reputation Risk | What is the quality of underlying data – statutory, employee, vendor etc?<br>What is the monitoring mechanism to track compliance ?<br>Do you possess an event log / audit trail for all data changes especially those of a sensitive nature ?<br>What is the quality of underlying data over history ?<br>With data sitting in multiple source systems how do you get "a single employee view" ?<br>Can we track the processes and competencies of 'approved persons'?<br>What is the quality of Employee Background checks ? | Manage, integrate and cleanse data ( current & historical) on an ongoing basis rapidly and accurately<br>Maintain an event log / audit trail capturing all the changes<br>Data Quality Dashboard designed & triggered at periodic intervals<br>Data integrated from multiple source systems to provide a "single employee view"<br>Data cleansed within the source system<br>Identify parts of the business that are open to compliance / governance risk and take corrective integration & cleansing action<br>Conduct a RACI assessment<br>Monitoring BGC quality |
| 2 | Operational Risk | Can we visualise sick / absence rates , identify causes & take actions to correct?<br>Can we predict "who, when and why" of regrettable attrition ?<br>Can we differentiate between "good and bad churn" ?<br>Can we sharply identify high / low-performing individuals & teams across role hierarchies, grades, locations, & functions ?<br>Can we identify rightsizing opportunities to build a more agile and flexible organization?<br>Can we predict "top, average and bottom " performer characteristics ?<br>Can we do more with less ?<br>Do we have the tight organization design from a go-to-market & customer facing perspective ?<br>Are we optimized in terms of headcount & people cost ?<br>Are we paying optimally for talent ( fresh & existing) | Save cost & reduce risk from temp staff, identify skills gaps and plan for 'right level' of temp vs. perm<br>Predict critical attrition enabling preventive action<br>Predict top, average and bottom performer characteristics and then change your hiring strategy .<br>Run what-if scenario models that enable rapid visualization of rightsizing opportunities<br>Develop process to people to cost maps through RACI to rapidly visualize process & cost optimization opportunities<br>Develop sunburst visualizations that enable rapid identification of high & low performing individuals & teams across the organization<br>Reduce resource in over-managed areas, relocate to over-stretched areas |
| 3 | Talent Risk | Where are the key roles and in which of them do we have a nominated successor ?<br>Where are the talent gaps across role hierarchies ?<br>What would be the future talent requirement 2-5 years from now ?<br>What are the key drivers for "future leader" talent ?<br>What are the key drivers for critical talent retention ?<br>What is the success ratio of talent retention programs ?<br>What is the level of "hiring effectiveness" ?<br>What is the cost per hire mix & ROI in talent acquisition ? | Succession planning for key roles<br>Talent forecasting across roles, mix and geographies<br>Workforce planning for talent deployment<br>Enhance hiring effectiveness through metric dashboards ; predictive modelling of top performer characteristics<br>Enhance effectiveness of retention programs<br>Identify parts of the business which are exposed to staff turnover in key roles |



**Exhibit 6.2** HR risk questions—operational/reputational/talent

- **Structured data filters for automating compliance checks and risk assessment**

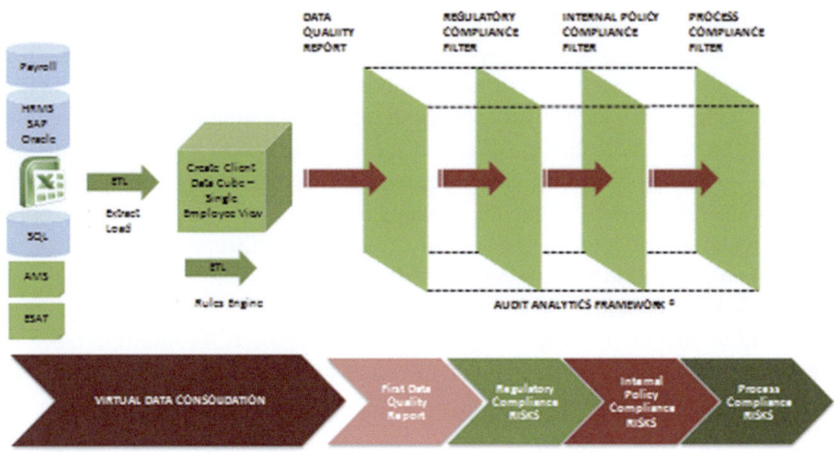




**Exhibit 6.3** HR risk analytics work flow

regulatory/internal policy/process compliance. Key risks are then automatically flagged off for mitigation (Exhibit 6.3).

## 6.5 Assessing Risk

Risk is a central element in any kind of planning. A statement about the future carries with it the risk of being somewhat to totally wrong. Even grand financial models miss some aspect, which can lead to disastrous investments. Today, there are many more external forces driving companies now than in the past, and that involves recognizing risk. Stability is gone for good; it has been replaced by volatility, extending far into the future. Unquestionably, human capital management is a high-risk game in this uncertain market. More than ever, human capital planning must now include risk assessment and management.

As we have seen, risk assessment has three steps.

**First**, the scan lists every factor that can potentially have an impact on the organization. For human capital management, those factors are edited to those that could have the biggest negative or positive effect on the organization's people, operations, structure, and external relations in the foreseeable future. Then, the question is asked: What will be the impact if these occur?

At the corporate level, examples of potential risks could be immediate loss of revenue, inability to deliver competitively, harm to the organization's reputation, legal penalties and loss of future revenue. On the positive side, if a new product release exceeds expectations, great—but will the company be prepared to service that increased level of uptake?

**Second**, each risk is rated on a scale of, say, 1 to 5 (Not Likely–Most Likely) with regard to its likelihood of occurring. How do you decide the likelihood something is going to happen? You have to look beyond the experience of people in the organization and research current media reports. That is where the threat lies—so listen to the maniac fringe. Visionaries and others operating at the outskirts often see ahead more clearly than do those in the establishment, who have something to protect. Managers have some control over internal factors, but they have little or no control over those outside the organization. If one of these threats or opportunities materializes, what might be the extent of the disruption? How long will it take the organization to respond? Further, do you have the ability to implement effective risk mitigation measures?

The **third** step involves applying the optional responses. From importance and likelihood, you decide how to mitigate the effects of those risks. For example, how will you handle the following?

- Avoid the risk by postponing or not implementing something—or just wait?
- Transfer the risk to a third party—in which case, who could do it better?
- Minimize risk exposure through a robust control environment? What should be the nature of these controls?
- Accept the risk if the cost outweighs the benefit—but what is the threshold?
- How best to balance between control and growth/entrepreneurial spirit which often entails taking calculated risks?

The organization's task is to develop a risk mitigation plan that prepares you ahead of any problem's arrival. It is similar to a disaster recovery plan. That is, if the worst happens, you are ready to clean up in the most expeditious manner. This approach reduces damage and confusion and helps the organization move on with a minimum of distraction. In short, while the unprepared flail about in the bushes, trying to get back on the trail, you distance yourself from the pack.

One of the most effective ways to prepare for the unexpected is to develop a playbook, much as is done in the game of football. The playbook lists the defensive and offensive plays that are ready to be used, given certain circumstances. The People Analytics toolbox enables you to "scenario model" options and thereby test and evaluate decision impacts in a simulated environment.

## 6.6 Managing Risk

The risks facing an organization are diverse, changeable and possibly hidden. They may come from inside the organization (compliance, safety, negligence) or outside it (credit, supply, customers). So it is no surprise that consistent, thorough risk management takes plenty of discipline and application.

**ANALYTICS RESPONSE**

- **Log risks "live" straight from the meeting room**, with all key people present, for review later on. Interactive approaches in the new cloud technologies and applications today make it easy to capture risks quickly and accurately and can be used in conjunction with special workshop tools.
- **Log agreed actions** to be taken in order to manage risks.
- **Map the pattern of risks** against your organization chart, then drill-down from the total weighted risk facing the organization to specific areas of risk in any part of it.
- **Visualize the balance of risks to gain new insights rapidly**. Who has responsibility for the most significant or most likely risks? Which departments are major sources of risk? Which stakeholders are connected with major risks?
- **Compare your risk profile with other variables** such as revenue or headcount per area.
- **Scale risks and connect them to linked perspectives** on your organization.
- **Generate a monthly risk report**, with a link to update change risks or add new ones.
- The new applications have the capability to generate a full **audit report on who has made changes and when**.

As an illustrative example, in this risk audit of a real estate company, the following key risks were identified and then captured in a risk matrix as seen below.

**CASE 1—HR Risk Diagnostics in a Real Estate Company**

## 6.7 Situation and Context

The company in question took pre-emptive action to first scan for key risks, rank them on business impact and then take actions to mitigate the same. This was done with a universal dataset as opposed to a typical sampling methodology made possible by an analytics solution that could apply diagnostics on the data and identify data anomalies immediately.

**Applying HR Risk Analytics as a pre-audit process can fundamentally enhance Risk mitigation**

## 6.8 Analytics Objectives

- Diagnosing key areas of HR risk including organization design and culture
- Putting out insights based on visual intelligence
- Institutionalizing internal controls to drive the desired culture.

## 6.9 Key Benefits

- Shifting from sample-based approach to universal set analysis for evidencing compliance effectively
- Identifying investigation areas in advance to enable proactive management action to mitigate risk
- Enabling effective resource utilization by leveraging automation to "do more with less"
- Key areas of operational risks and organization design risks were identified and visualized.

## 6.10 Key Risks Identified

| | Dimension | RAG | Findings | Areas for Investigation |
|---|---|---|---|---|
| 1. | Organization Design | | 34% employees "orphans"<br>17 Managers have 1 employee each reporting in | What is the engagement level of these employees ?<br>How are they being performance managed ?<br>How are their grievances being addressed? |
| 2. | Span of Control | | 6 Groups of 100+ employees reporting in to 1 Manager each with 9 Groups of 50-100 employees reporting in to 1 Manager each | What is the engagement level of these employees ?<br>How are they being performance managed ?<br>How are their grievances being addressed? |
| 3. | Depth | | 76% (4870) employees at M1 – All in one category<br>34% Employees in Level 1 with 45% in Level 4 & 5 ;<br>Bulging in the middle layers | What is the quality of communication from Leadership to junior employees ?<br>What is the quality of supervision in M1 category ? |
| 4. | Attrition | | Information in dataset not available in spite of Fields existing in the dataset: Absconding Date / DOL | Why are key fields not populated?<br>How is attrition being monitored / tracked ? |
| 5. | Performance Culture | | Lack of "Pay for Performance" Rewards ; Variable Pay is only by nomenclature with most categories drawing a fixed amount of INR 700/- per month ; no evidence of Rewards being linked to Performance | Are Reward strategies driving "pay for performance?<br>What is the co-relation between pay and performance ? |
| 6. | Data Quality | | Missing / incomplete data across critical fields: DOC, Previous Employment History, Address, Hiring Qualification, Sub-Department, Blood group etc | Are statutory deductions happening ?<br>Are nominee information in place ?<br>Have background checks been done ?<br>Are references being verified ?<br>Are joining documents being validated ? |
| 7. | Hiring & On-boarding | | 47% new hires getting confirmed only between 10 – 30 months while probation period seems to be 6 months or 12 months.<br>Early attrition seen in many cases | When are employees being confirmed ?<br>Is there a probation period and how is this being tracked ?<br>What is the hiring qualification / skill mix ? |
| 8. | Rewards | | Skew across dimensions: High variation in Compensation with similar tenure, qualification & category ; High Reward spend allocation in Support Departments etc | What is the ATC mix across categories ; location ; Budget sub-Department ; Gender ; Hiring Qualification etc.<br>What is the co-relation between Tenure and ATC across categories ? |
| 9. | Resourcing | | Headcount distribution skewed across Departments ; Locations ; Categories ; Skills base ; 99% Employees Full time leading to "high cost" of resourcing | Are employees overstressed ?<br>What is the headcount distribution across Departments, Locations & categories ?<br>What is the permanent / contract headcount mix ? |
| 10. | Demographics | | Gender Diversity mix low across categories ; Hiring Qualification mix 30% UG's ; 35% G's ; 57% of the data set are below 25 years of Age. | What is the optimal Age, Tenure, Gender, Hiring Qualification mix? |

### Key Organization Design Risks

- 34% of employees identified as "orphans", with no reporting managers
- Six groups of managers have>100 employees as direct reports with 17 managers having one direct report

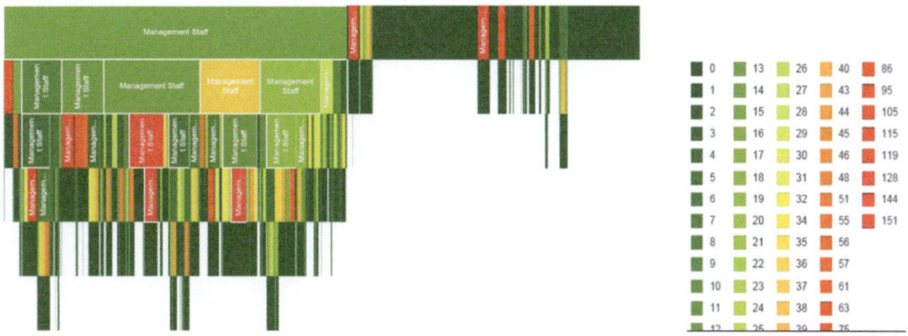




**Exhibit 6.4** Span of control skewed with six groups of 100+ employees and nine groups of 50+ employees reporting in to one manager each; significant number of "orphans"—no reporting managers

- Risk of low supervision and oversight leading to poor performance management and low engagement leading to high attrition

### Key Operational Risks

- In–out time discrepancies, working hours and thresholds breached
- Personal details missing
- Absence rates high, leave carry forward incidences high
- Lack of pay for performance culture (Exhibit 6.4).

# 7 Shape Culture and Drive Engagement—Real-time Actionable Insights

## 7.1 Context

From Glassdoor reviews to the "Great Place to Work" awards, the corporate world has developed a keen interest in gauging, rewarding and publicizing the health of company cultures. However, beyond offering great opportunities for PR, fostering internal engagement and employee satisfaction is good business. A study by consulting firm Kotter shows that companies with performance-enhancing cultures that "facilitate adaptation to a changing world" see a fourfold increase in revenue growth. Further, for those in the hunt for great talent, a widely quoted 2012 study by Corporate Responsibility Magazine revealed that 69% of respondents would take the reputation of the organization into account before applying for a job even if they were currently without one.

Highly qualified millennials, it turns out, are more focused than ever on aligning with a company's values and ethics. According to The Guardian journalist Matthew Jenkin, change is being driven by the so-called millennials; 62% of whom would prefer to join organizations that create positive social impact, half prefer purposeful work to a high compensation, and 53% would put in greater effort if their contribution was positively impacting other's lives.

Yet despite our increased understanding that corporate culture is an essential part of any management strategy, it often proves elusive to measure, manage and maintain. To put yourself on the path to creating a healthy company culture, it is necessary to look at what defines corporate culture, its impact on profitability and the ways traditional culture frameworks, voice of employee (VoE) programmes and People Analytics driven by deep learning text analytics technology can help yield scalable shifts for all kinds of organizations.



R. Ghatak, *People Analytics*, Management for Professionals,
https://doi.org/10.1007/978-981-19-3873-3_7

## 7.2 Defining Corporate Culture

While the idea of corporate culture may be hard to pin down, there has been extensive research on the different elements that shape and influence it. One particularly useful framework is the "Johnson and Scholes Culture Web model", which focuses on an organization's cultural paradigm, a term that defines the often unconscious understanding of a company's shared values and assumptions. There are six components he speaks about, which overlap, interact and continuously help employees understand how they are seen and valued within their corporate identity.

The six components are: stories, symbols, rituals and routines, power structures, organizational structure and controls. These aspects provide a road-map that will enable you in determining the culture you seek to foster in each of the spheres. Only then can you start strategically gathering data and coming up with patterns for analysis.

## 7.3 Questions to Answer

With a view towards moulding, embedding and then shifting corporate culture, business and HR leaders must come together to respond to some critical imperatives. For instance:

- Finding ways to proactively trigger employee signature moments that create high impact on a consistent basis
- Ensuring that rewards policies and philosophy enhance or bolster our culture drivers
- Driving a pay for performance culture through the performance management process as opposed to encouraging mediocrity
- Taking the risk to reduce productivity in the immediate term towards investing behind a culture of learning for the longer term
- Identifying the culture triggers that lie behind problem events such as fraud or compliance/ethical standards. This leads to some key questions: is taking exemplary action on offenders and reinforcing desired behaviours enough, or does supporting ethical ways of doing business require transforming culture norms that enable or even encourage dysfunctional attitudes and behaviours?
- Identifying and tackling cultural barriers to integration in M&A's before they become disruptive
- With the competition for good talent, intensifying with culture triggers clearly impacting the employer brand, it then grows to become the key driver towards attraction, selection and retention of top talent.

This is where HR leaders should closely partner with CEOs to take a data-first and evidence-based approach towards first embedding and then reinforcing the desired culture. To do this in a sustainable manner, companies must regularly first seek to understand and then analyse employee behaviour while revisiting other related processes and policy frameworks in the company.

Corporate culture can no longer remain hidden from the world. In the age of social media, it is no surprise that we see and read about many companies' cultures being written about, shaped, transformed and measured for the world to see on platforms such as LinkedIn, AmbitionBox and Glassdoor. We also see it in various "Great Place to Work", "Best Employer Surveys" and other such forums which may be a bit of hype on the one hand but on the other provide interesting insights on practices and trends related to organization culture in leading organizations.

## 7.4 Culture and Engagement—Organization Actions

Some organizations are taking action more than others towards actively shifting their corporate culture by leveraging People Analytics:

- **This retail company** has set up an in-house analytics team to work on a culture project that would acquire the best of talent and win in the marketplace. The team takes a multidisciplinary approach to designing programmes to define and reinforce its culture pillars
- **A large coffee retail chain** analysed the string of social media posts shared by employees and ex-employees to derive insights on its culture as perceived by employees on the back of which an action plan was put in place to address the gaps if any
- **A finance company** has identified core behaviours as a part of its culture pillars, after a deep analysis of current gaps and then set about scorecarding those behaviours to measure the changes over time
- A large software company from its climate surveys has identified elements of trust, empathy and respect as core culture attributes that employees hold very dear and believe is what differentiates them from competitors. The company then started measuring these attributes and included it in the balanced scorecard.

Once an organization develops clarity on the direction it needs to take regarding culture change on the back of data and analyses (survey dipsticks, focus group discussions, ONA analysis, etc.), it is critical to then get into action mode. Translating thought and philosophy to action on the back of these insights helps both to build traction and enhance the probability for successful transformation.

A healthy corporate culture is not just about boosting productivity, it is also about avoiding unnecessary costs and inefficiencies. At its worst, a neglected culture is like a disease: it slowly spreads, eating away at the organization's metaphorical arteries, weighing down motivated employees and leading to low productivity and ultimately system-wide failure.

It has been seen across organizations and cultures that when life is made difficult for employees or when they feel insecure or undermined, they tend to take out their frustrations and angst on peers and subordinates. A toxic culture has the tendency to spread across the organization rapidly and if left unchecked could cost the organization heavily in terms of health care, employee turnover and churn and productivity.

If you consider that it costs at least 30–75% of an employee's salary to fill a position and that a significant proportion of your top talent will look for a new job if they feel their corporate culture is going downhill—investing in the right engagement strategy to shift your corporate culture is not just essential to company morale, it is essential to your organization's health and business performance.

## 7.5 Employee Engagement—Shifting Your Corporate Culture

Culture and engagement are inextricably linked. Culture is essentially about how work happens in organizations; engagement is about the feeling of employees about how work happens. Engagement is an area that needs to be monitored proactively and in real time within organizations. It is a lead indicator of sustainability across organizations and is a crucial measure of organizational health and a key window into the potential for change and transformation.

Engagement includes within it an emotional element as well as commitment that are crucial factors which determine organizational success. Highly engaged individuals and teams reflect a shared and meaningful purpose in their work that lay the foundation for any organization to meet its goals and objectives.

This focus on engagement is influenced by a few factors: first, the competition for millennials who are not only seriously talented but also less loyal than earlier generations. Second, with digitalization becoming the norm for most organizations, there is a requirement for tech savvy and digitally native talent pools. Third, an organization's culture and employer value proposition is open to one and all, so potential candidates can do their own research by checking out social media sites or talking to peers and company employees or alumni to get the inside story on culture and work environment. Fourth, when employees are engaged and motivated, customers are more likely to be happy and stakeholders will benefit from the Organization's success.

- Employee engagement is a key imperative for leadership across levels and needs to be monitored and measured in real time as opposed to once or twice a year
- Despite the emergence of many tools for frequently evaluating employee sentiment, most organizations do it either annually or once in two years
- Managers and leaders are now accountable for engagement, but HR has to be proactive, implement the right analytics tools, provide business leaders both quality data as well as critical insights for decision-making, nurture a culture of listening and ensure that reward and recognition consistently tie in with the need to have an engaged work force that stays committed to shared organizational goals.

A starting point for putting together an employee engagement strategy begins with capturing the "**voice of employees**" in a meaningful way on the back of a set of contemporary tools and technologies that pull together real-time data that can lead to actionable insights.

## 7.6 Voice of Employees

Today, engaged and committed employees are central to an organization's success, shifting the power from traditional communication methodologies to the digital employee interface. As a result, HR managers are now required to anticipate their employee's needs, desires and expectations in order to ensure talent retention towards sustainable competitive advantage. This is where voice of the employee (VoE) comes into play. VoE is not a "nice to have", but a critical ingredient to understand the digital employee lifecycle and create meaningful experiences for digitally empowered employees with a view to driving a sustainable engagement strategy.

To become a people-centric organizations focused on shaping culture and driving engagement, it is critical to leverage the voice of your employees. The importance of People Analytics lies in collecting, analysing employee feedback, deriving crucial insights from it that would then go into making the employee signature moments count, thereby creating a unique employee value proposition resulting in a powerful talent magnet that becomes a unique differentiator from other organizations.

## 7.7 Leveraging the Voice of the Employee (VoE)

**Step 1: Gather Actionable Data**—with your company Cultural Web in place, it is the time to turn to your employees for an objective audit of how well it aligns with the existing cultural paradigm. The resulting data can take a myriad of forms—from traditional surveys to internal chat rooms or anonymous feedback forms—but one thing is clear: the richest insights will always be found in the form of unstructured feedback: comments prompted by open-ended, informal questions.

**Step 2: Compare and Contrast**—using your Cultural Web framework, identify the key gaps and contradictions in the way your company wants to be perceived and the way employees are currently engaging with your corporate culture and brand.

**Step 3: Adjust, Iterate and Repeat**—while conducting this kind of analysis manually can only be done once or twice a year, at most, text analytics will allow you to keep a constant finger on the pulse of employee engagement and sentiment. This is true even as your company grows, pivots, downsizes, adds perks and benefits or implements new corporate hierarchies and processes. Corporate culture is a living, breathing thing, and it requires continuous attention and care if you want everyone to stay in sync with your company's values and objectives.

## 7.8 You Cannot Afford to Lose Your Talent

Now that your initial feedback loop is set up and various channels of unstructured feedback are continually streaming in, you can adapt quickly as issues arise. In our fast-paced marketplace, agility means you will have a better chance at keeping your brightest minds engaged, happy, productive and, most importantly, on your payroll.

## 7.9 Engagement and the Data Challenge

1. Ensuring that the data is collected in real time and across multiple sources or cohorts, where appropriate is critical to identify employee engagement issues, both tangible and intangible
   - Is the data being collected, then actionable; that is to say can organizations leverage the insights from the data to initiate key interventions?
   - Is the data the only source or could other data be collected from multiple sources? Gathering data from multiple sources would make the data more reliable and therefore the insights more relevant and actionable
   - Is there a way to get a helicopter view of this data that might bring out areas of concern or positive trends which could then be shared across the organization?
2. Analysing the content of employee surveys to ensure that it covers the key engagement drivers while drawing relevant correlations to arrive at key insights
   - Are surveys covering all stakeholders within the organization with sufficient time being given to enable its completion?
   - Are survey response rates optimum? Are you getting a good enough sample size in terms of responses to work with? If not, have you tried to understand the reasons why?
   - Review of survey results to ensure they have been collated and analysed appropriately with communication, back to employees on the findings and insights along with actions to be taken while ensuring the monitoring and reporting processes are put in place (Exhibit 7.1).

However, it is not enough to base actions on the findings of a single annual survey. It is critical to have multiple streams of data—both structured and unstructured, flowing in across several channels and touchpoints. In the section below, we will discover contemporary tools and technologies that enable organizations to "listen" actively to their employee feedback in real time bringing in actionable insights that lead to sharper and more reliable decision-making.

## 7.10 Contemporary Tools to Capture VoE—Text Analytics

Nothing provides more insight and context on your employee's experience than open-ended feedback. However, staying on top of this unstructured feedback and

| | Positive Impact | |
|---|---|---|
| Negative Impact | Low | High |
| Low | Small Opportunity/ Threat<br>• R&R<br>• Communication<br>• Perf. Mgmt.<br>• Fun @ Work<br>• Work Environment | Opportunity Area<br>• Policies and Procedures<br>• Career and Personal Growth<br>• Compensation |
| High | Threat Area<br>• Senior Management<br>• Job<br>• Supervisor | Both Threat & Opportunity<br>• Satisfaction |



**Exhibit 7.1** Illustration—engagement survey: driver impact analysis

keeping an eye out for emerging trends can be difficult when you are collecting an endless stream of responses—exit feedback; performance reviews; 360 feedback; engagement survey feedback; meeting feedback, etc.

The text analytics solution uses advanced natural language processing and machine learning technology to do this heavy lifting for you. This powerful feature continuously evaluates and organizes your open-ended feedback, so you can discover the unexpected in the voice of your employees.

Text analytics allows you to mine the unstructured feedback that resides in text form through an automated solution. Applying text analytics to unstructured and open-ended feedback enables rapid extraction of patterns and insights around feeling, morale and sentiment for coming up with suitable interventions for enhancing the employee experience and thereby shifting the corporate culture.

Employee feedback may be collected in a couple of ways:

- Structured—examples include closed-ended, single-select or multi-select questions with a list of answers in multiple-choice format. The responded needs to choose an answer among the options provided
- Unstructured—this is gathered through open text questions to which the respondent must answer in text form.

Unstructured feedback supplements structured closed-ended feedback as it allows the respondent to describe and expand on his/her opinion, thereby bringing in several more data points which may have got missed out. The sources of this data apart from open-ended surveys could be live feeds from social media sites (Twitter, Facebook, LinkedIn, Glassdoor) but also e-mail communication, chat logs on messenger or yammer and so on.

Unstructured data takes a huge amount of time to collect and analyse if one uses traditional survey methods; that is why hardly 20–25% of such data gets to be analysed at all. This is where text analytics fills the gap by working off advanced search engines and along with network analysis can cull out deep insights in rapid time via word or concept clouds to make sense of large unstructured and open-ended data.

## 7.11 Leverage Artificial Intelligence for Actionable Insights

Text analytics leverages both machine learning and natural language processing to monitor and track the unstructured data feeds from multiple sources like social media, for instance continuously and in real time. Managers can utilize their time better by focusing more on enhancing employee experience and business partnering as opposed to collecting and interpreting data in traditional ways.

Let us explore some of the benefits of text analytics:

**Analysis across multiple sources or channels**—this enables you to get a 360° view of your data, gathered from various touchpoints such as surveys, forms, reviews, e-mails, social networks.

**Analysis across a sentiment spectrum**—it can automatically analyse the nature of the piece of feedback or comment in terms of its positive, negative or neutral nature, or even categorize them as suggestions or questions.

**Analysis through prioritization of feedback**—this enables you to prioritize the feedback you collect across multiple channels and rank them accordingly, so you can focus on the ones that are most critical, thereby applying the principle of addressing the critical few versus the trivial many.

**Reveal the critical insights via relevant dashboards for key stakeholders**—this allows you to create dashboards that throw up only the most relevant insights that could then be shared with business leaders to support them in taking more objective decisions based on hard evidence.

**Filter your Data**—this allows you to go deep and segment your data, thereby diving into the detail.

**Compare the feedback over specified time periods**—this enables you to compare the data or feedback gathered over time periods, thereby allowing you to see patterns and trends in the data over time, enabling you to monitor improvement or decline across key parameters.

**Thematic clustering**—the data gathered can also be clustered around various key themes to enable you to bring out the insights clearly.

**Some clear benefits of text analysis have been seen:**

**Fast and quick:** manually sorting out through thousands of exit interview forms or employee survey response could take weeks to do manually, but text analysis using machine learning can get it done in a few minutes.

**Reliable:** given that data is analysed across multiple source channels, it comes out as more reliable. Further, the reliability quotient gets enhanced by virtue of the fact that the tool starts to get more intelligent and process more data, thereby being able to identify both patterns and outliers.

**Lack of Bias:** text analysis through machine learning tells you the feedback as it is, without prejudicing it or diluting it in any way. The analysis is also fact based.

**Scale and coverage:** you are able to scale to analysing data gathered through multiple sources and channels from physical forms and surveys to e-mails to social media platforms like Twitter, Instagram, Facebook, chat rooms, etc.

**Over and above Text analytics enables organizations to:**

- Bring out key patterns and trends—machine learning is used to automatically segment all of your employee's unstructured feedback to highlight underlying patterns in the data
- Highlight key risks through an early warning system—trigger red flags by highlighting key risks that become visible in the unstructured data through spotting negative keywords, phrases or outliers (Exhibit 7.2).

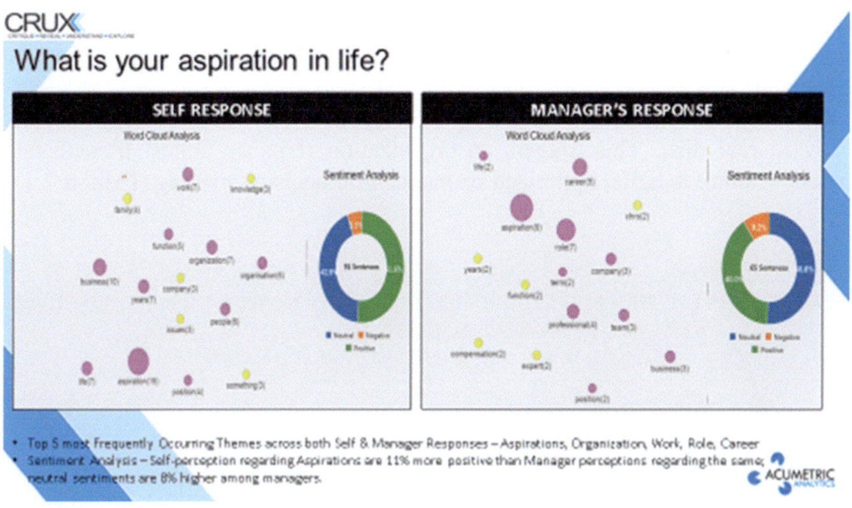




**Exhibit 7.2** Text analysis of key feedback themes in a large Indian Conglomerate: illustrative

## 7.12 Contemporary Tools to Capture VoE—Chatbot

Artificial intelligence-leveraged "chatbots" are starting to get deployed to determine mood and sentiment levels of employees in real time. Employee experience and engagement drivers around the following parameters can now start getting monitored real time:

- Manager support
- Career growth
- Values and ethics
- Recognition and rewards
- Role factors
- Team working and collaboration
- Cross-functional working
- Work environment

Real-time employee data can now be captured right through the employee lifecycle from on-boarding to exit. Mood and sentiment analysis of responses along with slicing and dicing of such responses across multiple variables now enables organizations to proactively identify "at-risk employees", thereby enabling timely and effective management action with the objective of retaining them and keeping them engaged.

**Select Touchpoints and Questions—Illustration**

Get started by confirming touchpoints in your employee lifecycle and the questions to be asked at each intervention. Now, sit back and relax, while the chatbot talks to them at these periodic intervals.

See below an illustrative question, the responses for which are captured and analysed real time. This triggers an organization response almost immediately, thereby leading to agile, optimized people-centric decision-making (Exhibit 7.3).

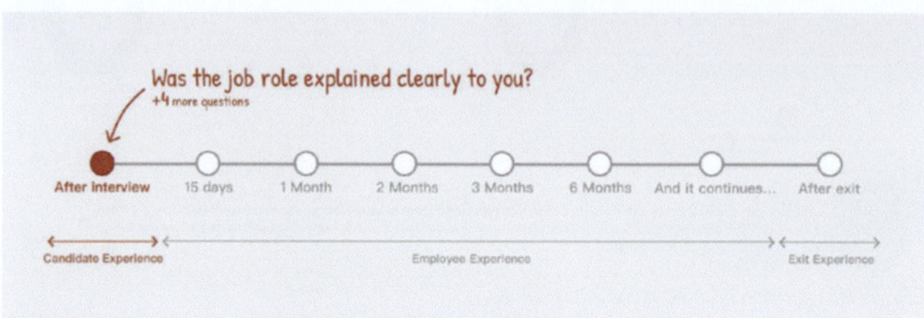




**Exhibit 7.3** Illustration of real-time feedback across multiple employee lifecycle touchpoints

Let us face it; everybody hates surveys; with survey fatigue kicking in, let the chatbot take charge of this in a humanized and personalized way. She/he will interact with your employees at their lifecycles over chat and send you daily + fortnightly reports.

This real-time feedback enables you to "listen in" on the voice of employees and start acting almost immediately.

**For organization to have a continuous pulse on employee engagement, the following actions need to be undertaken with suitable resource allocation done:**

- **Run multiple surveys** and then interpret the results for rapid visualization
- **Frequently collect** ongoing engagement data leveraging artificial intelligence and natural language processing tools—**chatbots and text analytics**
- **Reduce cycle time** from data collection to analysis, interpretation and action
- **Enhance performance on the back of rapid feedback** with impact of decisions and actions becoming clearer to managers far quicker by spotting risks well in time, so mitigating actions could be taken
- **Integrate the data from unstructured feedback with other structured data** from other areas both within and outside HR (for example rewards, performance and demographics or sales, customer and financial data), so your insights around engagement or morale could be seen together with operations for enhancing operating performance.

## 7.13 Real-time Feedback

Some forward looking organizations such as Adobe and GE have now junked year end appraisals. The "annual appraisal" process and the philosophy behind the same have been replaced with more "real-time" instantaneous feedback on competencies and behaviours. This is a paradigm shift in "performance management" practice and implies that "real-time, spontaneous and instantaneous feedback" not only is more accurate, free of bias or prejudice but also ensures greater transparency and engagement of the work force.

The question is how has this been made possible? Powerful SMAC technologies driven by AI and NLP with the ability to capture real-time feedback have provided organizations with the option of literally tracking, monitoring and getting feedback at a frequency of its choice. It could be real time, daily, weekly, fortnightly or monthly. With smartphones being made fairly affordable, it enables organizations to load these applications and shoot out "questions" or ask for "feedback" almost at every touchpoint even for a distributed workforce. These applications also have the ability to mine the data coming in again almost instantaneously, thereby churning out a slice and dice of the data by dimension, location, grade or other demographics again accessible by People Managers on their smart devices.

This is almost like a daily/weekly ESAT or pulse survey, enabling the organization to monitor morale and drive engagement on an ongoing basis.

**Case 1: Organization Transformation: Culture Building through "Culture Analytics" Implemented at a Manufacturing company for all its "People Managers": =/>3 Direct Reports**

## 7.14 Situation and Context

In the middle of rapidly changing times and with the need to transform its internal culture with a view to responding to external business challenges, this company sought to make the transition to start measuring leadership behaviours of its People Managers including leadership. This was driven from the very top with the CEO/CHRO and rest of the leadership team opening themselves up for assessment and feedback as well. The company deployed "People Manager Behaviour Scorecarding" for fostering a more open culture by focusing on "manager quality". There is an old adage: employees do not leave organizations; they leave managers.

People Manager Behaviour Scorecarding was one of the avenues for fostering a more open culture at this company with a turnover of approximately 1 billion $. This was an organization-wide intervention aimed at inculcating culturally desired behaviours, which are the drivers for culture change, in individual managers who are key actors in shaping organization culture through every behaviour and action they demonstrate. The desired culture forms the impetus for higher business performance.

For the first time "culture pillars" and their behaviour drivers were sought to being "measured" and culture/organization development interventions were being sought to being made on the back of "quantifiable and data-driven" insights rather than gut feel and perception. It was earlier believed that behaviours were too fuzzy and nebulous to be measured; however, the leadership team believed otherwise and with help from Ratan, an external consultant, an instrument was developed which captured key leadership behaviours. Of course, the key "culture pillars" were first arrived at after brainstorming by the leadership team over two days at an offsite; which then provided the foundation for "culture analytics" to then come into its own. This was a classic instance of an organization development intervention putting "people and culture analytics" at the heart of the transformation.

As part of the culture change journey at this company, the following set of culturally desired manager behaviours was arrived at:

Builds talent
Inspires performance
Fosters collaboration
Drives excellence
Surfaces and resolves differences

## 7.15 Scope

Having articulated the specific actionable behaviours that comprised the above behavioural dimensions, the company moved to create the "People Manager Scorecard". This was an **online manager feedback forum/survey tool** that allowed measuring the degree to which all People Managers with three or more direct reports demonstrated these behaviours. This survey was done once a quarter for @200 People Managers across all verticals.

The subsequent versions of the scorecard were in an expanded 360 degree format helping the participating manager to receive feedback from a wider audience of raters. They now received feedback from their direct reports as well as peers and manager.

The intervention invited a large sample size of employees to respond to questions relating to demonstration of core leadership behaviours by their reporting managers. The questions were scored, and the findings were shared with the top 100 plus managers who had a minimum of three direct reportees. The managers apart from receiving their personal scores also had visibility of the mean score of the cohort (only scores/no names or employee details to retain anonymity) so that they could compare their own scores with the average score of the cohort and figure out for themselves where they stood. The respondents included the MD and the Management Committee members who were evaluated by their direct reportees.

## 7.16 Analytics Insight Objectives

The People Manager Scorecard aimed to address the organizational need to actively build a strong, positive and vibrant culture of excellence at the company.

**It is an opportunity**

- For managers: to get feedback; develop and grow as People Managers; build and work with strong teams; be role models and actively bring about the desired culture
- For employees: to give honest, candid feedback; help their managers be better managers; be self-starters that contribute to the desired culture.

**It is a responsibility**

- For managers: take the feedback positively, which is for growth and development, not punishment; encourage team members to give feedback, not punish them for it
- For employees: give feedback for growth and development, not to criticize; be honest, candid and fair in your responses.

The objective of the People Scorecard Survey was to provide periodic feedback from direct reports, peers and manager to the participating managers on their working style, so they can improve it.

## 7.17 Analytics Insight Programme Framework

All managers who had three or more employees reporting to them were eligible to receive feedback through the scorecard. These participating managers seek feedback from their direct reports, their peers and reporting manager.

The survey used two sets of instruments:

- Direct Reports and Manager Survey Instrument
- Peers Survey Instrument.

The post-survey steps comprised of the following three actions:

- Understanding the scorecard
- Action planning
- Reviewing.

**Key Outcomes—What was in it for the company?**

- A proven methodology that enabled the organization to "culture transform" itself.

Organization Health Survey scores improved by 10% points

- An online survey methodology that captured "culture driver" data across People Manager cohorts, highlighting the RAG status across the businesses.

Highest ever survey participation % recorded @ 90%

- Measurable improvements in people and talent management.

Critical talent attrition reduced by 20%

- A coaching culture leading to a more motivated, confident and capable workforce.

Then, 12 internal coaches identified

- A toolset that enabled "People Managers" to improve their "people scores".

People scores for top leadership improved by 16% points over two annual cycles

| | Overall | | G | | H | | I | | J | | K | | L | |
|---|---|---|---|---|---|---|---|---|---|---|---|---|---|---|
| | 910 | | 11 | | 34 | | 347 | | 8 | | 31 | | 78 | |
| Dimension | Fav (%5+6) | Δ | Fav (%5+6) | Δ | Fav (%5+6) | Δ | Fav (%5+6) | Δ | Fav (%5+ | Δ | Fav (%5+ | Δ | Fav (%5+ | Δ |
| Engagement Score | 80% | 8% | 55% | -8% | 76% | 7% | 79% | 10% | 88% | -12% | 81% | 23% | 87% | 14% |
| Career & Personal Growth | 60% | 3% | 27% | 5% | 68% | 12% | 63% | 8% | 71% | 41% | 48% | 4% | 60% | -2% |
| Communication | 67% | 6% | 45% | -10% | 68% | 5% | 66% | 9% | 50% | 10% | 52% | -6% | 68% | 10% |
| Compensation | 48% | -4% | 27% | -28% | 68% | 11% | 48% | -2% | 13% | -37% | 35% | -1% | 49% | -2% |
| Fun@work | 51% | 0% | 18% | -15% | 61% | 14% | 47% | 1% | 38% | -12% | 48% | 12% | 49% | 2% |
| Job | 71% | 1% | 73% | 9% | 74% | 9% | 72% | 5% | 63% | 3% | 61% | 15% | 77% | -4% |
| Performance Management | 52% | 4% | 18% | -2% | 70% | 18% | 51% | 5% | 43% | 13% | 39% | -2% | 55% | 1% |
| Policies and Procedures | 62% | 0% | 18% | -42% | 74% | 5% | 62% | 4% | 63% | 3% | 55% | 13% | 66% | -2% |
| Rewards & Recognition | 61% | 11% | 40% | -10% | 71% | 6% | 61% | 10% | 38% | 18% | 55% | 7% | 64% | 13% |
| Senior Management | 76% | 16% | 50% | 5% | 79% | 14% | 77% | 17% | 86% | 46% | 61% | 15% | 75% | 13% |
| Manager | 72% | 6% | 64% | 14% | 82% | 13% | 73% | 12% | 63% | 33% | 77% | 15% | 71% | -3% |
| Work Environment | 66% | 2% | 55% | -8% | 74% | 26% | 67% | 3% | 88% | 18% | 58% | 20% | 69% | -7% |

Fav: %age of Agree (5) + Strongly Agree (6) responses   < 55%: Concern   55-74%: Improvement Opportunity   ≥ 75%: Sustain

**Exhibit 7.4** Engagement drivers across functions

## 7.18 Key Benefits

- Delivered a talent retention benefit of 20%
- Low cost of ownership
- Equipped People Managers with the tools to engage proactively with their teams
- Created sustainable cost reduction, improved productivity and increased profitability
- Enhanced leadership to connect with their teams and frontline employees
- Helped build a sustainable leadership pipeline across most key roles (Exhibits 7.4 and 7.5).

A case example of how a manufacturing company leveraged engagement and morale surveys, polls and dipsticks on an ongoing basis to track and measure the morale of its workforce.

**CASE 2: Sustainable Engagement and Talent Retention**

## 7.19 Situation and Context

In most companies, data collection around engagement usually happens once a year through a survey where the focus is largely around participation. This organization was keen to take pre-emptive action as it was on a diversification

| Dimension | overall Fav (%4+5) | overall Δ | A Fav (%4+5) | A Δ | B Fav (%4+5) | B Δ | C Fav (%4+5) | C Δ | D Fav (%4+5) | D Δ |
|---|---|---|---|---|---|---|---|---|---|---|
| | 1334 | | 18 | | 101 | | 24 | | 269 | |
| BUILDS TALENT | 74% | 1% | 83% | NA | 72% | -2% | 72% | -3% | 79% | -1% |
| INSPIRES PERFORMANCE | 72% | 0% | 81% | NA | 66% | -6% | 72% | -7% | 77% | 0% |
| FOSTERS COLLABORATION | 78% | 0% | 91% | NA | 75% | 0% | 83% | -6% | 85% | 2% |
| SURFACES AND RESOLVES DIFFERENCES | 72% | -1% | 85% | NA | 70% | -6% | 75% | -2% | 78% | -3% |
| DRIVES EXCELLENCE | 74% | 0% | 84% | NA | 70% | -2% | 78% | -6% | 78% | -3% |
| Overall | 74% | 0% | 84% | NA | 71% | -3% | 76% | -4% | 79% | -1% |

| Dimension | E Fav (%4+5) | E Δ | F Fav (%4+5) | F Δ | G Fav (%4+5) | G Δ | H Fav (%4+5) | H Δ | I Fav (%4+5) | I Δ | J Fav (%4+5) | J Δ |
|---|---|---|---|---|---|---|---|---|---|---|---|---|
| | 43 | | 29 | | 61 | | 637 | | 30 | | 122 | |
| BUILDS TALENT | 82% | 6% | 84% | 0% | 69% | -3% | 70% | 0% | 69% | -1% | 78% | 10% |
| INSPIRES PERFORMANCE | 81% | 4% | 75% | -8% | 67% | -2% | 69% | 0% | 77% | 9% | 75% | 7% |
| FOSTERS COLLABORATION | 92% | 6% | 91% | 4% | 77% | -1% | 74% | 1% | 83% | 9% | 80% | 3% |
| SURFACES AND RESOLVES DIFFERENCES | 86% | 10% | 83% | -4% | 70% | 1% | 67% | -2% | 81% | 12% | 74% | 7% |
| DRIVES EXCELLENCE | 88% | 6% | 84% | -2% | 73% | 0% | 70% | 1% | 81% | 9% | 82% | 9% |
| Overall | 86% | 6% | 83% | -2% | 71% | -1% | 71% | 1% | 78% | 7% | 78% | 8% |

Δ : Change in Favorable scores over 2011.
*All scores are Weighted Scores*

Favourable Score: 76% or higher | 66%-74% | <66%

**Exhibit 7.5** Dimensions scores

spree and needed to ring-fence their key talent and so decided to operationalize employee engagement and manage it in a responsive, intelligent and sustainable way—measure and monitor engagement on an ongoing basis.

## 7.20 Sustaining Engagement and Employee Morale—A Diversified Manufacturing Company

- Conducted multiple survey dipsticks and fed the data back for quick analysis
- Created their own survey tool and imported its results into their analytics toolbox
- Collected low-level engagement data more frequently and intuitively via polls and dipsticks
- Used tablet or "Buzz-box" surveys to guarantee anonymity (on request)
- Used the feedback to course correct with managers becoming more aware
- Engagement trends data was seen with other data to draw relevant insights around other aspects such as performance, rewards and operating productivity, etc.

## 7.21 Steps Taken

The survey was deployed, conducted, and findings are presented in a period of 6–8 weeks.

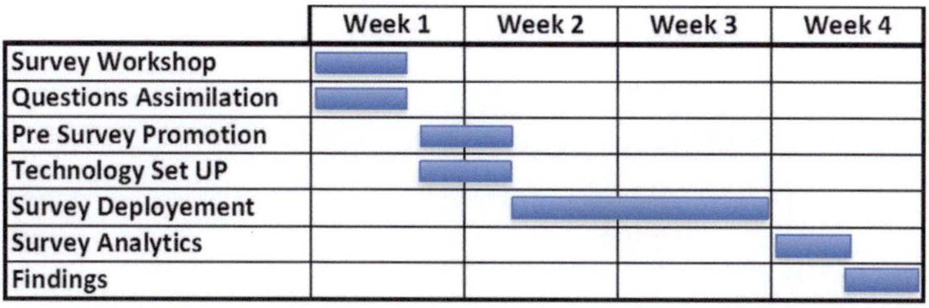


**Key Outcomes—What was in it for this organization?**

- An online methodology that enabled it to health check itself on an ongoing basis
- An effective way to identify "hotspots" and take pre-emptive action to mitigate them
- Improving retention rate of critical talent through pre-emptive action

As a result, talent risks were identified early and mitigated proactively.

**Case 3: Bank that developed a business case by linking employee engagement to customer loyalty**

## 7.22 Situation and Context

The bank was losing its high net worth customers to competitors and was determined to turn the situation around. It soon realized that apart from product and operational factors, a critical ingredient lays in the matter of employee engagement and sought to draw a linkage to the service profit chain, thereby seeking to make out a business case linking employee engagement to customer loyalty.

Rita, the Private Banking Relationship Manager, saw an opportunity here to work with HR to build on team engagement as she believed that it may lead to higher cross-sell and enhanced service levels, thereby impacting both revenue and customer loyalty.

## 7.23 The Service Profit Chain

The relationships between profitability, productivity on one side, customer loyalty on the other and then people engagement are brought to life by the service profit chain. The chain links up in the following manner: an organization's profitability rests on volume and value growth which are driven largely by customer loyalty. Loyalty is a positive fallout of customer satisfaction, which by the way is essentially an outcome of the value of services provided to customers. Value in turn is created by engaged, committed and productive employees. Employee engagement

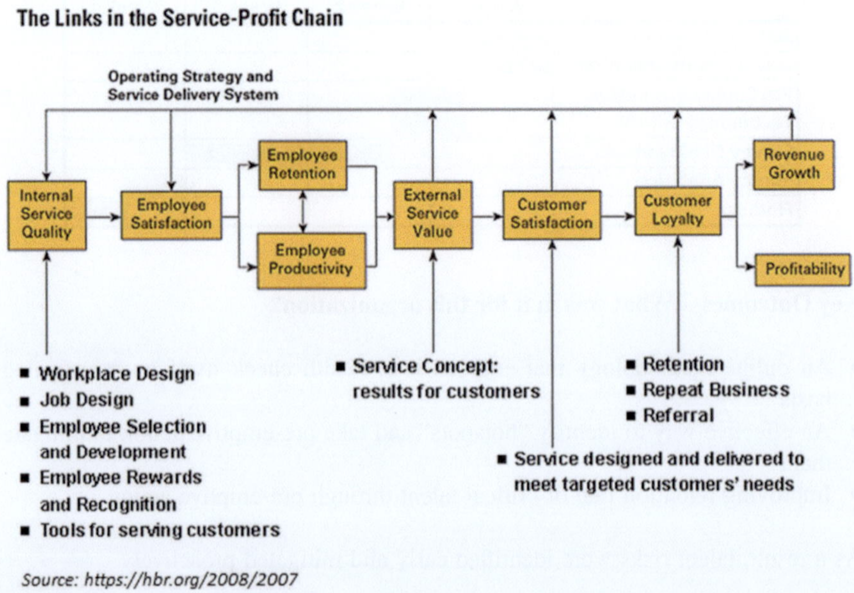


**Exhibit 7.6** Service profit chain

is in effect an outcome largely of support, development and policy frameworks that enable employees to deliver sustainable results to customers (Exhibit 7.6).

## 7.24 Hypotheses

**Business case was sought to be established between external service value and customer loyalty**

- Customers with high ESV scores are *more likely to stay* with the bank for its service and expertise, than for its product range
- Customers with high ESV scores are *more likely* to make additional purchases from the unit generating satisfaction, than its dissatisfied customers
- If customers are not likely to make additional purchases from the unit, because of a lack of personal need, the ESV score would strongly correlate with *likelihood to make* customer referrals (positive recommendations of the company to others), leading to acquisition of new customers for the brand.

*Note: Customer satisfaction is a measure that is coloured by product and operational policy drivers, in most cases not in the control of customer-facing staff.*

The team led by Rita and supported by HR then sought to measure the following drivers of employee engagement and came up with the following findings:

1. **Diversity of skill sets entailed in the role**

Engagement for individuals across a variety of roles was found to be driven by the range of skills and competencies the role required. The more the skills required, the more enriched the role becomes or is perceived to become as far as employees are concerned and that creates within the employee a perceived sense of value.

2. **Brand equity coupled with service quality and excellence**

Employees believed that organizations that were customer-friendly and made customers central to what they did were the better employers and reflective of an employer brand that they would like to be associated with. Again, the realization that they play a key role in meeting those customer needs further is reflective of the high levels of correlation found between employee engagement levels and customer satisfaction across various pieces of research.

3. **Functions and locations that communicate & collaborate towards meeting common goals**

Individuals and teams feel more comfortable in organizations that combine well across functions and have a continuous flow of communication, thereby ensuring transparency as opposed to an opaque-like structure or framework.

4. **Generational conflict**

Consistency of approach has the potential to bring people together, empathize with each other and support one another while on the flip side, if asked to follow directions without due explanation or which they believe has contradictions or has negative impact; it has an altogether dysfunctional impact.

5. **Impact Learning**

It was found that quality on-boarding had a tremendous impact both on engagement as well as on employee retention. The first 90 days are extremely crucial for both employee and employer, and any negative employee or organizational experience during this block of 90 days could lead to attrition that would impact the business. New joiners who experienced quality on-boarding and relevant learning early on can deploy their new skills and start contributing with impact. An early focus on learning is reflective of the organization valuing the employee both in their current role and recognizing their full potential.

6. **Empowerment and autonomy**

Empowering capable employees and allowing them the operating freedom to perform their roles optimally also helped to drive ownership. Needless to add, the organization also needed to provide support and resources to build self-awareness and capability.

7. **Reporting Manager Competence**

Engagement is also driven by both real and perceived technical and managerial competence of the immediate supervisor. Technical competence of the reporting manager coupled with the respect he or she is able to instil in their team members along with openness of interaction between the two cohorts was also found to be important factors.

## 7.25 Bank Used the Following Research Methodology

- Segment employee base at branch level: customer facing vs mid-/back office—prelaunch
  - Demographic and employment history required
- Segment customer types: transaction accounts vs. value segments—prelaunch
  - Customer value required
- Conduct dipstick data capture using online survey—4 weeks
  - 100% employee base
  - Sample of 1000 per customer group
- Run statistical modelling—4 weeks
- Preliminary findings—1 week.

## 7.26 The Team then Delivered the Following Insights from the Analytics Programme: Behaviours Driven by the Organization Culture

- Understanding the feelings an employee has towards their role (and the organization) with regard to personal value, respect and freedom
- Understanding the extent to which an employee understands the needs of the customer, therefore taking it upon themselves to create products and services to meet those needs
- Understanding the extent to which an employee will go to doing the best to remove barriers from getting the job done the "right" way
- Understanding team dynamics and performance
- Linking employee [engagement score] to customer [external service value score] with a significant correlation being drawn between employee engagement (score) and customer loyalty (external service value score) validated through data science tools. Employee engagement was then identified as a key predictor of customer loyalty, and within engagement, "key drivers" were ranked in order of priority and significance in its linkage to customer loyalty.

## 7.27 A Well-documented Case Study in the Matter of Employee Engagement and Customer Loyalty is that of a Retail Company

The company has been leveraging an analytics model to link HR decisions and business outcomes. As always, the biggest challenge was about getting management buy-in. Their analytics team sought to link various HR data (such as engagement, churn and wellbeing) to customer data (satisfaction and loyalty), supply chain data (inventory loss) and business/financial measures (such as sales per square foot and net income before tax). Once consensus was arrived at, a cross-functional team was put in place that developed a set of statistical models to test how the above data interacted with each other and what insights were derived.

Results and impact—a key finding from the analytics was the linkage established between engagement, customer loyalty and business/revenue impact. While the company may have sensed that engagement and customer satisfaction were closely linked, the company was able to validate that hypothesis by allocating a financial value to this relationship. For instance a clear linkage emerged between staff engagement and share of customer wallet—money spent by customer for each transaction. Through enhanced communication between staff and customers, the latter perceived an enhanced store experience and spent more per transaction. The company estimated that the revenue gap between the lowest and highest engaged store (in terms of staff engagement levels) was around one million $ per annum. With the business case, it established the HR team, then focused on replicating these practices across other store formats driving systemic transformation across the company.

This led to business leaders placing a value on employee engagement creating a "pull" effect making them want to learn levels of engagement of their own teams and what they could personally do to drive engagement levels. This is how in this company People Analytics has played a key role in enabling the business to drive sustainable change with clear business outcomes.

# 8 People Analytics in Mergers and Acquisitions

## 8.1 Context

An absolutely critical prerequisite for any merger and acquisition is risk assessment and due diligence protocols to first identify and then mitigate the key risks both for today and for tomorrow. There is tremendous business value for deploying analytics towards ensuring a seamless culture and structure integration apart from enabling the company to draw up a key risk mitigation strategy to address both present and future talent, operational and strategic risks. The success/failure of any M&A rests on the robustness of the due diligence and analytics protocols followed across the deal continuum.

## 8.2 M&A Deal Continuum

Every M&A has to tread on a six-step continuum from predeal stage to post-deal integration.

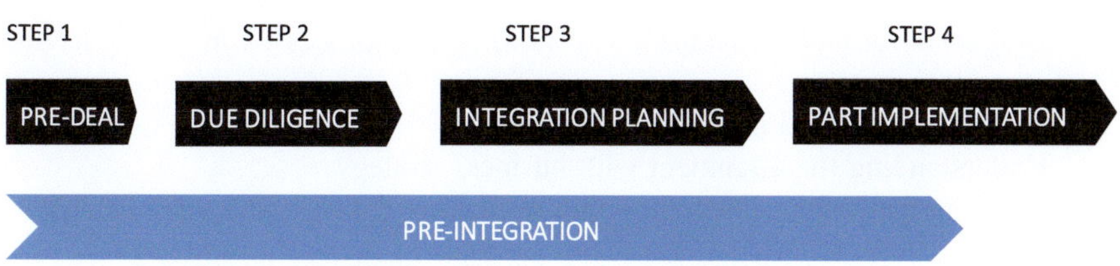




R. Ghatak, *People Analytics*, Management for Professionals,
https://doi.org/10.1007/978-981-19-3873-3_8

**In the Pre-integration stages, each step is a new level of commitment towards the deal and requires more data and analytics.**

**Predeal**: The company Identifies the strategy driving the M&A, locates and selects targets, determines potential business opportunity, defines critical success factors and notifies target company of intent

*HR's role: To provide inputs and guidance on HR impact and aspects, run deep-dive analysis on organization design, people practices, organization behaviour and culture fit based on data that is accessible, bring out people and culture-related aspects, set out an agenda for due diligence*

**Due diligence**: Information here is collated from the target and analysed, leadership teams are assessed, findings summarized, issues and risks debated and documented and go/no go decisions made

*HR's role: To collect and analyse HR-related information, identify issues, risks, costs and savings*

**Integration planning**: To set deal terms, used information previously collected to create plans to combine companies with minimal business disruptions, close the deal

*HR's role: To secure key talent from target, collect more information where necessary, create integration team for HR, create HR integration plans (e.g. culture, organization, people, retention programmes, HR processes, HR systems and policies)*

- **Evaluation of critical synergies with its linkages to the original acquisition strategy by the deal team involves:**
  - Lessons learned from project management
  - Diagnostic around organization design, people processes in a time bound manner
  - Suggestions around process improvements
  - Understanding the alignment with business strategy
  - Planning for culture integration and mitigating the risks that may emerge.

Acquiring companies remain essentially optimistic whether their deal was successful or not, yet two-thirds of deals fail to create real value.

> "55% of acquisitions fail to meet cost-saving targets"—Accenture Executive Survey, June 2006.
> "Our latest observations are that 50.5% of the mergers create value while the other 49.5% perform below their stock value before the merger"—AT Kearney online, July 2006.

## 8.3 Key Risks in M&A Integrations

Research in this area has brought out that risks related to culture and people alignment and fit present the most critical challenges during the post-deal period (Exhibit 8.1).

**However, organizations that are proactive take the following steps to mitigate these risks:**

- Recognize that the bulk of the barriers to change are people related.
- In all M&A activities—They consider how they would identify and manage the human impacts of change in order to deliver the business goals and strategy.
- They ensure that their change programmes were distinct from, but linked to, the more technical HR elements of M&A such as rewards, benefits and job alignments.
- They address both the day 1 issues (systems access, tools, etc.) and the longer-term integration needs of employees.
- Typically their change programmes address:
  Change definition (what, why, when, how)
  Change leadership style and capability of the acquirer and the target company
  Culture, behaviour and climate
  Key talent retention
  Communication and engagement
  Relationship/stakeholder management
  Organization design and structures.

**Exhibit 8.1** Key challenges in integration

## 8.4 HR Data Structures—Due Diligence

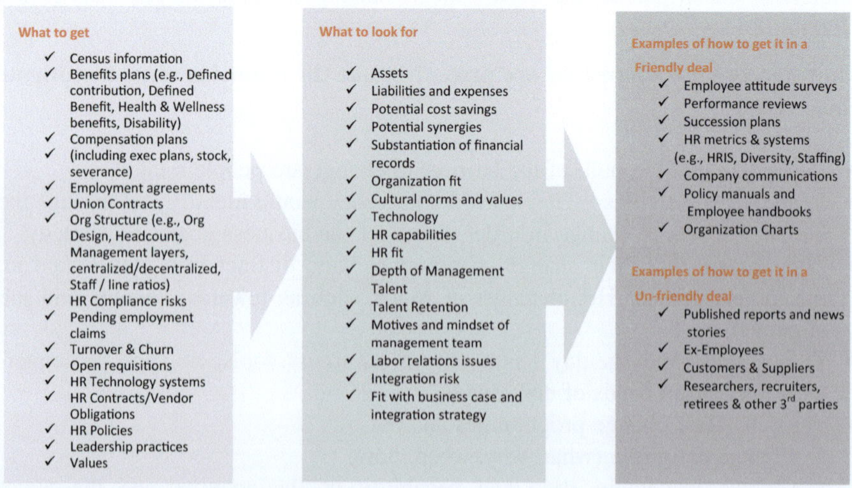


**The real value of People Analytics in M&A**

All of this data is then analysed with a view to taking decisions and coming up with specific strategies related to integration. People Analytics is leveraged to make sense of the enormous people data repository the acquiring company has taken over. The analysis and decisions herein will determine the people strategies adopted for post-deal integration. The insights thereby collated will play a crucial role in deciding whether the integration turns out to be a success or failure.

Data resting in organizations could be both structured and unstructured and ways need to be found to analyse both these data types lying in multiple source repositories. This analysis will then provide the requisite insights for organizations to develop their integration strategy to enable them to take the optimum decisions to mitigate key risks related to talent, performance, compliance, costs, culture and so on.

Unlike earlier times, today there are a host of solutions and tools from cloud-based data warehousing to People Analytics solutions that can ensure first you are able to migrate data from multiple sources into a single data repository, second, ensure data can be analysed in quick time to be cleansed and standardized and third, throw up the dashboards and visualizations required to evidence the insights to senior management. With these tools, due diligence can actually be completed in reasonably quick time allowing you then to start seeing the linkages between the HR data and key business KPIs and outcomes. By crashing the cycle time on due diligence and also saving costs, contemporary People Analytics tools become a key input into the M&A space which commands a premium on time, cost, visibility, insight and foresight.

The value therefore lies in the crucial elements of employee data seemingly hidden within many business systems that become visible and get bubbled up to key decision-makers. Through analytics, you can connect the dots and leverage people and business data to identify key value creators or mitigate critical risks.

**HR Due Diligence for M&A—Critical Steps**

In the M&A context, there are two crucial steps to be adhered to:

- Premerger—Evaluate the worth and risk and weigh the trade-off
- Post-merger—Once decision is taken to merge or acquire, then draw up an implementation road map with clear and agreed milestones.

*For the evaluation stage, People Analytics may be leveraged to run pulse dipsticks on the target company's climate and health.*

**You can examine the following:**

- Quality of sustainable leadership, culture pillars and traits, succession plans for key roles, core values and behaviours along with of course the business and revenue model
- Role and people allocations; future leader and high potential talent; high-performing and underperforming individuals and teams
- Churn rate of high potential and key talent; their levels of engagement, etc.
- Units that seemingly are doing well but in reality are bleeding and leaving invisible footprints which today can be uncovered through analytics (employee and customer churn, higher cost of sale, lower productivity, lower margins, etc.)

**In post-merger implementation**, by addressing the knowledge gaps through a rapid analysis of the data points captured from multiple sources, from HCM systems like Oracle, Workday or Successfactors or from Excel spreadsheets or even business data from sales systems like salesforce.com or CRMs or ERPs, you can start taking more objective decisions related to integration, talent, performance, compensation and benefits harmonization, organization design and culture fit issues.

Ensuring that workforce data constitutes a crucial aspect of the due diligence process value add can be seen in three broad areas:

1. Hiring decisions getting smarter
2. Retaining critical talent
3. Creating business value.

Timely generation and delivery of such data to the targeted recipient helps derisk the M&A against talent, performance and reputation risk.

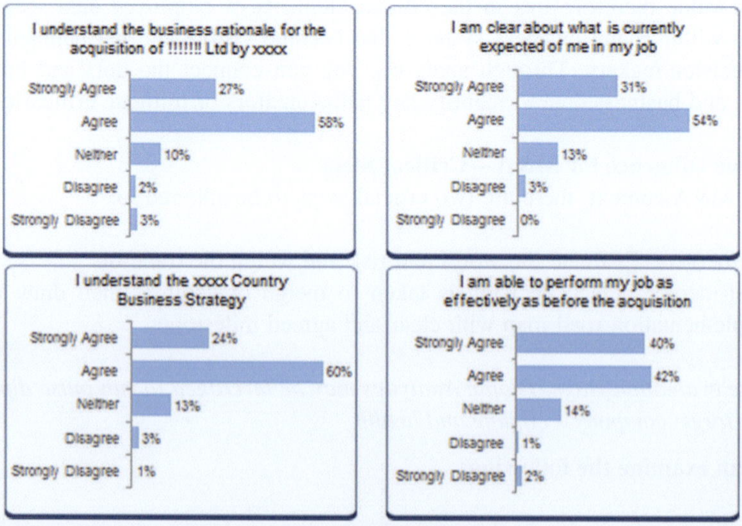


**Exhibit 8.2** Illustration of feedback from a pulse survey

For structured feedback, organizations use pulse and buzz-box surveys to dive into the insight regarding employee's understanding and perception of the deal and acquisition as illustrated in Exhibit 8.2.

## 8.5 Summing up

It goes without saying that the talent being acquired is key to either deliver or undermine the ROI of a deal. To safeguard the ROI, it is critical to come up with a risk management framework focused on a 360° view of things. Increasingly, analytics is being used to bubble up data that hitherto may not have been visible or remained hidden from due diligence. Talent and leadership risks or hidden cost liabilities are getting more and more difficult to hide due to the new-found ability of analyses, to leverage these tools to bring out the insights.

It is important to know that M&A deals are varied in nature. Some are asset transactions—acquisition of intellectual property rights or manufacturing hubs/factories—while others stake their future on the quality of human capital. The quality of your workforce is what drives future revenue growth and so investing behind tools that can analyse this asset more deeply and in more granular fashion, to enable future projections on business outcomes is the need of the hour. For acquiring companies, the relationship between workforce characteristics and medium to long-term business success is arrived at by analysing historical trends on revenue, profitability and costs and then making Excel-based projections; what this fails to take into account is the people side of the business.

Budget focused approaches to analyse headcount and employee cost implications may look simple, but it misses out on other key human capital drivers. For a typical people intensive enterprise, a suitable evaluation will require a much deeper understanding of the target organization's workforce dynamics—that is, the organization's talent frameworks, performance management processes, compensation philosophy and practices, cultural moorings, engagement drivers and compliance standards while understanding the linkages of these processes to business outcomes and performance over a period of time.

Workforce dynamics reveal how the key objectives of the deal can be achieved through changes in people decisions, policy frameworks, etc., after deal closure. The data around due diligence would also throw up decision choices around—talent (buy vs build), learning (roadblocks vs facilitation), high external dependencies on populating critical roles, retention challenges, practices and processes around talent acquisition, pay-for-performance and training programs, any of which could become an obstacle. In the case of a merger, differences in practices and policy frameworks need to be converted into broad synergies before going ahead.

Analytics is therefore at the heart of the change management focus of any acquirer in an M&A situation if the acquirer has any intention of making the deal a sustainable success.

# People Analytics Enablement Through Systems Thinking

# 9

## 9.1 Context

Organization strategy is almost always delivered through an operating plan that sets out what work needs to be done, by whom and at what cost. Analytics in the workplace is able to provide insights into how to resource it correctly; identifying the right types of people to do it; motivating them to engage in the work and constantly exploring innovations in how that work gets done to meet the business goals.

Analytics looks for patterns in employee attitudes and behaviours towards work activities required to achieve business goals. It goes on to predict the outcome of management interventions on employee ability to meet their personal objectives.

Analytics is most successful when applied to a business problem, solution of which gives the firm competitive advantage. The analytical process therefore needs to be consistent and agile to define the problem, gather data, interpret it and enable action.

The five-step systems thinking approach to People Analytics is an optimal insight to action process.

## 9.2 Five-Step Systems Thinking

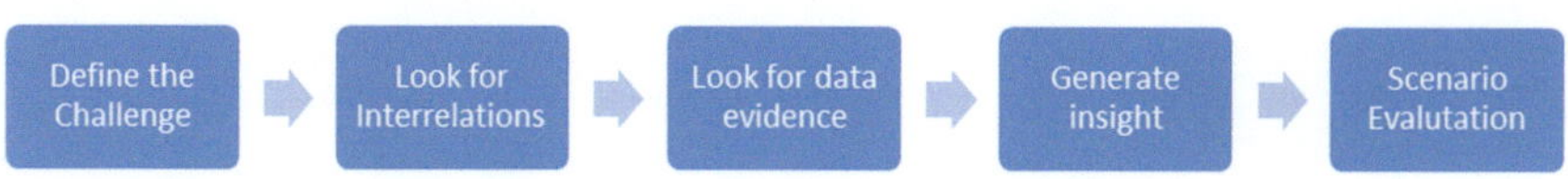


 
R. Ghatak, *People Analytics*, Management for Professionals,
https://doi.org/10.1007/978-981-19-3873-3_9

1. **Defining the Challenge**

   This is a critical first step requiring inputs across stakeholders. Given that every problem is a key cog of a network of interrelated problems, it is critical to explore the hierarchy to understand the scope of the challenge.

2. **Seeking some interrelations**

   The People Analytics framework uses system thinking to probe below the surface of the challenges, issues and/or opportunities. Interrelations are clarified by asking: What is happening? What has been happening? Are there similar events elsewhere? What are the contributors? What is there in our thinking that prevents change? How can we predict outcomes?

   The outcome of this journey of inquiry is a root cause analysis that generates sustainable solutions as they take into account the interrelated issues to the main problem.

3. **Looking for data evidence**

   Imperfect data and the collection of excess and unrelated data are reduced as the hypothesized model informs data needs.

4. **Insight generation**

   Various process mapping and quantitative techniques illuminate the causes and potential interventions with a focus on long listing actionable solutions.

5. **Scenario Evaluation**

   The shortlisted interventions are evaluated with what-if scenario modelling to predict overall outcomes and intermediary impact on associated issues to enable sustainable decision-making.

**The people and talent analytics journey** is about not only asking the right questions but also answering them rapidly, almost in real time. That is the cutting edge that will differentiate HR teams from one another and provide competitive advantage to organizations.

## 9.3 People Analytics Deployment

Most organizations struggle to answer the following three questions: What, When and How? When do they begin; what they need to do and how do they operationalize and give it life?

**In days**

**"See your business"** – rapidly visualize your data in order to kick-start your project and provide immediate value to the user community.
Stories hidden in your data can be revealed almost immediately.

**Benefits**

- Rapid visualization of data builds momentum for later stages of the project
- Low cost, high value initiation to project
- Lean, efficient development approach
- Extreme low investment required upfront; no IT capital expenditure required
- Creation of working tools from day one
- Project team gains thorough understanding of business early and rapidly.

**Activities**

- Creation of dashboards and charts using data visualization tools
- Visual analysis of data for answering ad hoc queries
- Immediate understanding of data quality
- Training and handover process begins.

In weeks

**"Share your insight"** – deliver data presentations to a wider community using web based tools and connect to live data to provide real time access to information.
Introduce a wider range of possible dashboards to meet user needs.

**Benefits**

- Dashboards shared with larger "user community" early in the project life cycle
- Integration of multiple data sources into a single data cube
- Trust in the data sources develops rapidly
- Live data connections make the system deliver insights with no manual intervention.

**Activities**

- Provision of a reporting platform to deliver charts and dashboards to wider audience
- Performance tuning to ensure higher user acceptance
- Real-time or near real time data being visualized through charts and dashboards.

Data visualizations can now be connected to live data and published to a wider audience through browser-based tools. The system will become more robust, data will become trusted, and learning among the analytics team members will continue to accelerate.

**In months**

**"Enterprise People Analytics"** – full data solution which delivers a single version of the truth in a high performance environment. Provides robust, validated data across the whole organisation. Only undertaken when the team has gained required knowledge.

**Benefits**

- High-performance reporting frameworks capable of handling large datasets in near real time
- Single version of the truth—one data source which joins all transactional databases
- Integration of any number of data sources
- Robust data validation
- Strong support for security and end-user permissions
- Getting started on predictive models.

**Activities**

- Design and development of a data warehouse
- Development of extract, transform and load (ETL) processes to load the data warehouse
- Data cube generation from multiple sources
- End-to-end data validation
- Creation of auditing framework to ensure high data quality
- Development of predictive models.

The end game of any People Analytics project—production of a single trusted data source—populated from all transactional systems used throughout the business. This provides the highest source of "robustness", performance and trusted data.

## 9.4 People Analytics Journey and Enablement

What are the next steps for People Analytics enablement, effectiveness and impact?

**Establish one cleansed file for the complete employee dataset**

- Identify errors and missing data and make corrections easily
- Design and broadcast web forms to collect missing data and then update the same

- Use data quality reports to drive consistency.

**Visualize hierarchy within the organization and set up HR operational analytics**

- Clarify reporting lines; produce instant organization charts
- Analyse heat maps for performance ranking, cost, risks, etc.
- Link datasets from traditional people sources and outcomes, e.g. sales, surveys, absence, performance
- Institutionalize first level dashboards across all key HR metrics.

**Extend into advanced analytics linking to business strategy**

- Go from people to roles, to Processes, Competencies, Clients and Objectives
- Track cost ratios, headcount ratios, identify drivers of best performance
- Link business outcome data to HR data.

Predictive analytics: Identify a "business challenge" and solve for it.

What are companies doing? Examples of positive momentum may be visible in the following areas:

**Sales Performance and Recruiting**

- Insurance companies have analysed the profiles of top salespeople and now know that screening candidates for grade point average or academic pedigree is no longer considered a strong indicator of future sales performance.
- An analytics model was developed by a technology company that was accurately able to predict those profiles of candidates who were likely to demonstrate negative or toxic traits (those who lie, cheat, or commit fraud) and drastically minimized the probability of hiring such profiles by deploying the model in a certain part of the selection process.

**Productivity**

- Organizations that hire on a mass scale such as ITes, consumer, retail and banks are starting to analyse the persona traits of high-performing employees, particularly the customer facing or revenue generating cohorts, understanding their social networks, how they work and collaborate internally, and how they engage with customers. These insights then go into predicting results and business outcomes far more accurately than study of any historical data or training or operational metrics.
- Some evolved HR functions are now analysing e-mail metadata to understand why some people are more collaborative than others or manage stakeholders better than others or more productive than others; then leveraging the insights to optimize on results.

- A large cosmetics manufacturer sets up a "sales productivity centre of excellence" to study hiring patterns, training, compensation and other people practices in the sales force to optimize productivity using people-related data.
- A well-known retail company found that by linking sales data to the hiring and selection of store managers, analytics improved profitability both at the store and across the organization. In essence, the data revealed how more analytics-driven hiring practices, higher offer acceptance rates and reduced time to hire drove store performance and profitability.
- Some manufacturing organizations are studying the patterns of unplanned absenteeism to predict when specific people are likely to take an unauthorized day off, prescheduling extra casual or contract labour to make up for estimated periods of absence.
- Some Oil and Gas companies are using a predictive workforce planning and analytics model to identify current and future talent and skills gaps in critical oil and gas occupations over a long-term horizon. The model takes into consideration some macroeconomic factors like oil price and exchange rates that correlate strongly to the demand and supply of skilled labour.

**Retention**

- Some organizations are now collecting data from LinkedIn and other social networks to predict the "high-flight-risk" candidates among their high-potential employees.
- Companies are experimenting with smart badges, using them to gather data suggesting that offices with larger shared workrooms, more light and more inter-company collaboration have higher retention and productivity.
- Some organizations are also developing predictive models focused on enhancing the employee experience through a range of data sources that throw up patterns for analysis that then enable decision-makers to get on top of issues such as high-potential talent retention and predicting flight risk.

**Compliance and risk**

- Banks are studying patterns of fraud and non-compliance and can now predict "persona traits" that will likely result in unethical behaviour.
- Some financial services companies use analytics to evaluate individual outliers, with a view towards identifying "rogue traders" and other compliance breaches as part of their risk management framework.
- Some large manufacturing and power companies also leverage analytics to identify probable safety hazards or behaviours that could have been demonstrated to prevent accidents.

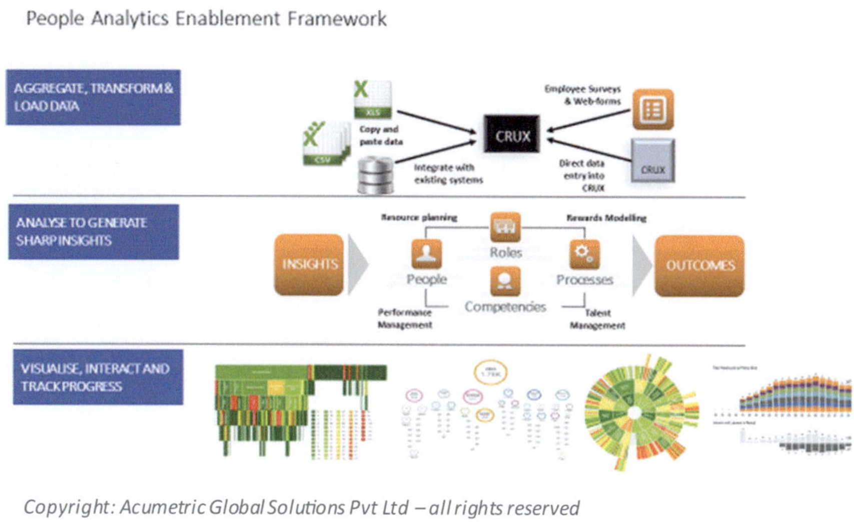


**Exhibit 9.1** Enablement framework and ecosystem

## Culture

- Some organizations collect data to assess the strength of its cultural values and the degree to which they have got institutionalized, through analysing a combination of internal and external data points including running text analysis of external sites such as Glassdoor.

Each of these instances reveals the opportunity to take people data (some from HR, some from business and some external to the company) to make better management decisions. Organizations are now starting to see the value of this upcoming domain and have started investing behind it both through capabilities and technologies.

The trend towards analytics-driven HR will continue gathering strength over the coming years. Today's People Analytics teams bring together data from a range of sources, including core HR systems, employee engagement data, survey data, external data (from LinkedIn, Glassdoor, and other systems) and text data from employee comments. Then they analyse these data points to understand company culture, find opportunities to improve retention or performance or diagnose key risks or other operational gaps (Exhibit 9.1).

# Organization Design, Rewards and HR Value Chain

# 10

## 10.1 Context

What are the key HR challenges that organizations typically face today and what are the various people and talent analytics responses that are recommended for organizations deploying and integrating into their HR delivery model? Organizational agility has become critical to enable organizations to respond fast to both "business as usual" situations such as differential pay allocations, process optimization, performance management and workforce planning as well as to "unique one-off events" such as transformation, restructuring or organization design interventions with razor sharp analytics solutions that enable agile and robust decision-making in real time. For this to be sustainable, a suitable ecosystem needs to be put in place with the right capabilities supported by relevant technologies and infrastructure.

## 10.2 HR Challenge #1

**Organization Design**

Digital disruption and dynamic global changes have forced companies to rapidly move up the innovation curve, adapt their products and services and focus their attention on local customers. This has prompted a resurgence of interest in business organization to be able to "think global and act local". Most companies believe that redesigning the organization is critical to not only optimizing on efficiencies but also to gain larger share of the consumer wallet. Companies are moving towards decentralization by going closer to the markets they operate in and delegating authority to local management, building business models that are product- and customer-centric and forming social networks of nimble and highly empowered teams that collaborate, communicate and coordinate work in unique and disruptive ways.

 
R. Ghatak, *People Analytics*, Management for Professionals,
https://doi.org/10.1007/978-981-19-3873-3_10

The emergence of the millennials in the labour market, the diverse nature of global teams and the need to innovate and work intimately with customers and vendors are triggering a never seen before kind of flexibility among highly customer-centric organizations. Their operating model is based on a network of teams working in tandem with traditional structures, with people flipping from team to team rather than remaining in rigid, formal hierarchies.

Organization design demands holistic systems thinking. It involves reviewing a range of options, each one backed up by numbers and charts. Processes must be defined, accountabilities mapped, headcounts rightsized. You also need to understand the impact on employees and track the benefits. Doing this quickly and accurately has been difficult or impossible.

**This is where People Analytics could be leveraged to**:

- **Challenge your existing organization design**: explore working your way around rigid structures to form specific "mission-critical" teams focused on unique problems or tasks or projects around customers, markets, technology or products and services and then once the project is complete the teams disband with individual team members moving into either different teams for solving a different set of problems or slipping back into a more formally structured role
- **Build real-time networks**: such a configuration pulls information from multiple sources to provide integrated data on customers, products, people in real time, enabling decision-makers to take quick decisions to respond to marketplace challenges. In today's ever-changing business environment, the need for agility supersedes all else
- **Do more with same or less**: the need is to optimize in today's environment and do away with all bad costs. Design your organization in a manner that drives process efficiencies as opposed to accumulating headcount and flab. Service and support functions ideally that serve the front-end business side of organizations ideally should be converted into shared services. How can you leverage analytics to identify underutilized spans of control to highlight inefficiencies?
- **Recast your Goals and link to Rewards**: focus on the team as opposed to the individual; flexible work teams are going to rule the roost in organizations, so the need of the hour is to figure out ways to better manage and reward them. Reward and recognize teams for project results, collaboration, supporting others; team innovation etc.; work out performance management processes around teams and stop giving importance to titles
- **Team-based processes and tools**: embed processes and tools that measure networking, collaboration and supporting others across team-based environments as work is going to become less structured, more amorphous, and team-based organizations are more likely to win and deliver results. The competencies and skill sets that people would need to develop are a far cry from the old traditional skill sets, and these new ways of working need to be adopted fast for companies to start winning in the marketplace

- **Inverted Goal Setting**: certainly, teams need to deliver results and would need to own that accountability—but, let them be self-managed; decide how to allocate and schedule their work among themselves and to communicate with each other; in a sense empower them to run on their own with minimum interference from the formal structure or hierarchy
- **Articulate a shared purpose and vision and then communicate down the line**: leaders should be leaders and not do jobs that are several notches lower; they must be left to think strategy, innovation, customer and growth; the day-to-day operating results should be left to the teams.

**Analytics Response**

- **Build and model organizational scenarios** whatever method you want to use and whatever level of detail you want to go to. There are cloud-based technologies today that enables easier workflow and better results
- **Build your baseline** using data from existing HRMS and other multiple sources—more quickly and effectively than you thought possible
- **Communicate your new design** by clarifying and recording goals, objectives, processes, decisions, competencies and activities
- **Define your new role tree** and assign employees to it, so you can see the impact of your design at aggregate and individual level.

As a microcosm of the larger organization design changes taking place, the Human Resources organization itself is undergoing rapid transformation to meet the new challenges (Exhibit 10.1).

| CAPABILITY | TODAY | TOMORROW |
|---|---|---|
| HR Business Partner  | HR Generalists are "jack of all trades" spending a disproportion amount of time spent on administritative and core process execution accountabilities. | HRBP proactively contributes to business strategy and business performance using data-driver insights. |
| Centers of Expertise  | Organisations have a fragmented approach to designing, developing and delivering talent and organisation strategies and programs that differ by business. | Leverage external leading practices to apply a consistent global approcah to creating and implementing common programs and policies |
| Shared Services  | Varying levels of call center and back office resources are available with local HR teams responsible to deliver core processes and training programs | Shared Services Solution Delivery Teams create and deliver consistent data driven insights through analytics, solutions, training courses, programs and core processes that are globally relevant and scalable. |
| Self-Service  | HR is heavily involved in assisting managers and employees in completing employment transactions and core processes including reporting and analysis. | People Managers and employees are accountable for an expanded menu of employment transactions |

**Exhibit 10.1** Evolving HR operating model

Human Resources will be reorganized into essentially three separate areas of focus:

- Business partnering
- Centres of expertise
- Shared services.

The transactional repetitive tasks would either be transitioned into a "self-service" model (employee and manager) or outsourced completely.

The HRBP will now proactively contribute to business strategy and business performance using data-driven insights.

The centres of expertise will now leverage external leading practices to apply a consistent global approach to creating and implementing global programmes, policies and solutions.

Shared services solution delivery teams create and deliver consistent data-driven insights through analytics, solutions, training courses, programmes and core processes that are globally relevant and scalable.

*A case example where a global services company sought to rationalize its central functions through modelling organization design scenarios basis span of control analysis in quick time to meet project time lines.*

**Case 1: Organization Redesign and Transformation for a Global Services Company**
**Situation and Context**

- A global services company sought to rationalize its central functions, to deliver better services at 20% lower costs
- The project team led by Deepak needed to transform its organizational structure and to map costs into roles
- The traditional solutions: Excel, Visio and Power Point were too cumbersome for the fast-moving project.

**Analytics Solution**

- Converted existing spreadsheets into new organization diagrams within a day
- Helped the client model and share the financial and resource impact of each scenario, allowing fact-based decisions on new structures.

**Key Outcomes**

- Decisions on change made in 2 weeks, where the project had previously been stuck for two months "in Excel hell"
- Span of control issues identified and corrected
- Decisions communicated simply by managers to their teams
- Cost savings targets achieved (Exhibits 10.2, 10.3 and 10.4).

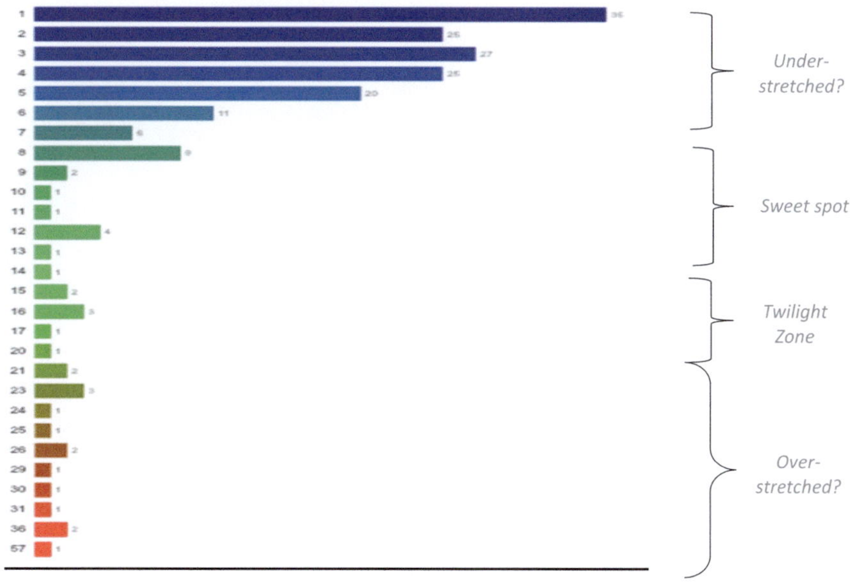




**Exhibit 10.2** Analytics helped identify large (and small) spans of control

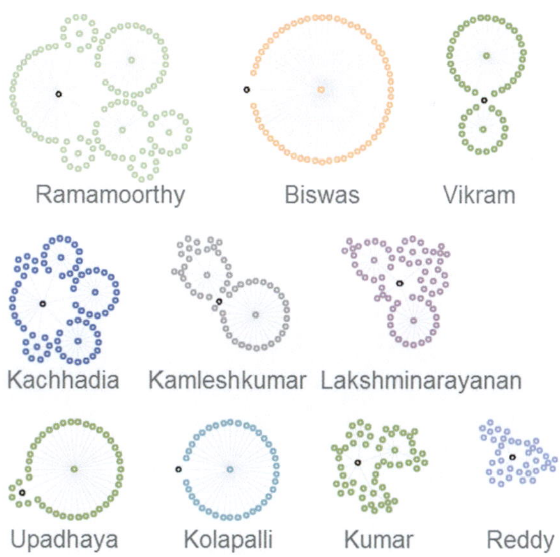


**Exhibit 10.3** Other views were used to explore the data—e.g. identify current fragmentation of reporting lines

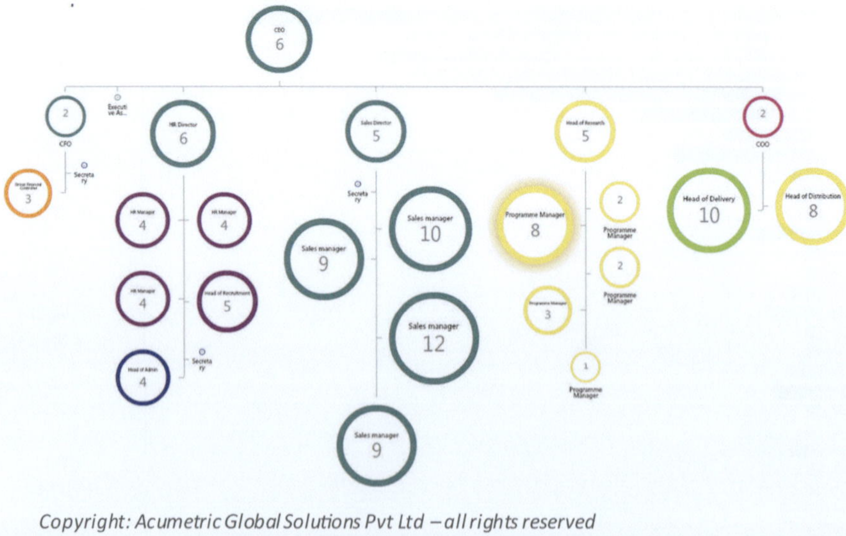


**Exhibit 10.4** Spans of control were resized across departments and teams

## What-if Scenarios were then developed

- What-if scenarios depicted reflecting change in headcount, structure and costs
- What-if scenarios using FTE's in roles, not named individuals
- Blue chart is current organization and orange chart is a what-if chart reflecting the changes projected post the planned restructure (Exhibit 10.5).

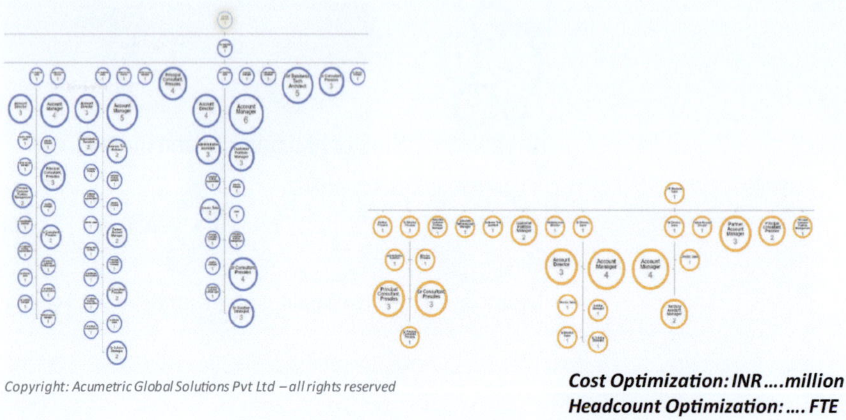


**Exhibit 10.5** **a** Current organization. **b** Post-restructure—what-if projection

## 10.3 HR Challenge #2

**Process, Accountability and HR Value Chain Optimization**

**The HR value chain depicts how HR processes lead to Organizational outcomes.** The tasks define how an organization actually works. But, they are often only recorded in job descriptions that are neither accurate nor exhaustive. As a result, there is no structure to the allocation of tasks, and no guarantee that job roles will "join up" to form coherent, effective work processes.

The HR value chain continuum is depicted below.

| Efficiency—processes and activities | Effectiveness—process optimization | Outcomes—organization goals |
|---|---|---|
| Workforce planning | Talent supply chain, matching talent to skills | Quality |
| Recruitment and selection | Performance, role fitment | Customer satisfaction |
| Rewards and benefits | Performance, retention | Revenue growth |
| Employee relations | Engagement, absenteeism | Morale, culture |
| Capability building | Competency levels, performance | Market share |
| Talent management | Talent metrics, timely acquisition, bench | Customer loyalty |
| Coaching | Realizing potential, performance, leadership | Market capitalization |
| Restructuring | Workforce costs and optimization | Productivity |
| Mobility | Internal career growth and fulfilment | Leadership succession |
| Organization design | Cross-functional team working, collaboration, managerial effectiveness, flexible organization structure for greater agility | Profitability |

On the extreme left column of the table, we find the HR processes. These are measured using the so-called efficiency metrics. Examples include:

- Cost of hire
- Time to hire/time to fill
- Learning and development actual versus budget
- Training time in days
- Time since last promotion.

The above KPIs measure HR processes and provide clues regarding the efficiency of HR. It does not say anything about how effectively it meets defined KPIs. The focus here is around cost optimization largely driven by squeezing the efficiencies out on the back of these metrics.

For example if HR teams can lower the cost of hire while keeping the *time to hire* metric stable, they are more efficient. This is a myopic approach with the focus being to optimize HR cost—and thus look at HR as a cost centre instead of focusing on HR as an investment and a function that adds value to the business.

In the second category in the middle column of the table, we observe the HRM effectiveness outcomes, which are commonly viewed as critical HR KPIs. Examples include:

- Engagement
- Retention/employee turnover
- Absenteeism rate
- Individual performance
- Team performance
- Quality of hire.

All these KPIs provide data around the workforce, involving both HR and line management.

For instance the conclusion drawn that when engagement is high, HR seems to be doing a great job versus when engagement is low. A similar inference could be drawn for retention and (inversely) for employee absence.

Part of HR effectiveness is how well the HR processes are executed by managers. HR can do a stellar job, but with bad managers, employees will be more absent, less engaged and much more likely to leave!

It is important to understand that most of our HR processes are aimed at achieving positive HR outcomes. For example:

- We do not want to spend too much time on bringing in new people, otherwise we will lose the best candidates, bringing our quality of hire metric down while increasing time to fill
- We are training our people to make them perform better and retain them
- We are adopting health and wellness initiatives to reduce absenteeism.

These kind of organizations measure and give credence only to HR outcomes that reflect a narrow and highly silo approach.

The last category to the right of the table is organizational goals. These are the strategic goals that the organization is focused on achieving. Examples of metrics include:

- Market share
- Profit margins
- Market capitalization
- Customer satisfaction
- Customer loyalty
- Total quality.

These are the kind of outcomes that add value to the organization and make the business more viable in the long term.

These organizations focus on the business contribution they make with all of their people policies and processes. These are truly strategic HR functions.

| HR organization | Focus | How |
|---|---|---|
| Operational | Cost saving | Through optimizing HR efficiency |
| Tactical | Process optimization | Through maximizing HR outcomes, cost saving is secondary |
| Strategic | Business results | Through analytics-driven effective HR processes and practices |

This is where analytics comes in. HR serves the business and should be focused on organizational goals. All HR outcomes and processes that HR focuses on should lead to these business outcomes.

Analytics is a great tool to measure the effectiveness of the HR interventions aimed at hitting these business outcomes. Analytics enables organizations to pull together tangible evidence that brings out the HR linkages to clear business outcomes.

**Analytics Response**

- Built on the back of a RACI matrix
- Costs are allocated to people, processes and customers
- Roles and accountabilities are then mapped on to the RACI
- High-cost islands in people, processes are identified which otherwise may have been hidden
- Cost of customer service and delivery is identified
- The above is done through drill downs to the last detail right across the hierarchy.

*A case example of an auto component company where the HR function uses analytics models to map its As-Is processes and analyse cost savings by moving to To-Be processes.*

### Case 2: Process Mapping—Business Case for Change

**Situation and Context**

The HR team knew that their processes needed to be improved, but was not sure where it would get the biggest benefit from change. It also was not easy to quantify how much time saving might be obtained by considering automation and self-service options. There were no existing records of what the HR processes were and how people at different levels (and costs) allocated their time to the processes.

**Analytics Approach**

The analysts worked closely with the HR team led by Smita, the HR Operations Manager. The HR team had already established their view of their people, their roles and organizational structures using analytics and visualization tools. In this section of work, they interviewed 11 key HR operations people about their roles and activities. They gathered all existing data on volumes of cases and time per case. After 6 weeks of work (8 days on site), they had a clear view of roles, activities and time spent. The organization could then see its process cost for each process. Then, the team mapped their new processes and the links to people, generating a view of savings per process and overall.

**Analytics Objectives**

- Map HR processes at a high level
- Clarify who is responsible/accountable, etc. for each activity
- Calculate the cost of each process step
- Develop the business case for change
- Communicate the activities within the business
- Build the capability in HR to make business cases for process change.

**Analytics Solution**

- Built on existing data available from its analytics tools
- Responsibility data captured through interviews
- Work volume data from HR service centre statistics (Exhibit 10.6).

Based on the RACI, the HR structure was redesigned, mapping people to roles (Exhibit 10.7).

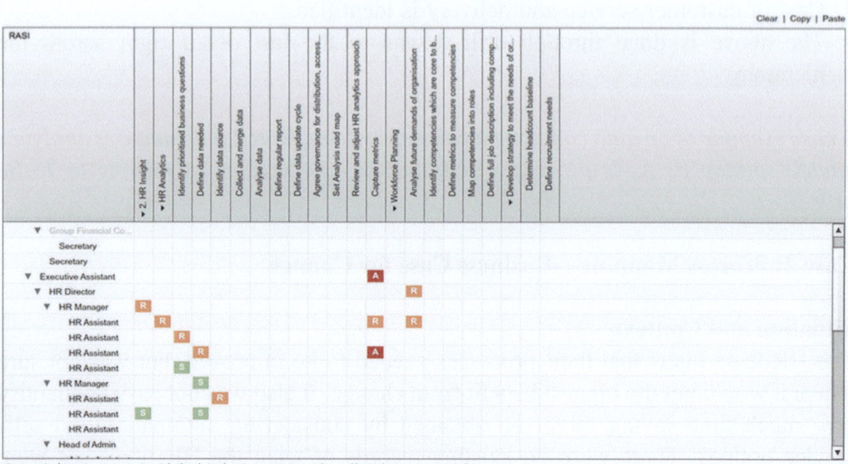




**Exhibit 10.6** Sample RAC/SI matrix is depicted below—to map responsibilities and accountabilities

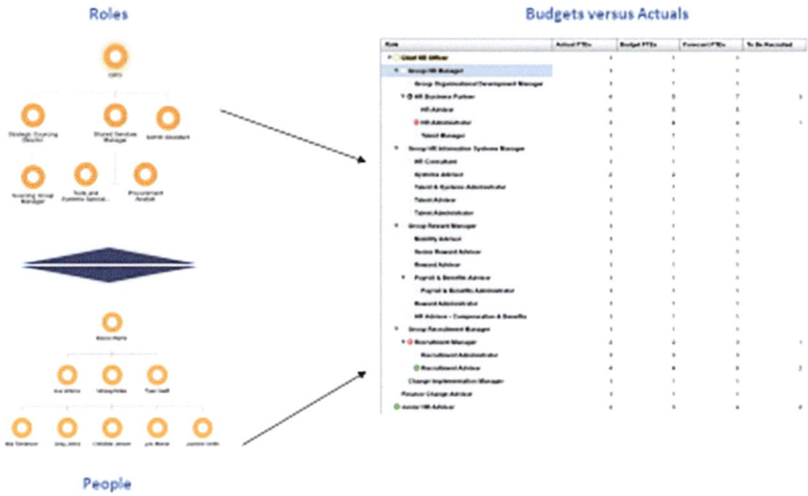




**Exhibit 10.7** HR organization structure redesigned, mapped people to roles and tracked actuals versus budgets

### Key Outcomes

- The analytics model allowed the business to surface and visualize processes as seen by the staff
- The difference between the "As-Is" and the "To-Be" processes was shown intuitively and visually
- With a 34% saving within existing processes with a clear business case being made out.

The HR team became capable of producing business cases for process change which had previously never been part of their skill set. Roles were mapped to people, and costs were tracked real time.

*Let us take another case example of a financial services company that was struggling to manage/optimize its high-cost processes such as "employee leave".*

### Case 3: Optimization of Employee Leave practices towards reducing operating expenses

#### Situation and Context

In this financial services company, taking two weeks leave was mandatory from an employment and compliance perspective. Employees not utilizing their full annual leave days and instead encashing it also cost the bank. Annual leave days accrued became a liability for the company since it needed to set aside money to account for those days. Further, employees that were made redundant or decided to leave the company were entitled to cash out their leave days.

**Key Challenges**

On average, the bank employees were taking 18 annual leave days out of 20 that were authorized every year.

What did this cost the bank financially? Those two days leave each employee was not taking was increasing liability by 15% year on year, which translated to about INR 12 million annually.

Who were the worst offenders? 50% of the company's liability sat with about 20 per cent of its employees. A majority of the worst offenders list were in management staff levels.

What other patterns of behaviour were observed? Analysis on this population found they were also the sickest population, taking 100% of their sick leave in all instances before the end of the year. The less annual leave an employee used up, the more sick leaves that he or she was taking.

**Analytics Solution**

- First, all leave data was consolidated in the HCM system so that it was the "single source of truth". Missing data points were filled. The monetary value of leave hoarding was sized up
- Organization-wide leave patterns were mapped for better resourcing and compliance
- Analytics was leveraged to identify the worst offenders when it came to saving leave days
- Wider employee profiles were created, by linking with other metrics like grade, tenure, gender, location, function, career progression, basic pay, employee engagement score, performance, business delivery, etc.

**Key Outcomes**

System-generated quarterly lists went out to line managers on leave balances for their direct reports. The company achieved 100% annual leave rates resulting in massive savings. Valuable qualitative insights were derived on employee behaviours leading to learning and development "carrot" interventions to mitigate the effects of the "stick" approach to leave hoarding.

**Case 4: Let us look at the case example of an IT leasing company that needed to understand 100% of the costs whether from the point of view of people or processes or customers**

See Exhibits 10.8, 10.9, 10.10, 10.11 and 10.12.

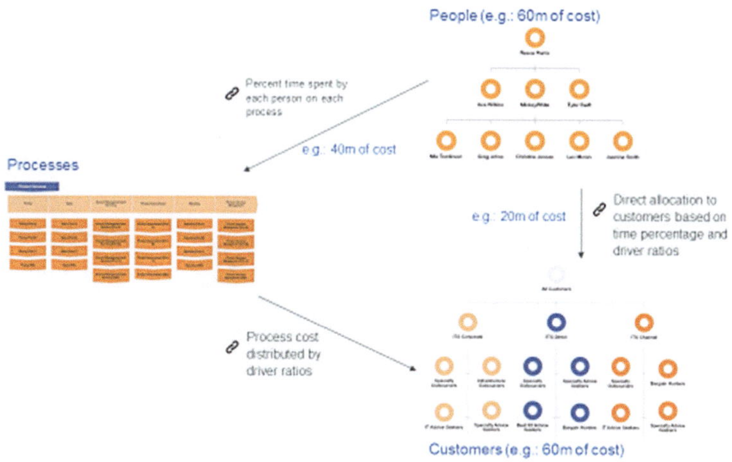




**Exhibit 10.8** People, process, structure mapping

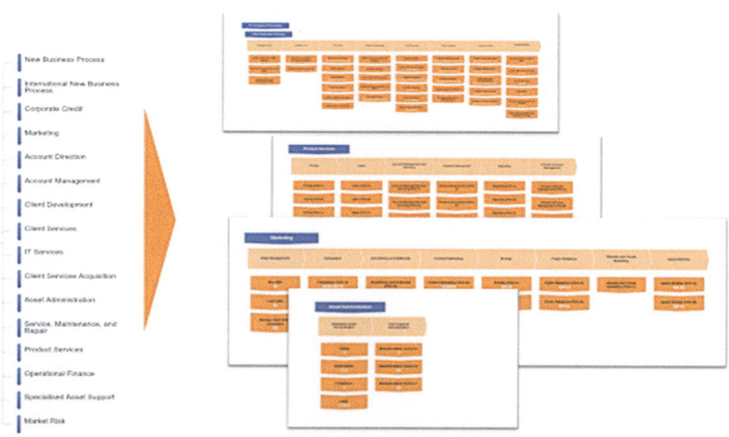



**Exhibit 10.9** Documented 16 business processes covering 153 process steps

**Exhibit 10.10** Linked only 33% of employees to business processes (170 out of 526); balance involved in non-revenue generating processes which emerged as a concern area

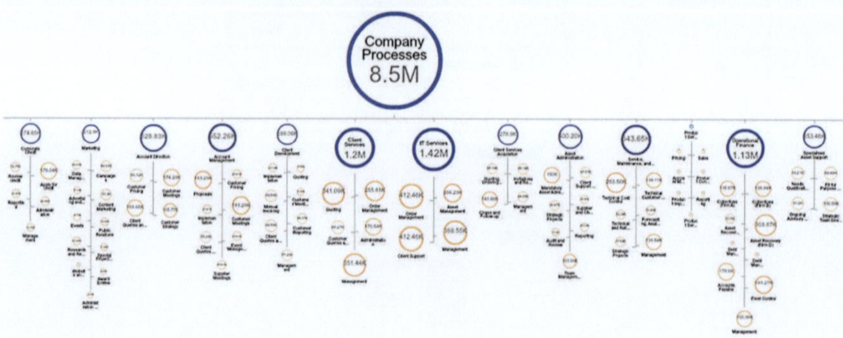




**Exhibit 10.11** Only 14% of overhead costs allocated to business processes (8.5 m out of 60 m) with balance 86% of overhead costs allocated against non-revenue generating processes, again a huge concern

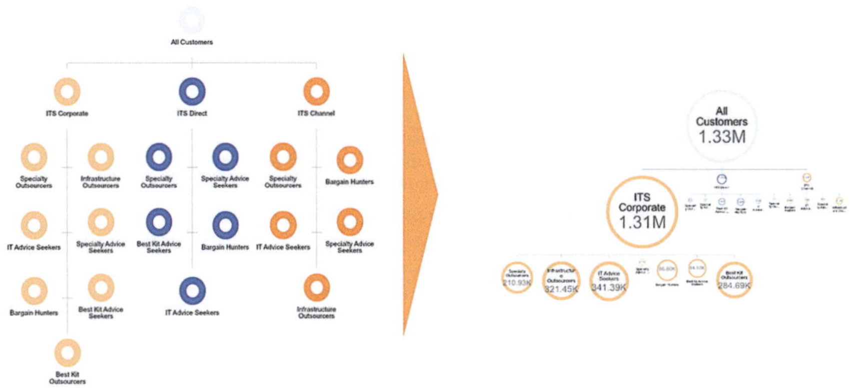




**Exhibit 10.12** Only 1.3 m in cost allocated to the customer level

## 10.4 HR Challenge #3

### Rewards Versus Performance Modelling

There is a need to embed a more direct link between pay and performance as the linkages are more often than not tenuous. Most organizations are still steeped in tenure and seniority principles as opposed to meritocracy and performance. Whether legacy or new age organizations or those going through transformation and change processes, it is critical to embed the "pay for performance" linkage clearly as part of this change.

### Rewards modelling

Organizations need to answer many questions when it comes to drawing up a total rewards strategy whether it be base pay, variable pay structures, retention programmes or benefits packages. Further, it gets more complex when there needs to be a clear linkage to performance drivers and business outcomes.

## Who is Motivated by What? Key Questions

| | Dimensions | Areas to investigate and analyse | Business outcome |
|---|---|---|---|
| 1 | Rewards modelling | • What is the compensation mean, median, mode across grades/levels?<br>• What % of high-performing employees are reflected as below median compensation within the grade/level?<br>• What % of low-performing employees are reflected as above median compensation within the grade/level?<br>• What % of "future leader" talent are above or below median compensation?<br>• How does the organization median compare with market median?<br>• How does the median compensation across critical roles compare with market median?<br>• How do you review salaries internally and with industry/market?<br>• How do you identify anomalies in both base pay and variable pay?<br>• How do you balance between internal parity and market competitiveness?<br>• What is the correlation between pay for performance differentiation within teams and team engagement/morale? | Operating cost growth |
| 2 | Retention programmes—monetary | • What is the correlation between retention programmes and actual retention of key talent?<br>• What is the correlation between retention programmes and performance at work?<br>• What is the correlation between retention programmes and employee engagement? | Growth cost |
| 3 | Variable pay | • Does a high % variable pay/incentive versus total pay contribute to better performance? I.e. higher incentives contributing to enhanced customer service?<br>• What is the correlation between variable pay/incentive and productivity?<br>• What is the correlation between variable pay/incentive and employee retention? | Growth cost service level |

| | Dimensions | Areas to investigate and analyse | Business outcome |
|---|---|---|---|
| 4 | Recognition | • What is the correlation between "visible and public recognition" of performance and employee retention?<br>• What is the correlation between "visible and public recognition" of performance and employee engagement? | Growth service level |
| 5 | Benefits packages | • What is the correlation between select benefit packages, i.e. dependant parent medical insurance and employee satisfaction/engagement across different "cohorts" across the organization?<br>• What is the correlation between select benefit packages and employee retention? | Growth cost |

## 10.5 Illustration: Incentive Design Considerations

One of the critical considerations in defining the incentive plan is to understand the organizational context within which the plan needs to be structured; a few clear elements emerge as the considerations which the plan needs to be able to address:

1. The structure should drive value creation in medium/long term
2. The plan needs to ensure it acts as an effective retention tool for employees
3. The plan should provide competitive pay outs vis-à-vis performance
4. Plan should be cost effective and economically viable.

**The following areas need to be evaluated and analysed before coming up with an incentive plan:**

- ***Understanding company's broad strategy:*** the strategy of the business, key performance, metrics and objectives, both in the short and long term
- ***Understanding the overall pay and incentive philosophy:*** appreciation of the company's overall philosophy with regard to compensation, executive pay, competitive positioning, pay components and mix, etc. Understanding of the incentive structure and extent of alignment with performance and retention objectives
- ***Plan Vehicle:*** multiple alternatives need to be evaluated basis the objectives that emerge from the discussions with management and the board. The proposed plan could also be a combination of multiple incentive instruments if multiplan

approach best suits and aligns with the company's overall business and HR strategy
- ***Selection of Performance Measures:*** the critical element of the plan would be to determine the appropriate performance parameters to ensure that the reward quantum is linked to the actual value drivers for the business. Also the fact that the costs of the reward plan would lead to additional P&L impact, it is important to identify metrics that offset these costs
- ***Performance and Payout Matrix:*** determination of the performance targets and the range of payouts at different levels of performance achievement. The payout levels need to be determined basis:
  - Overall orientation of plan, i.e. plan needs to be primarily performance or retention focused
  - Level of stretch in performance targets
  - Affordability of the business to pay.

**Analytics Response**

- Built on the back of data science tools and statistical models
- **Percentile, range and scatter diagrams can be used to dive into the insight**
- **Pay for performance linkages across job bands and roles**
- **High wage-cost islands in people and roles identified right through the hierarchy**
- Rewards versus performance differentiation visualized right through the organization—top to bottom
- Individual manager versus team performance gaps highlighted.

## 10.6 Rewards Modelling—Some Examples

1. **Pay Mix**
   Typical pay mix would show various split of fixed versus variable at various levels in an organization, once combined with pay mix actuals which is based on the actual payment (avg.) or targeted pay mix would lead to an indication of the max earning possibility by the employee and equal spend by the employer (Exhibit 10.13).
2. **Benchmarking**
   Visual representation of compensation positioning—internal and external will provide view on positioning of the company against the market where A to F are the job levels (Exhibit 10.14).
3. **Variable Pay Comparators—Field versus Aggregate**
   Comparison of field avg. achievement versus business unit achievement would help you compare the units which have a diverse achievement spread.
   For example: mobility has business achievement which is higher than field average achievement which means that is high spread of under achievers which

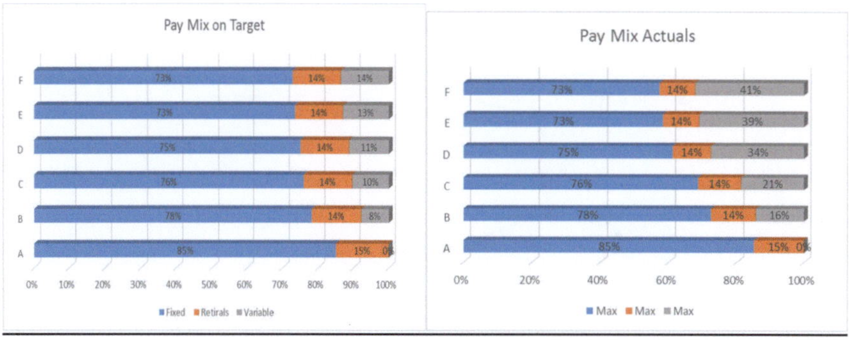




**Exhibit 10.13** Pay mix

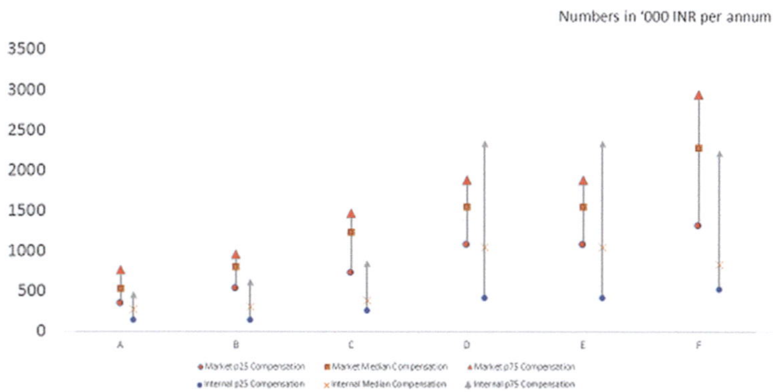




**Exhibit 10.14** Compensation benchmarking

is pulling field achievement down, while the business performance is high due to some star performers who are pulling the overall achievement higher (Exhibit 10.15).

4. **Cost of Services**

   Depicting the cost of services as a % of the revenue generated in a typical services company.

   It also helps you compare the cost of services across business unit and thereby interpret the business units which are capable of generating higher revenue at lower costs, thereby making out a case for higher investment.

   PS—same can be replicated for products as well (Exhibit 10.16).

5. **Sales Incentive versus Revenue Achievement**

   The scatter below depicts the relation of the revenue achievement to incentive earned on revenue achievement. It helps validate the incentive plan design with

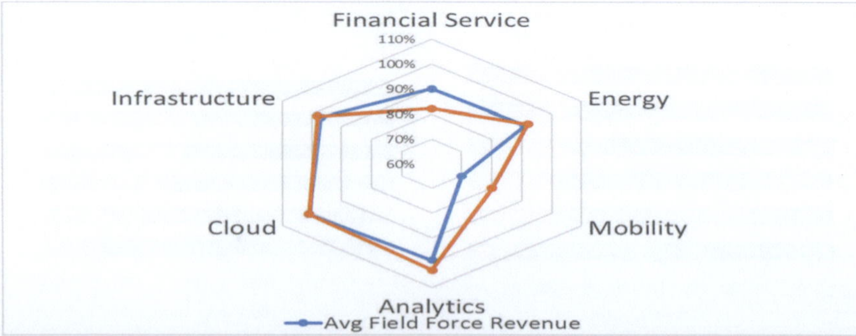




**Exhibit 10.15** Variable pay comparators field versus aggregate

| Business Units | Sales HC | Rev in Mn INR | Fixed Comp in Mn INR | Incentive Paid in Mn INR | Total Payout in Mn INR | Fixed Comp. as a % of Rev | Inc. as a % of Rev | COS |
|---|---|---|---|---|---|---|---|---|
| Financial Service | 108 | 487 | 8.2 | 1.1 | 9.3 | 1.70% | 0.20% | 1.90% |
| Energy | 151 | 710 | 10.9 | 2.3 | 13.1 | 1.50% | 0.30% | 1.80% |
| Mobility | 27 | 150 | 2.2 | 0.3 | 2.6 | 1.50% | 0.20% | 1.70% |
| Analytics | 79 | 419 | 5.5 | 1.3 | 6.8 | 1.30% | 0.30% | 1.60% |
| Cloud | 74 | 292 | 5.2 | 1.1 | 6.4 | 1.80% | 0.40% | 2.20% |
| Infrastructure | 116 | 570 | 7.5 | 1.8 | 9.3 | 1.30% | 0.30% | 1.60% |
| Total | | 2628 | 39.5 | 7.9 | 47.5 | 1.50% | 0.30% | 1.80% |



**Exhibit 10.16** Cost of services

reference to threshold, cap as well as the payout model, viz. linear payout, accelerated payout, etc. (Exhibit 10.17).

*A case example where performance* versus *rewards analytics was deployed to draw correlations between performance levels, pay levels and job bands in an Oil & Gas company.*

## Case 5: Performance versus Rewards Modelling and Distribution—Individual and Team

### Situation and Context

Refinery was underperforming, but key areas of underperformance were hidden and not visible to senior leadership; high people costs were reflected, but commensurate performance was not coming through.

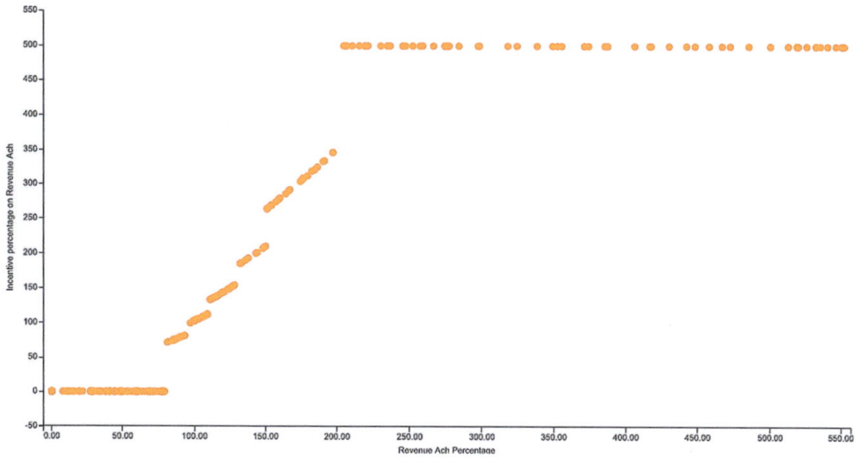




**Exhibit 10.17** Sales incentive versus revenue achievement

## Key Objectives

- To examine the interlinkages between performance and rewards across the job bands
- To draw insights from performance distribution trends across the role hierarchy
- To identify gaps in individual manager versus team performance

## Analytics Solutions

- Scatterplot revealing performance versus pay correlations across job bands
- Sunburst visualization revealing individual and team performance scores through the hierarchy
- Scatterplot highlighting differences between individual manager and team performance (Exhibits 10.18 and 10.19).

## Performance Score Distribution across the Role Hierarchy

Each field represents an employee. The 'top' of the hierarchy is at the centre. The green colours stand for performance scores larger than 1.1, orange colours between 0.9, 1.1, red colours below 0.9, and grey for not assessed.

*First results:*

- Most employees who also have responsibilities for subordinates score reasonably highly
- It becomes obvious that team xxxxxxxx has the biggest gaps between manager ratings and team member ratings

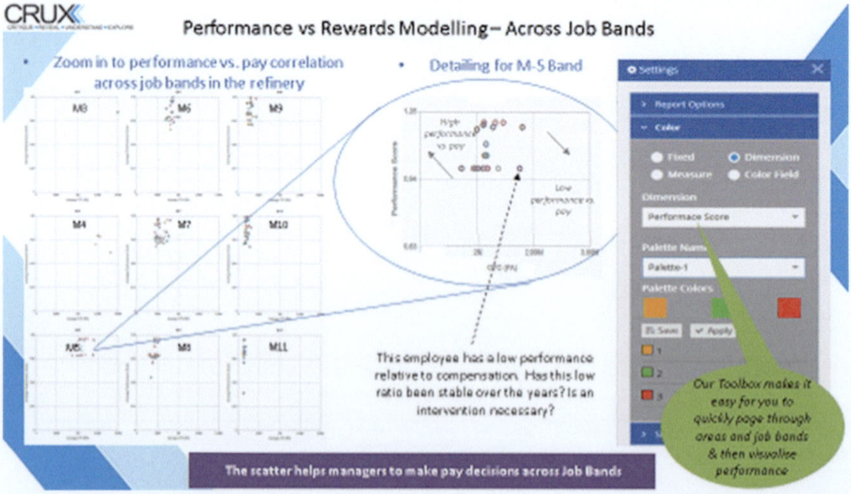




**Exhibit 10.18** Key performance versus rewards insights across job bands zoomed in to performance versus pay correlation for job bands in the refinery

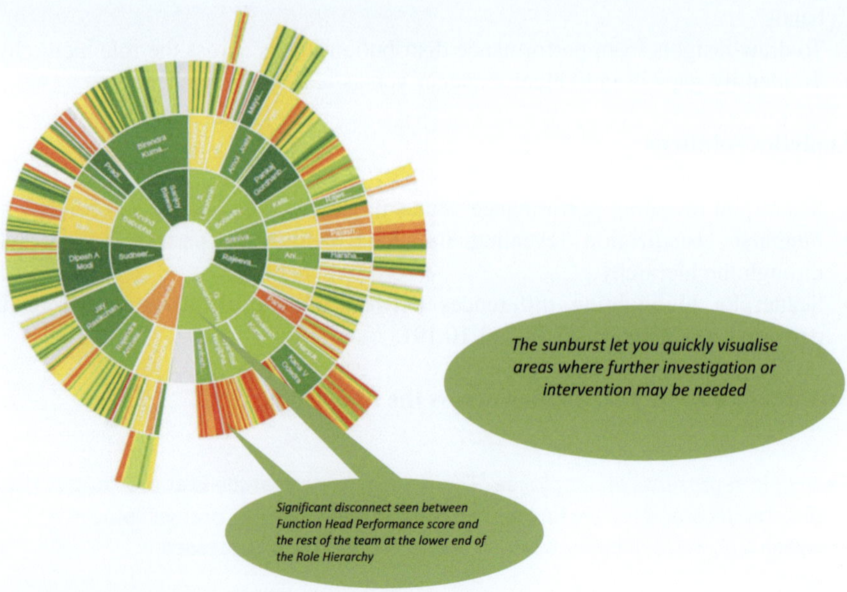




**Exhibit 10.19** Sunburst diagram of the ten largest teams in the dataset with individual performance scores

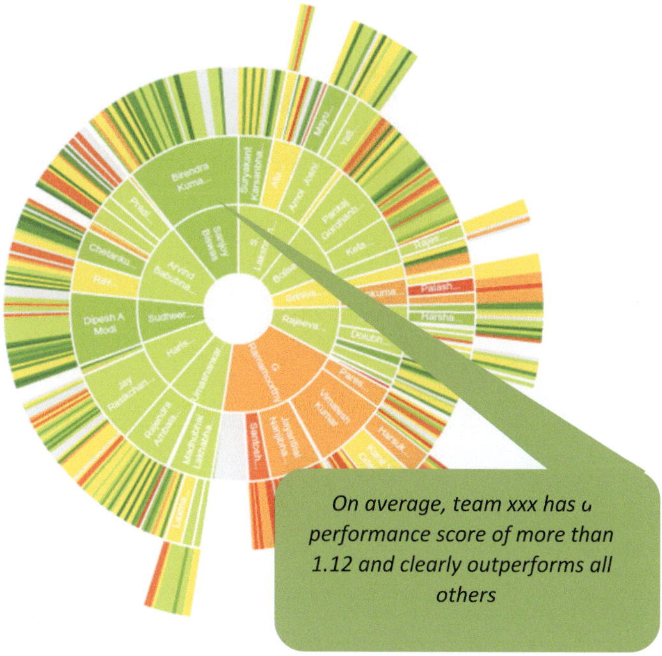


**Exhibit 10.20** Rolled-up sunburst with average performance of teams

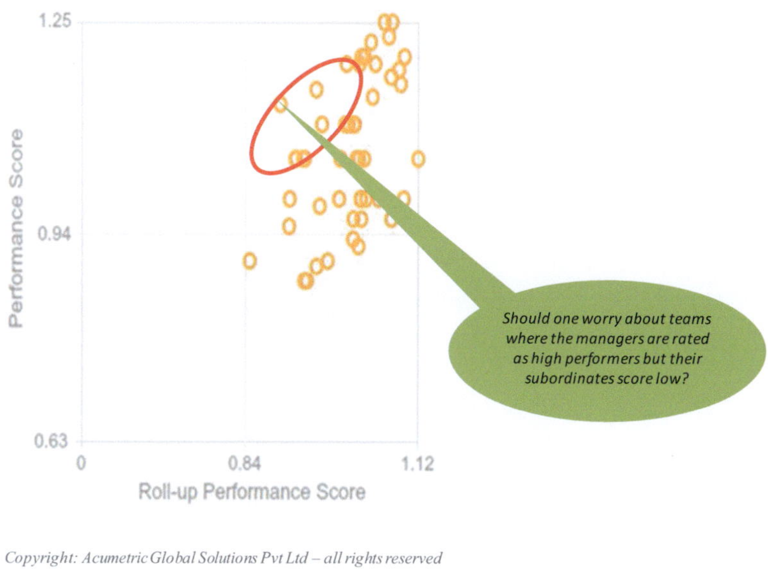


**Exhibit 10.21** Individual manager performance versus average performance of team

**Key Benefits**

- Identification of performance versus pay mismatch outliers across job bands
- Identifying and then clearly differentiating between high-, average- and low-performing individuals and teams right through the hierarchy
- Identifying gaps between individual manager and team performance (Exhibits 10.20 and 10.21).

# Metrics, Measurement, Scorecards and Power of Visual Intelligence

# 11

## 11.1 Context

HR teams are being pushed to become more metric driven focused on business outcomes. There is a need to balance both the "lead" and "lag" indicators and to leverage relevant measurement systems with a view to analysing "real", "large" and "big" data to drive key business deliverables. It is important to stay relevant in making the right choices in metrics/measures and focusing on the critical few that drive business outcomes as opposed to the trivial many that distract and do not link up with key organizational deliverables. The linkages and integration between people data and business data on the back of these models and technologies raise the bar on more effective and timely decision-making.

With HR becoming more KPI and metrics driven, the capability to track all of these data points real time coupled with key insights is what will drive competitive advantage for organizations as they need to now compete globally.

Coupled with measurement, HR teams need to develop the ability to build scorecards relevant to triggering agile, real-time decisions and leverage visual intelligence to design intuitive and brilliant dashboards that enables stakeholders to dive straight to the insight.

## 11.2 Design Measures

Measurements are all about goals and objectives. Are you meeting your objective or aren't you? How far away from your goal are you? Any objective or goal needs to be measurable. The robustness of your measurement will determine how

 
R. Ghatak, *People Analytics*, Management for Professionals,
https://doi.org/10.1007/978-981-19-3873-3_11

effectively you are able to meet your goal. The goal or objective and its measure need to be so intertwined that anyone should be able to view the measure and immediately decipher broadly the objective. This is called the "blindfold test".

| Objective | Measurement |
|---|---|
| 1. Reduce employee attrition by 10% | % employee attrition—meets blindfold test |
| 2. Reduce delivery times to customers by 10% | % error rate in purchase orders processed—does not meet blindfold test |

As a result, measurements must be designed in a manner that is relevant to the goal or objective that needs to be achieved. Some of the measurement design criteria are:

- Critical few versus trivial many—measuring what is critical and valuable
- Balance between financial and other measures—inclusive of process, learning, competencies
- Grounded—relevant data can be collected, stored and retrieved to design the measure
- Benchmark—can benchmark or compare with other data points over time periods
- Validated—accuracy and reliability of the data
- Time bound—timeliness of the reporting and reference across specified time periods
- Simplicity—easily computed and understood.

If the goal is amorphous and looks subjective, then critical success factors linked to the goal must be fleshed out. The example below brings out the flow:

| **Objective** | | **Critical Success Factors** | | **Measures** |
|---|---|---|---|---|
| | | Accurate Order | | Error Rate |
| Happy Customer | ⇨ | Fast Order Fulfilment | ⇨ | Wait Time |
| | | Friendly Service | | Customer Complaints |

**What are the steps required to be fulfilled as we begin the task of setting HR KPIs and metrics:**

1. Define the success criteria for HR
   It is critical to link HR KPIs to business outcomes and strategy. Traditionally, HR functions have focused on measuring operational metrics by and large looking at improving their operating efficiency; however, the time has come to reorient the focus and attention on to business drivers.

2. Data-driven insights
   Employee experience needs to coexist with customer experience; that is to say without great employee experience, loyalty and commitment it is unlikely, you will be able to delight customers. Measuring employee experience is key towards identifying gaps that could be bridged or signature moments that could be made to count. How do you bring the voice of employee data into the sphere of decision making; what tools go into capturing the data in real time and then enabling you to crunch out the analytics in real time to interpret the same and provide meaningful insights for management action.
3. Strategic support to business drivers
   How can we go beyond operational metrics and arrive at measures that truly add value to the business and organization? How can we look beyond just HR efficiency and tactical measures to business effectiveness with more strategic measures.

## 11.3 Define Measures—What is Involved

After designing a measure and selecting the most relevant, the next step is to operationalize it. There are essentially six ways to operationalize a measure.

- The definition should include a brief description with formula on its computation
- Unit of measure reflects the mathematical format in which it needs to be shared
- Data requirements that go behind the measure; a key input into the measure
- Source data repositories to locate the data requirements
- Reporting frequency for the measure
- Every measure should have an owner who can identify a SPOC for periodic reporting.

## 11.4 Implement and Evolve Measures

On operationalizing the measures, the output can be collated, reported and leveraged to make key decisions. Based upon the applicability of the output to management decisions, the team may review and redesign the measures appropriately.

- Reporting to ensure that the recipients of the report get to see it in a timely manner
- Decision support—based on the output, management may reassign roles, reallocate workloads or headcount towards ensuring higher productivity

- Improve Measures—measures will continue to evolve basis the business imperatives and the robustness or otherwise of the data being collected.

## 11.5 Types of Measures

It is imperative to have a mix of both lead and lag measures with a view of throwing up data points as inputs into people and business decisions. Lead measures throw up alerts which if timely acted upon can result in decisions that could impact the current business outcome. Lag measures help us track the final outcome which is a critical input into decisions that could impact future business outcomes.

**Level 1 Metrics—Scan, Plan, Produce**
(Reporting basic frequencies and percentages of HR operational variables)
Examples of measures:

- **Headcount and attrition:** by region, business, process, centre, grade, age, gender, tenure, etc.
- **Training, L&D:** programme enrolment, registration, completion
- **Performance tracking:** appraisal, review, accomplishment, absences, grievances, disciplinary
- **Recruitment tracking:** vacancies, skills matching, competencies, time to fill
- **Payroll:** injury, illness, time and labour
- **Voice of employee survey analysis:** overall satisfaction; satisfaction by various cuts, key driver analysis by survey variables*; key driver analysis by non-survey data variables*, sentiment analysis*.

**Level 2 Metrics—Predict Outcomes**
(Linkage modelling using factor analysis and various predictive models in conjunction with advanced statistical tools and packages such as R and SAS)
Example: **Recruitment and Retention linkage:**
Heavy Tech Talent Sourcing → Stability of Top Talent in R&D → New product development cycle time → Customer/Employee engagement + Retention programmes.

| Types of measures | Definition | Example |
|---|---|---|
| Leading | Intermediate outcomes that predict or drive bottom-line performance results | Employee turnover rate |
| Lagging | Bottom-line performance results resulting from actions taken | Employee satisfaction score |
| Input | Amount of investments, assets, equipment, labour hours or budget amount used | Number of cashiers |
| Output | Units of product or service rendered—a measure of yield | Number of value meal orders fulfilled |
| Outcome | Resulting effect (benefit) of the use and application of an output | Customer satisfaction score |
| Objective/quantitative | Empirical indicators of performance | Wait time |
| Subjective/qualitative | Performance and evaluations of major customers and stakeholders | Customer complaints received as a % of total customers served |

## 11.6 Frameworks and Scorecards: Asking the Right Questions

Another critical aspect on getting the framework right is the ability to ask the right questions and scorecard the right metrics, key to business outcomes. Often organizations mistake analytics for data and reports; however, the real core of analytics is “insight”, which leads into delivering “business outcomes” (Exhibit 11.1).

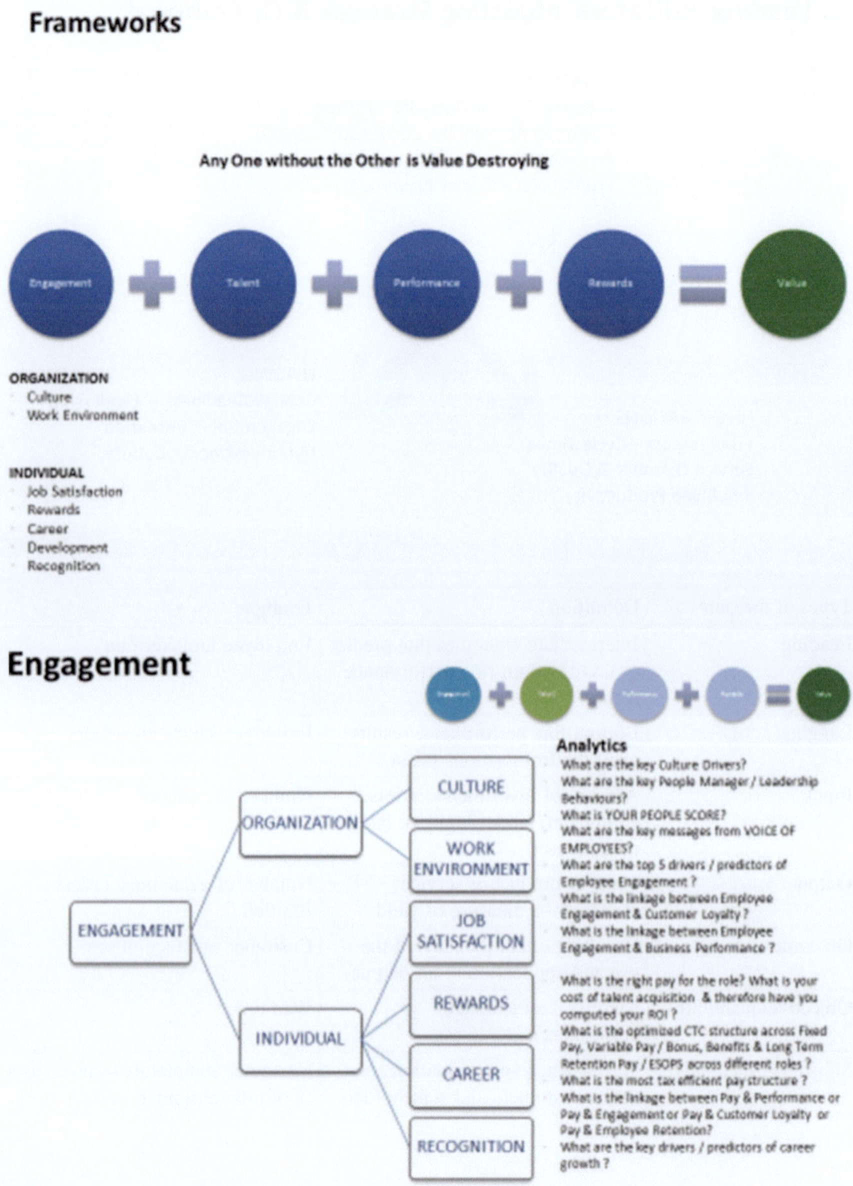


**Exhibit 11.1** Scorecarding frameworks

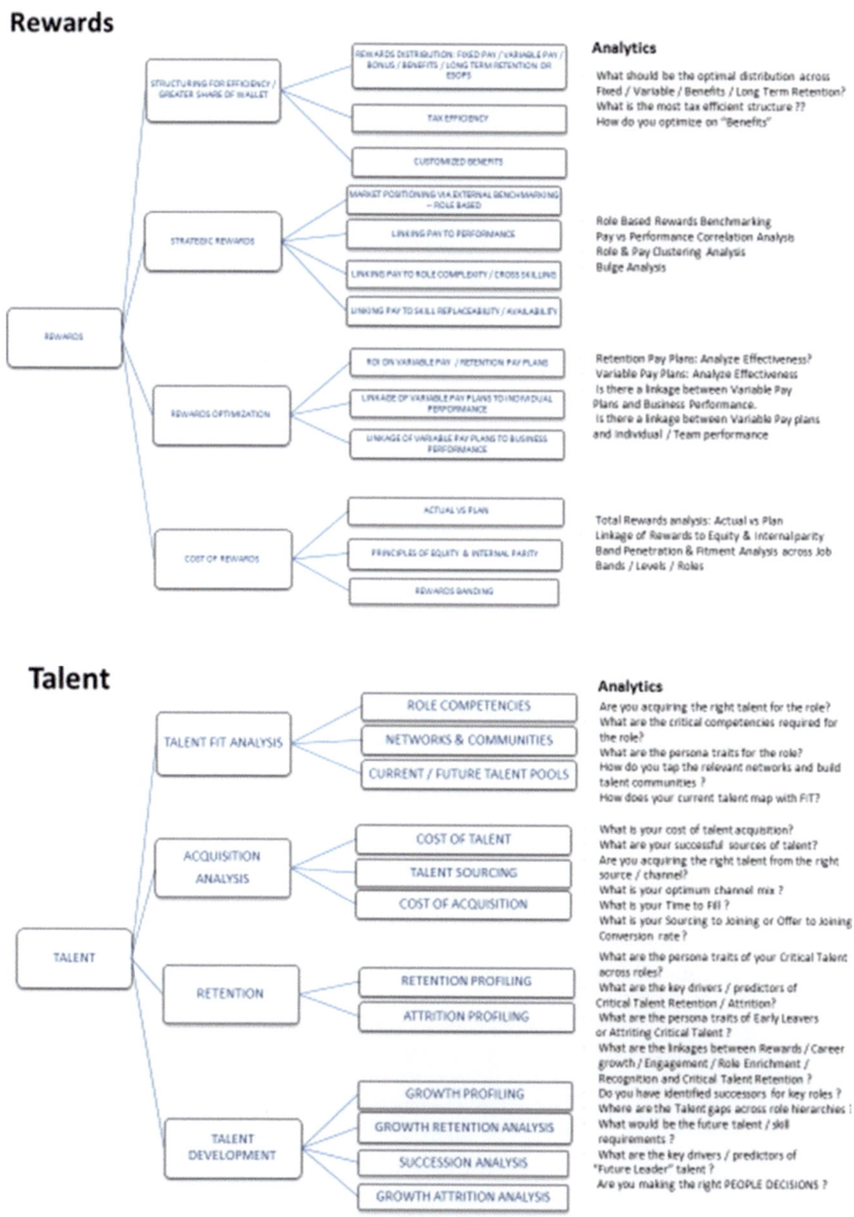


**Exhibit 11.1** (continued)

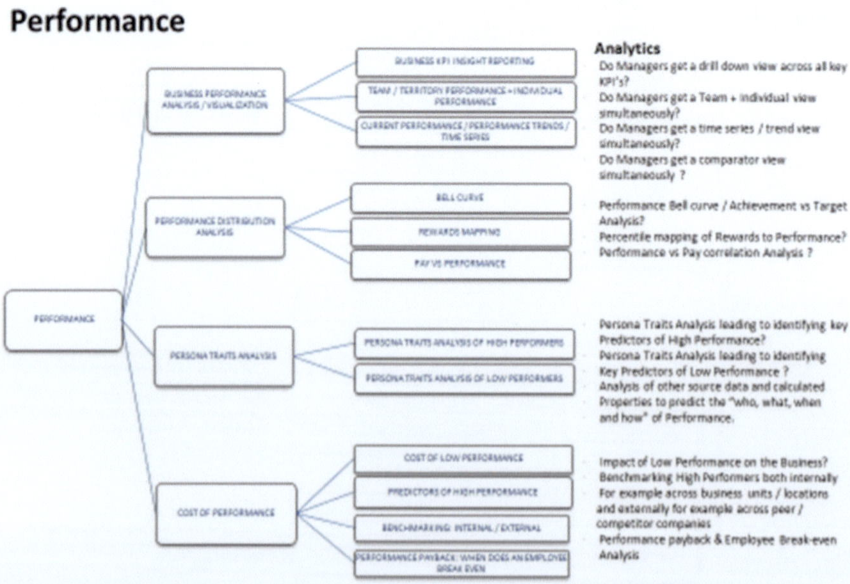


**Exhibit 11.1** (continued)

## 11.7 HR Scorecards: Types of Measures that Could Be Tracked Regularly

| S. no. | Parameter | Areas to investigate | Business outcome |
|---|---|---|---|
| 1 | FTE and cost per area | How many people do we have in each area? How many do we pay in each area? | Efficiency |
| 2 | Temp versus permanent | How much do we rely on temporaries in each area?<br>For how long do we deploy them on average?<br>What is the temporary versus permanent ratio across the business? | Cost risk |
| 3 | Span of control | What is normal span of control and which areas are high and low? | Efficiency |
| 4 | Staff or manager performance | How does performance vary across areas, functions, teams and reporting managers? | Growth |
| 5 | Sick/absence rates and causes | Can we visualize sick/absence rates, identify causes and take actions to correct? | Cost |

| S. no. | Parameter | Areas to investigate | Business outcome |
|---|---|---|---|
| 6 | Retirement/attrition risks | Where do we face risks from staff turnover or retirement? | Cost risk |
| 7 | Line manager performance versus employee engagement | How does the line manager impact employee engagement?<br>How does the line manager impact team performance? | Growth risk |
| 8 | Employee engagement versus customer satisfaction | How does employee engagement impact customer loyalty?<br>How does employee engagement impact service levels? | Growth risk reputation |
| 9 | Line manager performance versus team performance | How do we understand high-performing and low-performing teams? | Growth cost |
| 10 | People risk management | What risks do we face on regulatory compliance, discrimination and grievance cases? | Reputation cost |
| 11 | Succession planning | Where are our key roles and in what % do we have a nominated successor?<br>Which are the roles for which we have certain successors and which are those roles for which we have potential successors or in watch list?<br>What are the succession risks we face across the business? | Growth risk |
| 12 | Corporate culture and employee behaviours | What attitudes and behaviours prevent our people delivering customer value?<br>What attitudes and behaviour result in employees committing acts of fraud or non-compliance? | Growth reputation cost |

The key question is how to bring it all together. How can you compare measures across multiple dimensions? (For example "what is employee engagement by performance level by tenure by grade by function by country…"). Ideally, you would be able to drill, cut and slice the data to get answers straight away—not wait for someone to build another dashboard or run another query.

**Analytics Response**

- **Built to work with people data** from the ground up
- **Custom-built database** that graphs your people data quickly and easily, showing your hierarchy
- **Powerful visualization tools** offer new views and new insights
- **Schema-less model that "just works"**. Getting data in, cleaning it and adding to it
- **Answer complex questions**—and simple ones too—with a wide range of graphs, dashboards and organization charts. What is my headcount? Who is accountable for what? Do we have the right skills, in the right numbers, in the right places?

## 11.8 Visual Intelligence and the Power of Visualization

Converting data to insight comes with the power of visualizations. It is all about turning information into visual intelligence. The question is, do analysts possess the capability to differentiate between actionable, relevant data from interesting but irrelevant data that is not central to the problem that needs to be solved.

The effective implementation of a real-time dashboard enhances decision-making and performance management.

**Visualized Dashboards—Critical Design Requirements**

1. Visually easy to understand
   - Visually pleasing
   - Clear and unambiguous
2. Drillable
   - With minimal clicks can get to the lower level data and root causes
3. Drives action with clarity on what is good or bad
4. Supports prioritization
   - Important KPIs on top
   - RAG status
5. Gives context
   - Corporate objectives driving KPI tree structure
   - Ownership of KPIs
   - Time series
6. Single version of the truth
   - Data comes from single source
7. Web based
   - Enabling collaboration and ease of access
8. Security protocols
   - Ensure only authorized group has access

9. Timely
   - Enables proactive action as issues arise
   - Reports are updated on a real-time basis in line with decision-making and performance management processes.

| Design framework | User understanding | Create visual intelligence |
|---|---|---|
| Who | Role requirements of the dashboard user | Regional sales manager with four territory managers |
| What | Specific business activities: "success/failure" measures showing trends and KPIs | Drill into how teams are performing by financials, sales rep, product, customer, etc. to show which issues are high impact and require attention |
| When | How often are decisions made | The ability to report on historical YoY, MoM, WoW and DoD changes helps identify how external forces and internal changes are affecting performance against targets |
| Where | How responsive do decision-makers need to be | Taking an on-demand approach to historical reporting. Providing a forecasted view of nearly any KPI or metric and give the ability to drill into details, so you can understand what is driving changes when they are atypical |
| How | 1. Accurate<br>2. Available<br>3. Accessible<br>4. Actionable | 1.Single-verified data source<br>2. Always-on access<br>3. Scheduled versus triggered<br>4. Goal tracking |

*The illustrative example below brings out the power of visualization and its impact on relevant business metrics.*

**Case 2: Salesforce Performance Visualization**

**Salesforce Performance Analytics in a Pharmaceutical company—Team and Individual drill-downs**

**Situation and Context**

The company did not possess a visualized dash-boarding capability with the reporting being largely through Excel reports which nobody really analysed as it was too dry and tedious. Neither could patterns be drawn from the data, the way it was reported, nor could decisions be taken. It was essentially information that was being reported; culling out critical insights that would lead into decision-making was almost impossible.

**Salesforce Dash-boarding and Visualization: Illustration**

The company went beyond traditional reporting tools like Excel and explored strong visualization tools that leveraged visual intelligence to deliver an automated dash-boarding capability that could drill-down to the last individual in the value chain.

**Sales Team Performance**

- Monthly sales (target versus actuals) comparison on individual level for a line manager
- YTD sales achievement % on individual level for a specific line manager
- Month on month team performance indicator (3 scale rating) basis their overall scores (Exhibits 11.2 and 11.3).

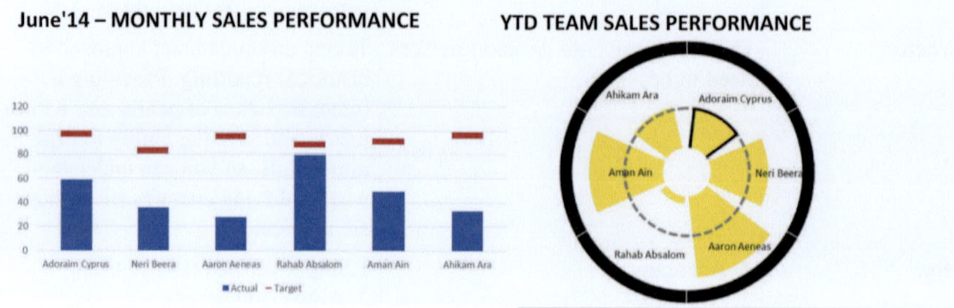




**Exhibit 11.2** Sales performance dashboards—team and individual drill-downs

**Exhibit 11.3** Team performance dashboards—team and individual drill-downs

**Sales Performance: Individual Drill-downs**

- Monthly sales (target versus actuals) comparison on individual level for a line manager
- Individual drill-down YTD sales (targets versus actuals) for an individual team member
- Individual drill-down of performance indicator (KPIs) for an individual team member.

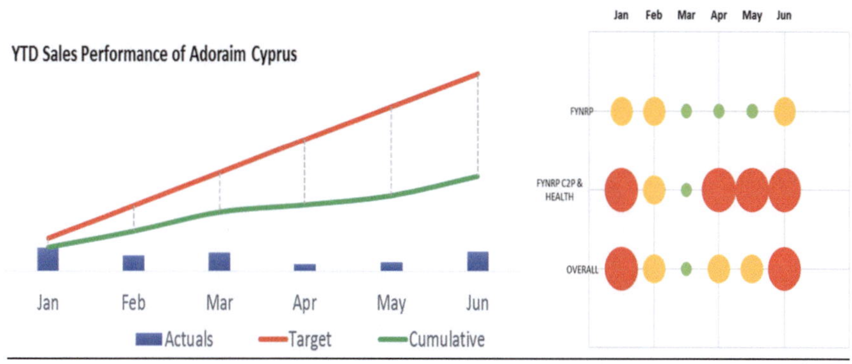




**Monthly Sales: Comparative Performance with Hierarchical Drill-downs**

- Monthly sales (target versus actuals) comparison on individual level for a specific line manager on specified parameter
- Monthly sales (target versus actuals) comparison on individual level for a specific line manager on a specified parameter
- Hierarchical presentation of individuals drill-down on overall performance indicator
- Cumulative targets versus cumulative actuals versus actuals depiction for a specific line manager on specified parameter.

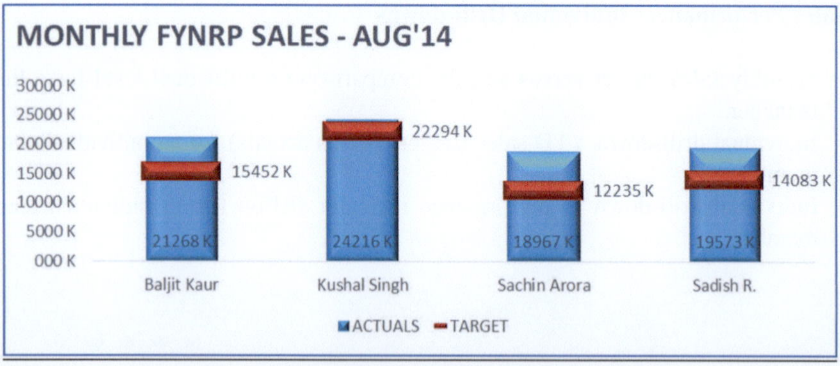
MONTHLY FYNRP SALES - AUG'14
30000 K
25000 K
20000 K
15000 K
10000 K
5000 K
000 K
21268 K
15452 K
24216 K
22294 K
18967 K
12235 K
19573 K
14083 K
Baljit Kaur
Kushal Singh
Sachin Arora
Sadish R.
ACTUALS
TARGET

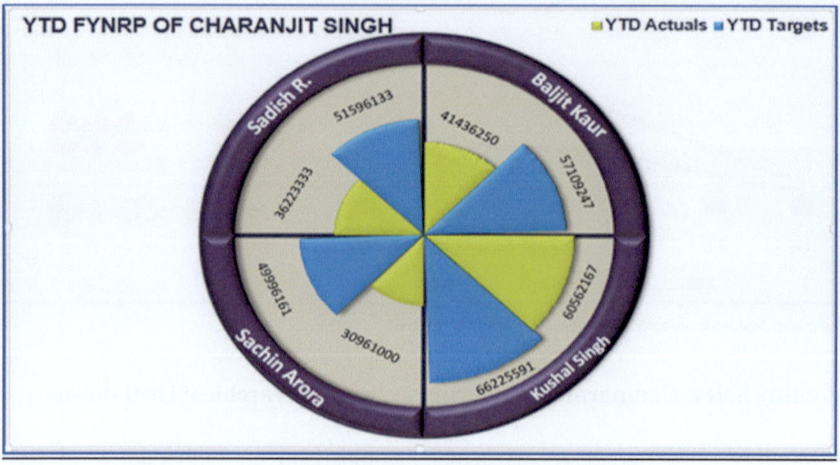
YTD FYNRP OF CHARANJIT SINGH
YTD Actuals
YTD Targets
Sadish R.
Baljit Kaur
Sachin Arora
Kushal Singh
51596133
36223333
41436250
57109247
60562167
66225591
30961000
49996161

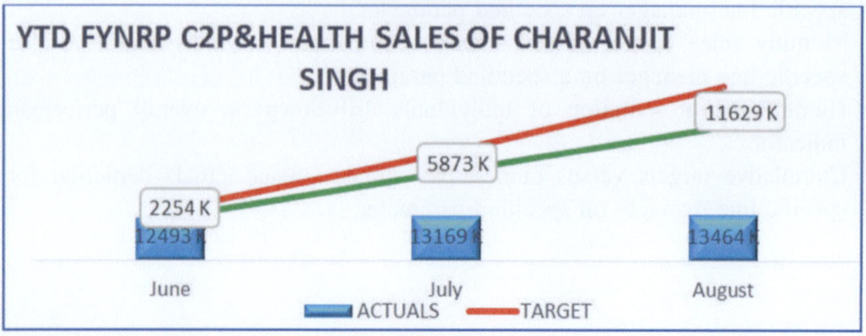
YTD FYNRP C2P&HEALTH SALES OF CHARANJIT SINGH
2254 K
5873 K
11629 K
12493 K
13169 K
13464 K
June
July
August
ACTUALS
TARGET

## Key Outcomes

- Real-time dash-boarding capability customizable with drill-down options
- Powerful visualizations enabling insights as opposed to information
- Hierarchical dataset drilling down to the last team, person in the value chain.

# 12 Role and Deployment of Statistics and Data Science in People Analytics

## 12.1 Context

The People Analytics possibilities are not a recent phenomenon. Even in the last decade, organizations have been collecting HR metrics to measure critical KPIs that matter, such as "retention rates", "employee engagement" or "time to fill". During that period, KPIs were pretty basic, relying mostly on simple charts and resorting to generating insights only for specific projects. Then things started changing with globalization, talent mobility, business models reinventing themselves and of course the data explosion. It was only a matter of time before statisticians started making an appearance in the HR function along with a relatively new domain of "data science".

Initially, it were the technology companies that made the first inroads into adopting and leveraging People Analytics and bringing data science approaches to solving real business problems. One of the initial, impactful and far-reaching People Analytics projects took place at Google, where a team of statisticians came together on a project code named "Oxygen". This new project, in a nutshell, was about figuring out first what went into being a great manager and then discovering the best way to create them; like a factory assembly line; churning out the best in the business and not leaving it to chance. Statistical models came to be used to analyse performance data, feedback survey data and descriptive data around top manager award nominations. Using these methods, the team made an attempt to isolate habits and patterns of high-performing managers. Within the year, the team had identified eight critical characteristics an effective manager must demonstrate. Some of these traits are pretty common across organizations so nothing surprising there, for instance: "Being productive and results-oriented"; "Empowering your team" and "Having a clear vision and strategy for the team". However, what is surprising was the one trait that Google identified as least important: "Technical Expertise". Apparently, basis the data analysed employees seemingly valued



R. Ghatak, *People Analytics*, Management for Professionals,
https://doi.org/10.1007/978-981-19-3873-3_12

far more, managers who made time for one-on-one interactions, took an interest in what was happening in their lives and who dealt with problems by asking questions rather than slipping into solution mode. The analytics team came to understand that that while it was important for the manager understand the work of the team member, but the crucial differentiating factor between being a good manager and a great one, was about creating a deep bond with your team members individually and as a group.

With all of the above insights and takeaways being based on a data-driven approach allowed the company to put all these findings into application. Based on the analysis, Google updated their development programmes, initiated personal coaching for managers with poor performance or teamwork and started working on creating better management teams.

While Google was in many ways a pioneer in leveraging "People Analytics", using statistics for people management is not the exclusive arena for technology firms. Most big companies now rely on data-driven insights to manage their people, as also some brick and mortar companies where the problem is largely around losing their capable workforce due to retirement.

Let us take the instance of a large conglomerate, with over 100 years of existence. The company had some people challenges: their workforce was rapidly ageing of which a few roles required some very specialized skill sets extensive training to get to full competence. With a view to addressing this, predictive models were constructed based on statistical tools to estimate the number of employees who would retire year on year. This enabled HR to put in place a workforce plan that identified talent and skill shortages for the future so that the company could plan ahead and take steps to address the same proactively.

However, it is not always smooth sailing,and there have been bumps along the way for People Analytics: BIAS. For instance it has been observed that flawed psychometric tests and models commonly used for hiring or career growth may be inherently biased, rewarding knowledge, behaviours and practices common in certain cultures, yet not in others. This is true, especially when companies use a "one size fits all" approach and use tests and instruments that may give great results in one culture versus applying the same tools to cohorts across other cultural groups. An example would be a test developed with data of Asian employees only. Within this group, the personality traits that correlate with good performance might not be the same traits that describe successful European employees, simply because personalities tend to differ from a cultural perspective. Not factoring these kinds of biases could derail the objectives of a psychometric test and throw up spurious correlations or mismatches in culture fitment.

However, on balance, the benefits of analysing people data within a company are becoming more and more relevant, as organizations are now using data to actually solve performance issues and business problems from a HR perspective. For instance, associations between infection rates and people issues reported in different hospitals were used as a means to identify training or hiring issues that could lead to unsecure protocols being utilized by a healthcare company. A financial services company analysed the common traits of fraudulent individuals along with the type of environmental or hiring factors that might contribute to such behaviours. With this, the company expects to significantly mitigate risks of fraud going forward.

All companies rely on people for their day-to-day operations and considering the fact that human resources is one of the major expenses of major corporations, you probably assume, correctly, that People Analytics is a major powerhouse for companies. Further, as it happens with powerhouses, companies are willing to pay millions to gather the deep insights a statistician, a la data scientist can bring to the HR team. Many data companies are already investing big on these trends, providing personalized solutions for the human resource operations of companies. Some organizations have invested behind their own in-house People Analytics teams, capabilities and technologies focused on enhancing the employee experience, jump-shifting productivity, designing more consumer facing and leaner organizations, improving learning outcomes and even to optimize the hiring process to improve joining strike rates. Some others have developed unique interactive visualizations that not only highlights critical KPIs but also performs some basic analyses to identify interesting correlations between performance and employee compensation or engagement.

The rapid spread of People Analytics demonstrated by the business benefits across organizations has increasingly led to statistics and data science frameworks being adopted across many sectors. As a result, it is only a matter of time before many of the regular operational aspects of the human resource function become closely linked with the use of statistical tools and concepts.

## 12.2 Statistical Learning

In statistical learning, the predictive functions are arrived at and primarily derived from samples of data.

Just like machine learning, statistical learning is also about building the ability to infer from the data that in some cases represents experience.

**Application of Statistical Learning in Human Resource:**
Analytics as a term is an outcome of two words: "analysis" and "statistics". It describes any analysis based on the use of statistical tools and concepts. Therefore, HR analytics is a data-driven approach to managing people at work (Gal et al. 2017).

The world of HR, people, culture and engagement, can be extremely subjective and amorphous. Statistics helps to understand, capture, foresee and bring some structure and predictability into our ever changing world. It has the ability to minimize risk by estimating or projecting future uncertainties and surfacing hidden patterns or trends.

For example, using statistical tools, we can predict who is most likely to leave the organization, estimate whether we are rewarding different employees fairly and discover biases in our hiring process. Without it, we miss out on a lot of valuable information needed to make better people decisions.

**Exhibit 12.1** Mean, median, mode and outliers

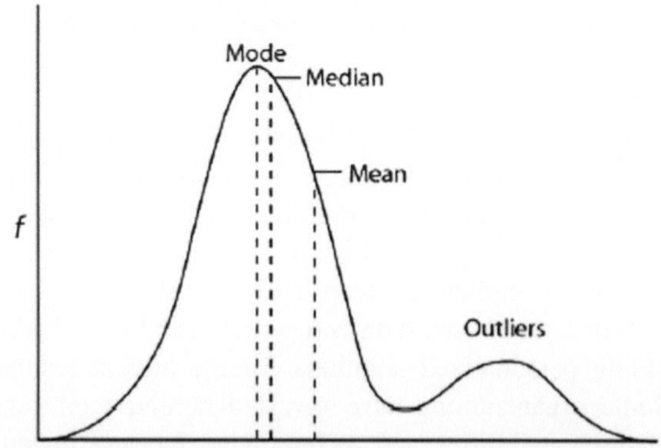




**Statistical concepts:**

- **Measures of central tendency:**
  There are mainly three types of measure of central tendency

  1. Mean
     The average value of the distribution
  2. Mode
     Value of a distribution corresponding to highest frequency or count
  3. Median
     The middle most value of the distribution.

Each of the measures have several advantages and disadvantages.

Apart from getting idea about a distribution, measures of central tendency have uses in missing value treatment (Exhibit 12.1).

- **Measures of dispersion:**
  Measures of dispersion have two broad categories:
  – Absolute Measures:

    1. Range
       Difference between max and min value of a distribution
    2. Standard Deviation

  – Relative Measure:
    Coefficient of variation
- **Histogram:** It represents the distribution of continuous data (decimal point values ) (Exhibit 12.2).

**Graphical Presentation: Histogram**

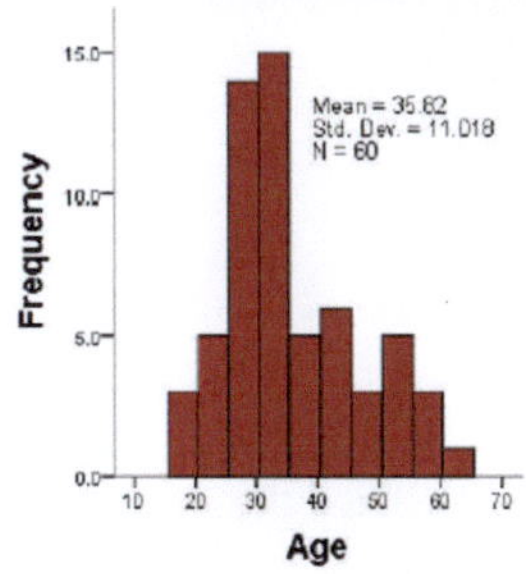


**Tabular Presentation**

| Class Interval | Frequency | Relative Frequency |
|---|---|---|
| 6 – 11 | 6 | 0.06 |
| 12 – 17 | 23 | 0.23 |
| 18 – 23 | 34 | 0.34 |
| 24 – 29 | 17 | 0.17 |
| 30 – 35 | 12 | 0.12 |
| 36 – 41 | 8 | 0.08 |
| | 100 | 1 |



**Exhibit 12.2** Histogram

- **Normal Distribution:**
  It is the distribution of a continuous random variable. It has several applications in HR.

**Performance Management** (Exhibit 12.3):
The bell curve is a graph of a normal/Gaussian distribution.
The distribution is normal if

1. The mean, median and mode are almost equal
2. The standard deviation should be low
3. Skewness and kurtosis should be close to zero
4. Median should lie exactly in between the upper and lower quartile.

We can standardize the value of a variable by changing its origin and scale to 0 and 1.

After such conversion, the newly created variable is said to be standard normally distributed. The general rule for such a distribution is:

**Exhibit 12.3** Bell-Curve

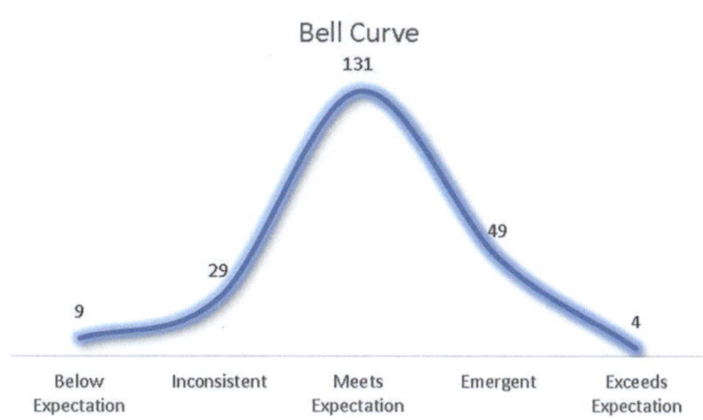

**Exhibit 12.4** Standard deviation

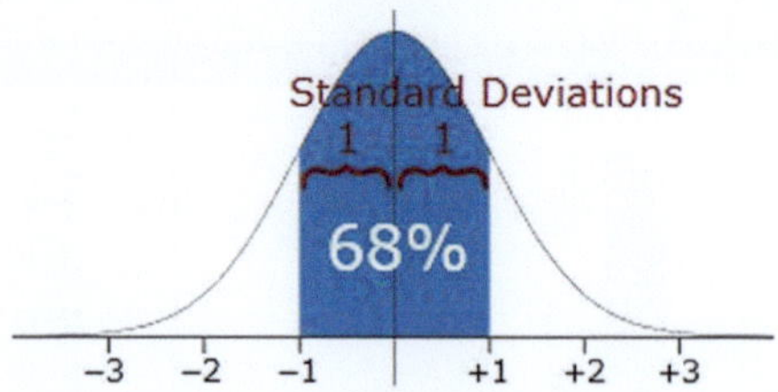




1. 68% of the population of the dataset will lie within 1 SD of the mean
2. 95% of the population will lie within 2 SD of the mean
3. 99.7% of the population will lie within 3 SD of the mean.

- **Standard Deviation as a unit of measurement**

Many a time, it is helpful to express data in multiples of sample standard deviation. This makes the data unit free (Exhibit 12.4).

We assume that we have 1000 employees in our organization, and we find that their average age is 31 years with a SD of 3.

Using the concept of standard normal distribution, we can conclude that

- 680 employees (68% of 1000) will be within the age range 28 (31 − 3) years and 34 (31 + 3) years.
- 950 employees will be within age of 25 and 37 years
- Only three employees will be either less than 19 years in age or more than 43 years.

**Microsoft Power BI** collects your data from disparate sources of data and converts the data into deep and integrated insights—the eco-system is a collection of applications, service frameworks and APIs. Power BI is system agnostic and can pull data from any cloud or legacy system or data warehouse and then visualize it brilliantly for the user to interact with it or share it with other users or stakeholders.

## 12.3 Overview of Tools in Power BI

Let us take a look at these basic tools that could be used to generate unique insights for the business:

- Visualizations
- Datasets
- Reports
- Dashboards.

**Visualizations**

**A visualization** is a powerful depiction of data in a visual, colour-coded form that crunches the insights into easily interpretable form that is easy to understand that enables you to zero in on to the insight rapidly (Exhibit 12.5).

Visualization serves to present data in a manner that lays out both the context and culls out the insights from the raw dataset of numbers.

**Datasets**

A dataset is compilation of raw data that Power BI uses to create its visualizations. Datasets can also be merged together from multiple sources to provide a unique collected dataset which could then be analysed (Exhibit 12.6).

For example, you can create an HR dataset by pulling in multiple data from performance management to learning management, to demographics databases to payroll data files by merging all these files to create a single data cube.

Power BI lets you focus on the data that you need tor analysis. It therefore allows you to filter the data. For instance, from your entire employee database you want to run an analysis only around sales function attrition so that only sales employee data would be filtered for creating the dataset for analysis. You can then come out with visualizations based on that subset (the filtered collection) of employees who were included in the attrition analysis. Filtering enables you to stay focused on the data that you need for analysis rather than blunder around without a core problem that you are seeking to analyse.

A key enabler of Power BI is the availability of data connectors that are included. Whether the data you want is sitting in multiple source repositories or legacy systems or on the cloud, the connectors help you easily plug into that data, filter it if required and merge it into your dataset.

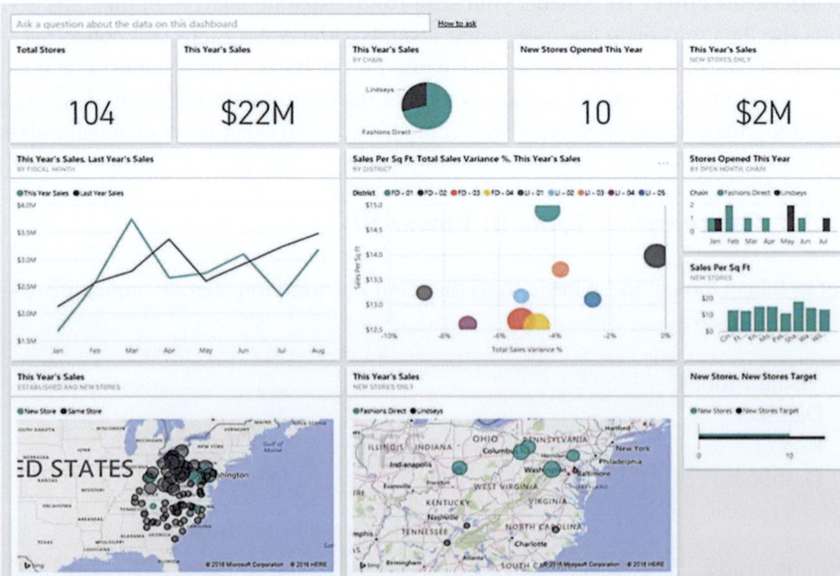


*Source:* Power BI Tutorial; 360 Reports
link: https://360reports.io/get-started-with-power-bi/introduction-to-power-bi/

**Exhibit 12.5** Power BI visualization—illustrative

| EMPLOYEE ID | EMPLOYEE NAME | POSITION | DATE OF JOINING | FINAL RATING (NUMERIC) | FINAL RATING (TEXT) | DIVISION |
|---|---|---|---|---|---|---|
| 1002 | Piyush Khanna | Manager Warehouse | | 0 | Not Rated | Operations |
| 1003 | Sanjay Rana | National Sales Head | | 0 | Not Rated | Sales |
| 1004 | Ajay Mittal | GM Finance | | 0 | Not Rated | Finance |
| 1005 | Mohamed Ali | Manager Sales | | 0 | Not Rated | Sales |
| 1006 | Amit Bhati | Business Head | | 0 | Not Rated | Finance |
| 1007 | Rahul Sharma | Manager Sales | | 0 | Not Rated | Sales |
| 1001 | Meletis Glentzes | Managing Director | | 0 | Not Rated | Operations |
| 1 | Sujoy Ghosh | GM Operations | | 3 | Meets Expectation | Operations |
| 2 | Jitendra Trivedi | Head Logistics | | 3 | Meets Expectation | Operations |
| 3 | Andondeye Godwin | Logistics Officer | | 3 | Meets Expectation | Operations |
| 4 | Moffats Thompson | Dispatch rider | | 2 | Inconsistent | Operations |
| 5 | Ejiofor Doris Uzoamaka | Logistics Officer | | 4 | Emergent | Operations |
| 6 | Chima Ekwonye Kenneth | Logistics Officer | | 3 | Meets Expectation | Operations |
| 7 | Friday Gabriel Umoke | Logistics Office | | 3 | Meets Expectation | Operations |
| 8 | Agboighale Jonathan Akhere | Planning Supervisor | | 3 | Meets Expectation | Operations |
| 9 | EMMANUEL OKPE | Branch Operations Manager | | 3 | Meets Expectation | Operations |
| 10 | PAUL | Branch Operations Manager | | 3 | Meets Expectation | Operations |



**Exhibit 12.6** Dataset—illustrative

With your dataset created, you can begin to visualize your data to carve out insights based on what you see. That is where the reporting element comes in to help you put together your story.

## Reports

A report is a set of visualizations that are seen together to tell a story on the back of hard data and actionable insights.

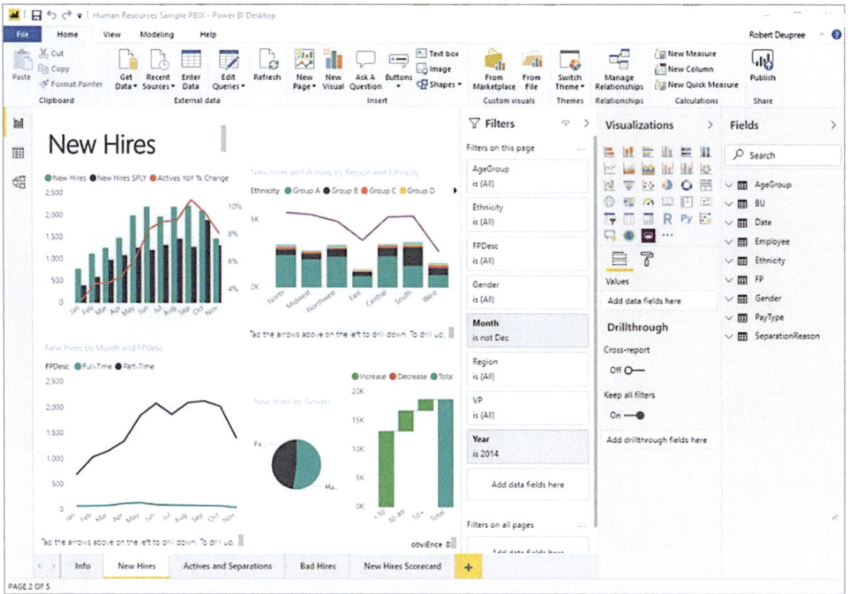


*Source:* Power BI Tutorial; 360 Reports
link: https://360reports.io/get-started-with-power-bi/introduction-to-power-bi/

**Exhibit 12.7** Power BI report—illustrative

Reports enable you to pull together multiple visualizations, on multiple pages if necessary, and let you sequence them in a way that best helps you communicate your story (Exhibit 12.7).

**Dashboard**

Dashboard is like providing a snapshot of your story; a group of select visuals that culls out rapid insights from the story that is being presented: ideally on a single page or canvas.

With the power of networking and connectivity, dashboards can be shared with other users or groups, who can then interact with them across multiple devices (Exhibit 12.8).

## 12.4 Power BI in People Analytics

People Analytics integrates the workforce data with the analytics of Power BI to provide the critical insights required, thereby providing you real-time visibility into your data allowing you to take decisions quickly and smartly.

*Source:* Power BI Tutorial; 360 Reports
link: https://360reports.io/get-started-with-power-bi/introduction-to-power-bi/

**Exhibit 12.8** Power BI dashboard—illustrative

Power BI HR dashboards

- Turnover: Annualized voluntary turnover rate, regrettable churn; % high potential employee retention; % new joiner attrition, etc.
- Learning and development effectiveness: L&D cost as % of total HR cost; % of operating expenses; training hours correlation with performance
- Talent acquisition: time to fill; cost per hire; open versus closed positions
- Productivity and cost: HR headcount versus total FTE ratio, labour cost as % of net sales; HR cost as % of total labour cost (Exhibit 12.9)

*Source:* Power BI Tutorial; 360 Reports
link: https://360reports.io/get-started-with-power-bi/introduction-to-power-bi/

**Exhibit 12.9** Power BI HR dashboard—illustrative

## 12.5 Excel Dashboards

If investing behind Power BI is a constraint, Excel is a quick and easy way to get started on creating dashboards. It enables you to crunch out dashboards from large datasets quite easily.

Familiarity with Excel comes with understanding of the following—Excel workbooks, Excel charts, PivotTables, data modelling, power pivot charts and Excel Power View reports (Exhibit 12.10).

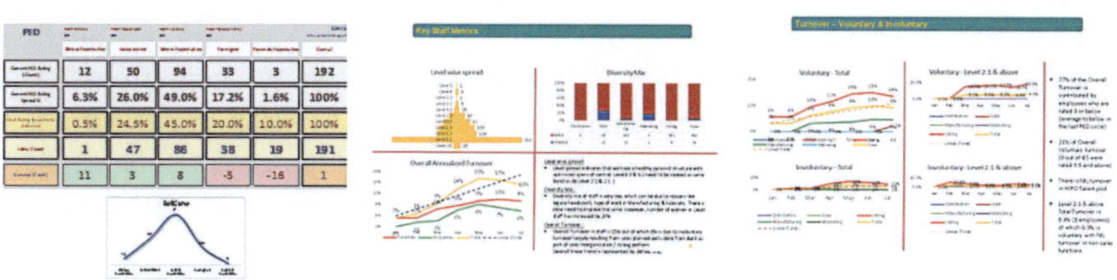

*Copyright: Acumetric Global Solutions Pvt Ltd – all rights reserved*

**Exhibit 12.10** Excel dashboard—performance distribution and HR KPIs

**Dashboard Benefits**

Dashboards allow managers to monitor and track critical parameters and metrics that go into taking decisions related to both business and people.

Benefits of dashboard are as follows:

- Visualization of KPIs and metrics.
- Risk identification and mitigation
- Depicting and comparing trends over time (time series)
- Track actual achievements of goals versus targets
- Goal and KPI alignment
- Ensuring interconnectedness across multiple and disparate data points
- Outlier identification and basis for statistical modelling and analysis
- Saves time by enabling you to rapidly zero into the insight.

**Important applications of Excel in Human Resources**

- **Managing your data**: Excel enables you to create tables on the back of preset layouts. It also allows you to sort and filter helping you to manage and store data.
- **Analysing the data**: A key role for an HR Analyst is to will always be to analyse data to cull out insights. The "Pivot table" functionality of Excel enables you to first sort your data, then do a count and finally compute the output.
- **Visualization of data**: Basic reporting can also be done via Excel, for instance, bar graphs, line charts, histograms, pie charts, etc. These data interpretations which were used to procure simple insights can now be used for mare meaningful analysis.

Some of the typical formulae that HR Analysts use in their daily work:

- **SUM**—Computes the total or sum of any number of rows and columns. For instance, = SUM (A1: A20) would sum all values in between A1 and A20 and so on. This function among others could help the HR function in computing the total salary or headcount of a company.
- **COUNT**—Counting the number of cells in an array that consists of numerical values. For example, = COUNT (A1: A10) would count the cells from A1 to A10. This function might help an HR Analyst run an attrition analysis for first getting a count for those employees who resigned. If filters were to be applied, this formula could also help the analyst to deep-dive further and run a gender or performance-wise split of attrition.
- **AVERAGE**—Computing the mean or average of the values selected. This functionality can help an HR Analyst quickly compute the average incentive earnings of an employee for a month or even a year, This, might be in critical input into planning for the salary budget.
- **VLOOKUP**—This functionality enables the analyst to search for something in the leftmost column of a spreadsheet and return it as a value. For example,

= VLOOKUP (lookup value, a table being searched, index, sorting identifier). Here, lookup value is the "value to seek in the first column of a table", "table—the table from within the table to seek out a value" "Index number—the column within the table from which to seek out a value", "Sorting identifier—[optional] TRUE = approximate match (default). FALSE = exact match". This formula is widely used by HR Analysts as it is used to merge data based on a common column. This enables them to merge data from multiple sources and store them in a single data cube.

- **CONCATENATE**—If the need is to combine data into one cell, then this functionality can be used, for instance, if we had a first name and the last name, in cells B1 and C2, respectively. Then, we will use, = CONCATENATE (B1," ", C2), which would combine the names into one cell, with the"" adding a space in between. This can be useful in situations like if you have two columns first name and last name, you can merge them and make a single column name.

## 12.6 Tableau Data Visualization

Tableau is one of the most immersive and interactive data visualization tools with the following core functionalities:

- Drag and drop feature
- Seamless data migration to or from file formats like XLS, CSV, XML
- Charts, heat maps, histograms and scatterplots with drill-down views (Exhibit 12.11).

**CRUX is a one of a kind plug and plays People Analytics platform that provides the HR leader and analyst the following key benefits:**
The only plug and play application that gets the business ready for People Analytics through the following key features:

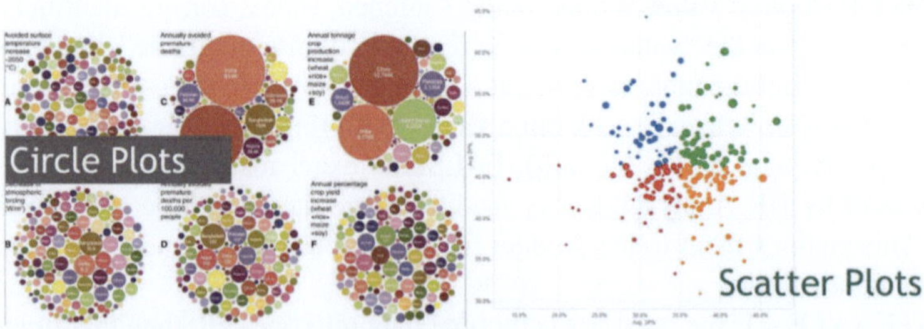


*Source: How Tableau HR makes data Human Video*
*link :https://www.tableau.com/learn/webinars/How-Tableau-HR-Makes-Data-Human#:~:text=Come%20find%20out%20how%20our,assessment%20information%2C%20and%20attrition%20analysis*

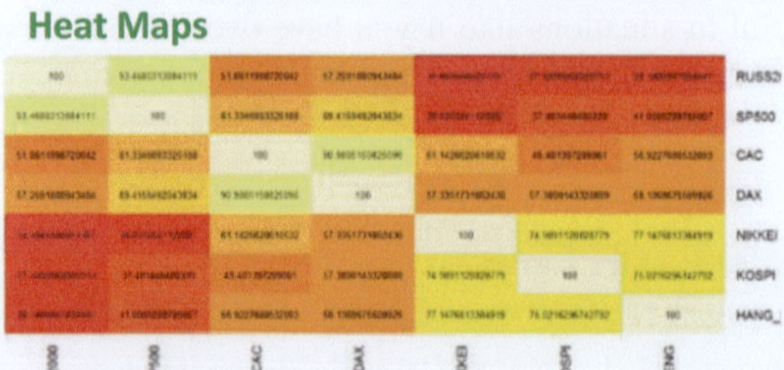


*Source: How Tableau HR makes data Human Video*
*link :https://www.tableau.com/learn/webinars/How-Tableau-HR-Makes-Data-Human#:~:text=Come%20find%20out%20how%20our,assessment%20information%2C%20and%20attrition%20analysis*

**Exhibit 12.11** Tableau visualizations in depth—illustrative

- Import, extract and merge data from any one or multiple systems/spreadsheets
- Instant data quality assessment reports with ability to transform large volume of data rapidly
- Structure the data in hierarchical format
- Web forms to collect missing data and new data for analytics
- Unique sunburst and tool tip visualizations with insightful dashboards
- View any KPI for every individual/team in the organization drilling down to the last employee.

HR metrics and reports typically reflect the efficiency of HR operations. CRUX is organization management analytics and diagnostics software that helps see and understand the value of the workforce. Powered by CRUX, your HCM system can offer this new perspective to HR directors and business heads, while also reducing the time to improve data quality required for People Analytics.

Most people data is stored in multiple spreadsheets, simple databases, and legacy systems. CRUX imports data into its engine in csv and Excel formats, thereby making it universal. CRUX goes beyond Excel functions where flat employee datasets are merged for charting and statistics. CRUX engine converts flat datasets into hierarchical formats to represent data in organization structures.

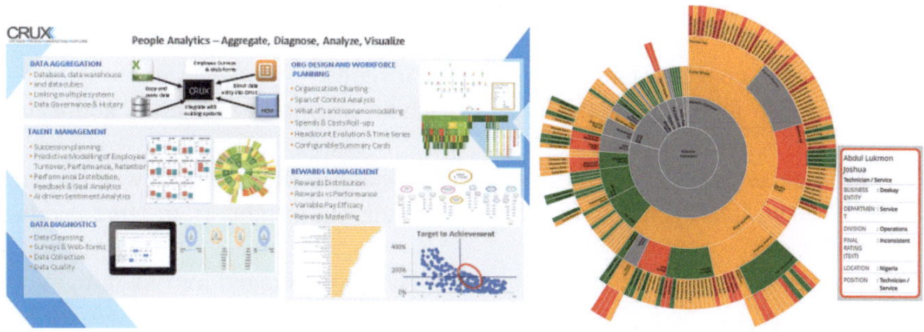


**Exhibit 12.12** CRUX data aggregation, visualizations and analytics/CRUX SUNBURST

CRUX queries are point-and-click, drag-and-drop to select variables and applying visualization and charting functions to the data. It is easy to understand visualization of dimensions and measures quickly enable insights. Histograms for span and depth of reporting can show resourcing problems in any organization structure. Variations in dimension variables focuses on data quality, gender, user ID, locations, departments, qualifications, competencies, training, etc.

Measures can easily be categorized into custom range buckets using filters, sales performance, compensation, performance rating, engagement surveys, compa-ratios, etc. Measures can also be visualized through roll-up formats (both count and sum), i.e. sum of total salary cost split department wise; location wise, business unit wise, manager or staff category wise, etc.

Keeping data updated regularly is a challenge within any data warehouse to safeguard master databases. It is almost impossible to quickly collect new data variables for the specific use of analytics. CRUX has standalone web forms to collect data from specific individuals and groups via its email configuration capabilities.

CRUX offers powerful hierarchy visualization, i.e. the organization tree split by levels; the sunburst with fully configurable tooltips; the icicle with spans of control ranges cutting across the organization hierarchy; application of measures by colour ranges; visual understanding of team and individual attitudes and behaviours.

CRUX reports can be viewed by, coloured by and split with multiple criteria shown in a single chart; the entire organization is reflected in a single visual right through the hierarchy, and of course, basic statistics can be run within the dataset (Exhibit 12.12).

## 12.7 Data Science

**Data science** in my view is simply a study around data—both structured and unstructured: it is management, storage, analysis, insight creation and prediction.

Some more perspectives include:

- Data science converts data into actionable insights
- Data science leverages analytics and machine learning to generate actionable insights
- Data science goes beyond traditional data analysis such as data warehousing and business intelligence with a view to culling out insights from large and big data
- Data science has predictive capabilities and can be leveraged for risk mitigation.

**Application of Data Science in HR**

The world of HR has entered into a space where fact-based and data-based analytics backed by statistical models and smart software tools and technologies and has become the need of the hour. The earlier tools of psychometric assessments and endless surveys are now being replaced by tools such as text analysis, network analysis backed by rapid visualizations all in real time throwing up actionable insights for agile decision-making. These tools can now through up early warning triggers for attrition, red flags around engagement or the lack of it as well as triggers around fraud for better risk management.

Data scientists can draw out correlations across multiple variables and bring out inter linkages across seemingly disparate data; can monitor, structure and transform large datasets, bring out unique and impactful visualizations to then arrive at high impact insights. From generating metrics that get you to look in the rear-view mirror, data science enables you to anticipate the future on the back of hard data analytics and predictive power.

Data science also enables HR leaders to analyse their workforce data more accurately and use it to make predictions about attrition and churn trends, future leader succession potential and investment around future skills and capabilities. From matching job descriptions to candidate CVs or social media profiles to predicting key skill requirements over time, data science enables organizations to get future ready as opposed to traditional analysis and metrics that only allowed you to take reactive action from looking at the rear-view mirror. This new orientation and domain are providing those organizations that have invested behind this capability a more robust framework that focuses on a different set of metrics and analysis around talent, performance, rewards and learning to drive competitive advantage.

**Data Science Tools**

While we have explored some new age analytics and visualization tools such as Power BI, Tableau and CRUX, let us now explore some of the tools that data scientists swear by such as R Studio, Python and SAS.

## 12.8 What is R?

- R is an open-source integrated suite of software functions for data computation, manipulation and graphical interface.
- A built-in programming language (called "S")
- More information on R project
  - http://www.r-project.org/
- There are now a number of books which describe how to use R for data analysis and statistic.
  - https://r-dir.com/learn/e-books.html
  - http://www.linuxlinks.com/article/20130216063859514/9oftheBestFreeR Books-Part1.html

**Why Learn R?**

- Open-source language
- Cross-platform compatible
- Advanced statistical language
- Outstanding graphs
- Relates to other languages
- Vast community
- Supports extensions
- Extremely comprehensive
- Flexible and functional.

**R is the weapon of choice for a legion of data scientists:**

- Cost of ownership—Open-source software that is free to download
- Versatility—Perhaps the only analytics software to run on MAC
- Can be Customized—Software code is flexible enough to make improvements
- Extensive Analytics capabilities—Used for text analytics, predictive modelling, time series, optimization, data mining, etc.
- Integration—Integrate with other software vendors: SAS, Oracle, IBM, Tera data, Tibco, Alteryx, SAP, HDFS, WEKA, Python, MATLAB, Excel.

R's uses cuts across the ability to analyse large to big data trends, run statistical models and compute around the dataset while also come up with visual and graphical interpretation of the data in unique ways. The predictive power of R is what attracts most data scientists to it.

**Installing R**

- R is a free software. It is hosted on many different servers around the world (-mirrors‖)
- One can be downloaded from any of them
- A list of all the available download mirrors is available here:
  – http://www.r-project.org/index.html

**Installing R Studio Desktop**

- Take control of your R code—R Studio is an IDE for R. It also has tools for plotting, history, debugging and workspace management
- Desktop R Studio—Download and run R Studio on your desktop.
  http://www.rstudio.com/products/rstudio/download/

**Application of R in People Analytics**
**The Data Science Process:**

- **Define a goal**. This means identifying what specific problem you are trying to solve. Without a problem or issue to solve, you do not have a goal.
- **Collect and Manage data**. The dataset needs to be relevant to the problem that is being sought to be solved through analysis. Data collection and management includes pulling data from multiple data systems and source repositories like a data warehouse or a HCM system and then merging them into a data cube. This is followed by ensuring data quality through cleansing and standardization of the data and then of course storing the data in a protected environment.
- **Build the Model**. With the definition of the business problem, a relevant data mining tool needs to be identified. Let us take the example of employee attrition—the prediction that needs to be made is around who are the individuals who could leave versus those who might stay. Based on this problem, the type of data mining tool and statistical model to be applied needs to be identified. With the dataset as input the relevant model gets applied and then visualized through unique graphical displays to reveal the insight for the stakeholder then to take action.
- **Evaluate and Critique Model**. Data mining needs to consider two key aspects: first, do you have all the relevant data for analysis or does new data need to be further collected to arrive at a more accurate or reliable output; second, which algorithm needs to be used and statistical model deployed to arrive at a more accurate prediction.
- **Present Results and Document**. The point at which you believe the model is sufficiently reliable to throw up relevant predictions, you should be getting ready to presenting the output and results., while what constitutes reliable or acceptable may vary across organizations the common factor is improvement: as long as the model ensures an output that enables you to proactively take decisions that take the business and organization forward.

- **Deploy Model**. The key objectives of constructing a model would be to:
  - Use the model on future data when it becomes available to predict or prevent something from happening before it occurs or
  - To better understand your existing business problem to tailor more specific responses.

## 12.9 Python and Python IDE

Python is an open-source language that is flexible, easy to learn and very useful for data manipulation and deep analysis.
**Why Python?**

- Free to use—Open source and freely downloadable
- Versatility—Multi-purpose language can be used to build an entire application
- Big data compatibility—Big data processing capability for its wide selection of libraries
- Predictive capabilities—Can be used to build predictive models
- Integration—A Python-based application stack can more easily integrate a data scientist who writes Python code.

**The traditional implementation of Python (nicknamed as C-Python) is available on:** www.python.org (Exhibit 12.13).
**How to Install**

- Make sure there is no prior Python installation
- Download Python 2.7 and 3.5 for your OS
- Move to the Directory
- Launch the installer and follow the prompts.

**Note:** After installing, the default path is updated to point to Anaconda.

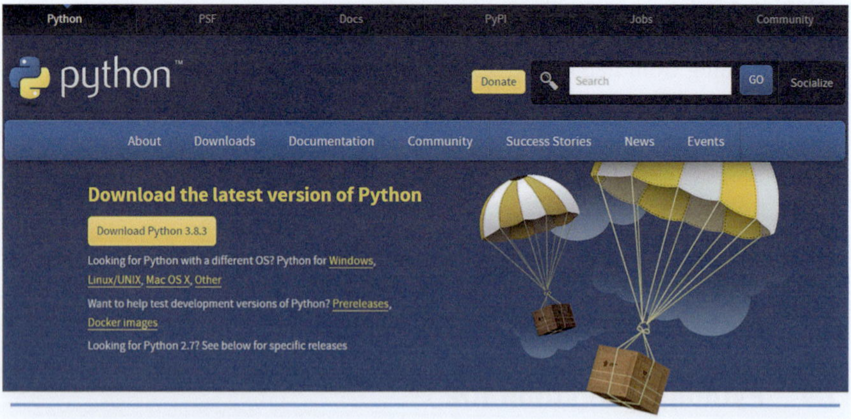


*Source; www.python.org*

**Exhibit 12.13** Python installation

SAS is an integrated software that is used by data scientists to do the following:

- Data entry, retrieval and management
- Report writing and graphics design
- Statistical and mathematical analysis
- Business forecasting and decision support
- Operations research and project management
- Applications development.

SAS is an extraction, transformation and loading (ETL) tool. The data (in raw format) is extracted from its storage location and then "Transformation" of the data takes place.

Transformation can pertain to treatment of missing values (e.g. putting "0" or "NA") when an observation is missing and all sorts of data analytics can be done here. The data (after cleaning) can be finally loaded to the data warehouse.

SAS is found useful by data scientists due to the following reasons:

- It is an ETL tool and can also be used for reporting.
- It can fetch data from remote locations and store it (the data) after transformation
- The unique feature of SAS is that it can be used as a forecasting tool
- Moreover, the SAS language is user-friendly and can be used in another platform, for instance "Mainframe" and "Statistical".

SAS tools may be leveraged in People Analytics to improve both functional standardsand deliver to client needs.

SAS has superior memory management capabilities. SAS can read data from any file format.

It has several built-in procedures for data summarization, visualization and graphics.

Having had a glimpse of various statistical tools and software technologies let us now delve into a case where some of these tools have been used.

## 12.10 Case Study: Usage of Statistical Tools for Predicting Employee Turnover

**Part1: Exploring the data**

The dataset has:

- About 15,000 employee observations and 10 features
- The company had a turnover rate of about 24%
- Mean satisfaction of employee is 0.61.

**% employees who stayed—76% and those who left—24%**

**Note: When performing cross-validation, it is important to maintain this turnover ratio.**

```
0 0.761917
 1 0.238083
```

**Overview of summary (Turnover vs Non-turnover)**

| turnover | satisfaction | evaluation | projectCount | averageMonthlyHours | yearsAtCompany | workAccident | promotion |
|---|---|---|---|---|---|---|---|
| 0 | 0.666810 | 0.715473 | 3.786664 | 199.060203 | 3.380032 | 0.175009 | 0.026251 |
| 1 | 0.440098 | 0.718113 | 3.855503 | 207.419210 | 3.876505 | 0.047326 | 0.005321 |

**Correlation Matrix and Heat map**

**Moderate Positively Correlated Features**

- project count versus evaluation: 0.349333
- project count versus average monthly hours: 0.417211
- average monthly hours versus evaluation: 0.339742.

**Moderate Negatively Correlated Feature**

- satisfaction versus turnover: −0.388375.

**Stop and Think**

- Which elements impact the target variable the most, in this case employee turnover?

- What are the variables that correlate with each other?
- Can these variables be examined more deeply?

**Summary**

From the heat map, there is a positive (+) correlation between project count, average monthly hours and evaluation. The implication here is that those who put in more hours and completed more projects were rated highly.

We see here in the heat map that employee turnover and satisfaction are highly negatively correlated. One can draw the insight here that people tend to leave a company more when they are less satisfied (Exhibit 12.14).

**Statistical Test for Correlation**

**One Sample T test (Measuring Satisfaction Level)**

Since satisfaction has the highest correlation with dependent variable turnover, let us test to see whether the average satisfaction level of employees that had a turnover differs from those that had no turnover.

**Hypothesis Testing**: is there significant difference in the means of satisfaction level between employees who had a turnover and employees who had no turnover?

- **Null Hypothesis**: (H0: ATS = ANTS) The null hypothesis would be that there is no difference in satisfaction level between employees who did turnover and those who did not

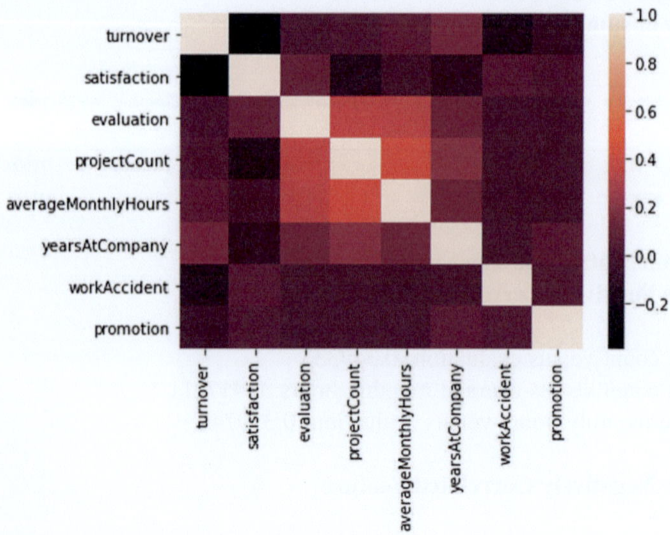




**Exhibit 12.14** Correlation analysis heat map

- **Alternative Hypothesis**: (HA: ATS ! = ANTS) The alternative hypothesis would be that there is a difference in satisfaction level between employees who did turnover and those who did not.

**The mean satisfaction for the employee population with no turnover is:0.66809590479516**

**The mean satisfaction for employees that have a turnover is:0.44009801176140917**

**Conducting the T test**

A T test could be done at **95% confidence level** and tested to see if it correctly rejects the null hypothesis that the sample comes from the same distribution as the employee population:

**T test Result**

The test result shows that the **test statistic "t" is equal to −51.33**. This highlights the deviation of the sample mean from the null hypothesis. If the t-statistic falls beyond the quantiles of the t distribution that corresponds to our confidence level and degrees of freedom, we can then reject the null hypothesis.

**T test Quantile**

The t distribution left quartile range is: −1.9606285215955626

The t distribution right quartile range is: 1.9606285215955621

**One Sample T Test Summary**

**The null hypotheses stands rejected:**

- T test score is outside the quantiles
- P value is lower than the confidence level of 5%.

Based on the T test analysis, a significant difference has been seen between the mean satisfaction of employees who turned over and the entire employee population. The super low P value of 0.00 at 5% confidence level is a good indicator to reject the null hypothesis. But this does not necessarily mean that there is practical significance. We would have to conduct more experiments or may be collect more data about the employees in order to come up with a more accurate finding.

**Distribution Plots (Satisfaction—Evaluation—Average Monthly Hours) Summary**

- **Satisfaction**—Employees with low and high satisfaction levels reflect a spike.
- **Evaluation**—There is a bimodal distribution for low evaluations (less than 0.6) and high evaluations (more than 0.8)
- **Average Monthly Hours**—There is another bimodal distribution of employees with lower and higher average monthly hours (less than 150 h and more than 250 h).

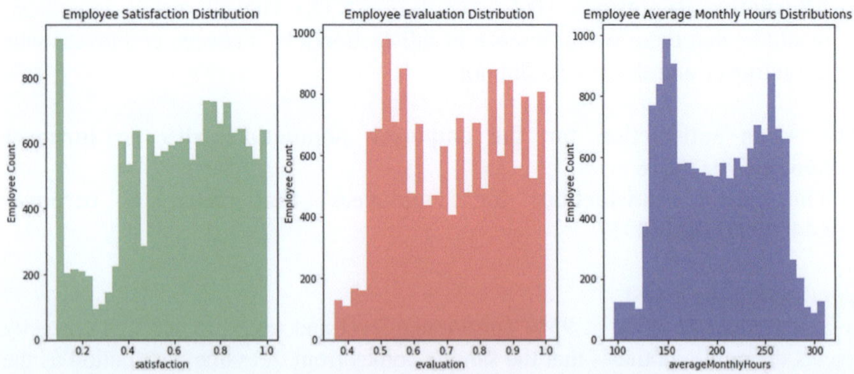




**Exhibit 12.15** Histogram—average monthly hours versus satisfaction

Similar distribution seen in evaluation and average monthly hours.

Those with average monthly hours that were low reflected a lower evaluation and vice versa.

If we look back at the correlation matrix, the high correlation between evaluation and average monthly hours does support this finding.

**Stop and Think**

- Why is it that we see a spike in low satisfaction of employees?
- Could employees be grouped in a way with these features? (Exhibit 12.15).
- Do we see a correlation between evaluation and average monthly hours?

**Salary versus Turnover**

**Summary**

- A large proportion of those who left either had **low** or **average** salaries.
- Barely any employee left with **high** salary
- Those with low or average salaries showed a higher inclination to leave the company.

**Stop and Think**

- For those with low or average or high compensation, do we see a difference in work environment?
- What made employees with high salaries exit the company? (Exhibit 12.16).

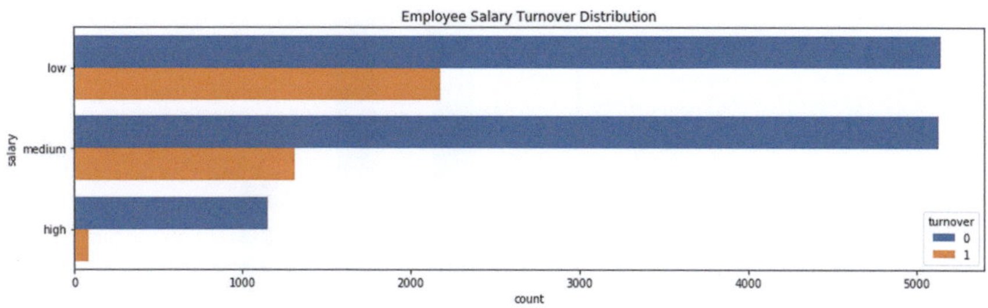


**Exhibit 12.16** Employee salary versus turnover distribution

**Department versus Turnover**
**Summary**

- The high turnover departments are sales, technical and support departments
- The least amount of turnover is reflected in the management department.

**Stop and Think**

With more data being made available, perhaps a more direct cause for employee turnover could be identified? (Exhibit 12.17).

**Turnover versus Project Count**
**Summary**

- Greater than 50% of employees who were assigned **2, 6 and 7** projects were found to have attrited.
- A large proportion of employees who were assigned **3, 4 and 5** projects were found to have been retained.
- A 100% of employees who were assigned **7** projects were found to have left the company
- Employee turnover rate was found to increase as project count increased.

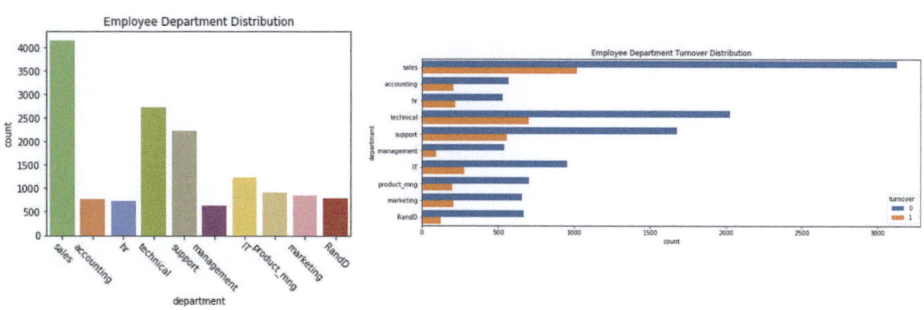




**Exhibit 12.17** Employee department distribution versus turnover

**Exhibit 12.18** Employee project count versus turnover

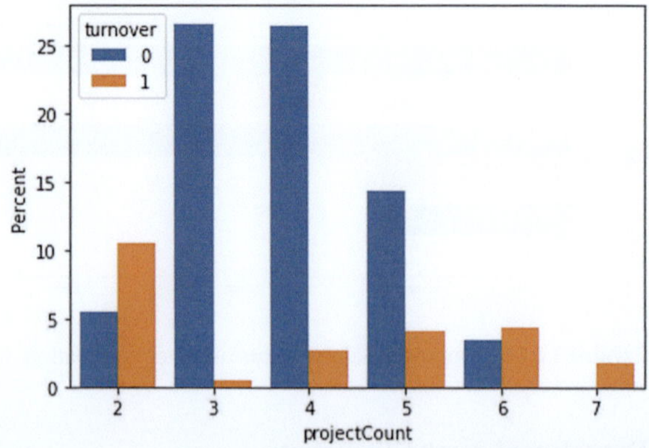




**Stop and Think**

- What could be the reasons for attrition at the very low or very high project count levels?
- Does it follow or imply that those with project counts 2 or less are either not allocated sufficient projects or are not valued, thus exiting from the company?
- On the flip side, does it follow or imply that those with 6 + projects are getting overworked with too many project assignments thereby getting burnt out with excessive workload and leaving the company (Exhibit 12.18).

**Turnover versus Evaluation**
**Summary**

- There is a bimodal distribution for those that had a turnover.
- Low-performing employees tend to leave more
- Very high-performing employees tend to leave more
- Those between **0.6** and **0.8** evaluations actually stayed more (Exhibit 12.19).

**Turnover versus Average Monthly Hours**
**Summary**

- Another bimodal distribution for employees that turned over
- Those who put in less working hours (**~150 h or less**) were found to be leaving more
- Those who put in excessive working hours (**~250 or more**) were again found to be leaving more
- Those who left were either underutilized or overstretched (Exhibit 12.20).

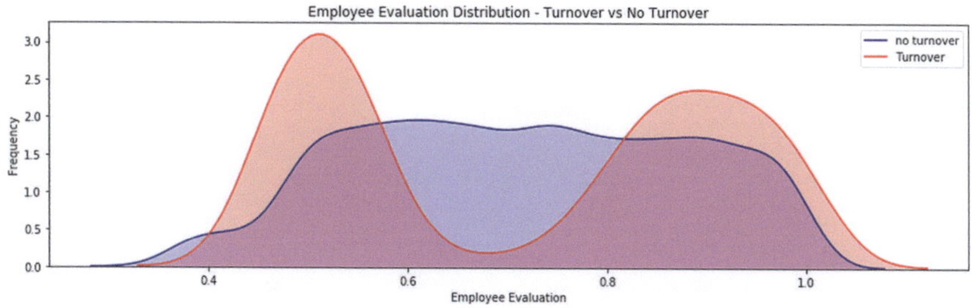




**Exhibit 12.19** Employee performance evaluation versus turnover

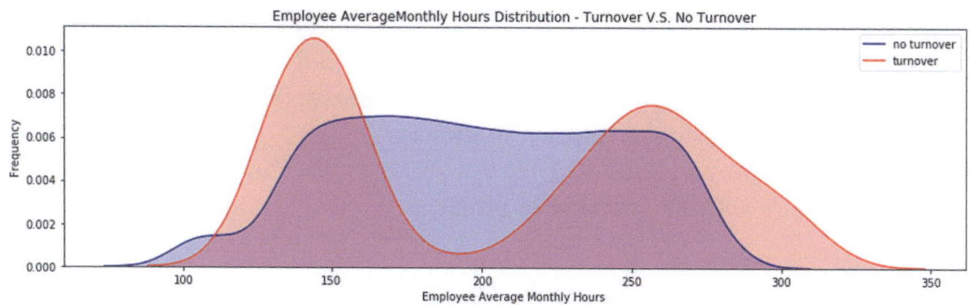




**Exhibit 12.20** Employee average monthly hours versus turnover

**Turnover versus Satisfaction**
**Summary**

- There is a **tri-modal** distribution for employees that turned over
- Those with satisfaction levels that were excessively low **(0.2 or less)** were found to be leaving the company more.
- Those with satisfaction levels that were low-mid **(0.3 ~ 0.5)** also were found leaving
- Those with satisfaction levels that were really high **(0.8 or more)** also were found leaving
- Interestingly enough, those with above average/high satisfaction levels **(0.6–0.7)** were found to have been staying (Exhibit 12.21).

**Project Count versus Average Monthly Hours**
**Summary**

- With project count increasing average monthly hours increased as well

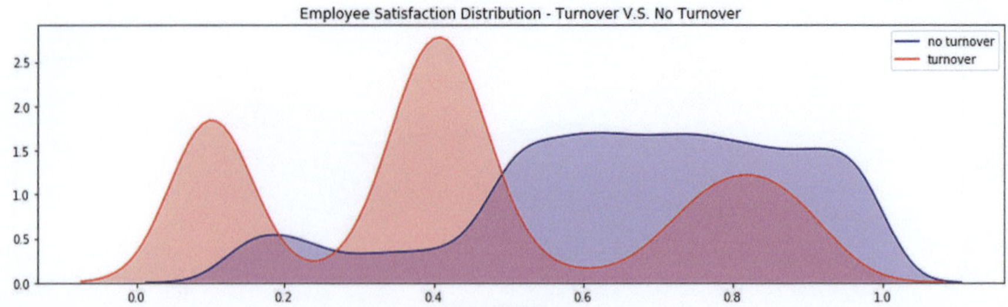




**Exhibit 12.21** Employee satisfaction versus turnover

- Something weird about the boxplot graph is the difference in average monthly hours between people who had a turnover and did not
- Looks like employees who **did not** have a turnover had **consistent** average monthly hours, despite the increase in projects
- In contrast, employees who **did** have a turnover had an increase in average Monthly Hours with the increase in projects.

**Stop and Think**

- What could be the reasons?
- Why is it that those who worked more hours left the company versus those who did not, even with similar project count? (Exhibit 12.22).

**Exhibit 12.22** Project count versus average monthly hours

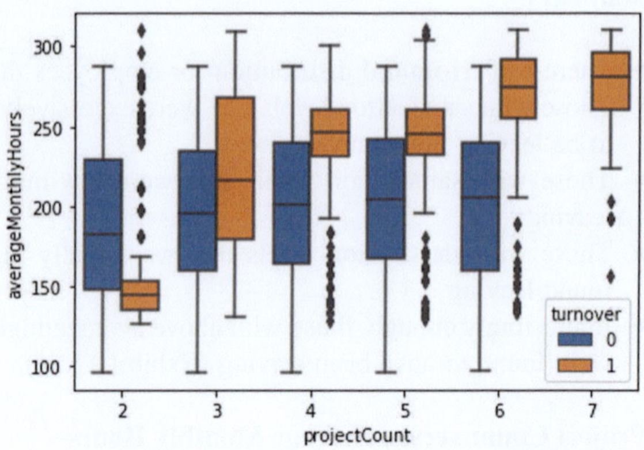

**Exhibit 12.23** Project count versus evaluation

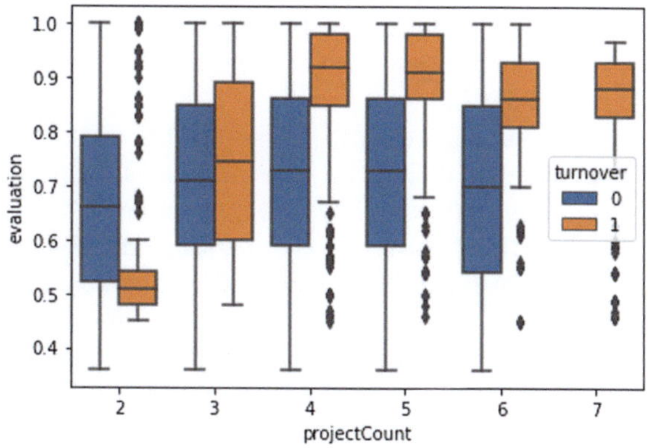




**Project Count versus Evaluation**

**Summary**

We find an increase in evaluation for those who delivered a higher project count within the turnover cohort. Then, again for the non-turnover cohort, they had a consistent evaluation despite the project count increase.

**Questions to think about**

- What is the reason for those who left having on average, a higher evaluation than those who did not leave, even with an increase in project count?
- Should not it be presumed that those with lower evaluations/performance levels would tend to attrite or churn more? (Exhibit 12.23).

**Satisfaction versus Evaluation**

**Summary**

- We find three separate clusters for those who left the company:

  **The first cluster (Hard working and Sad Employee)** reflected a satisfaction level <0.2 with evaluations/performance levels >0.75. This could imply that those who left the company were high performers, but did not either enjoy their work or felt they were not being rewarded or recognized enough in line with their contribution.

  Question to be asked—What could be the reason for feeling unsatisfied when you are evaluated as a high performer? Could it be an instance of work overload and feeling burnt out?

**The second cluster (Average Effort and Low Satisfaction)** reflected a satisfaction level between 0.4 and 0.5 with evaluation/performance levels between 0.45 and 0.55.

Question to be asked—Does this cluster reflect those who "underperformed" or "did not deliver up to expectations" and were largely indifferent to the company; reflecting low commitment levels?

**The third cluster (Hard working and Happy Employee) reflected a** satisfaction level between 0.7 and 1.0 with evaluation/performance levels >0.8. This essentially implies that employees in this cluster were a "perfect it" enjoyed their work and were evaluated highly for their contribution.

Question to be asked—Could this be an instance of their aspirations (around career growth or value addition or rewards or recognition) not being met internally and because they found another job opportunity that better fit in with their aspirations? (Exhibit 12.24).

**Turnover versus Years at Company**
**Summary**

Is there a linkage between tenure within a company and employee turnover?

- More than 50% of those who left had a tenure of **4 and 5** years
- Clearly, this cluster of employees should be analysed to understand the reasons for attrition.

**Exhibit 12.24** Employee satisfaction versus performance evaluation

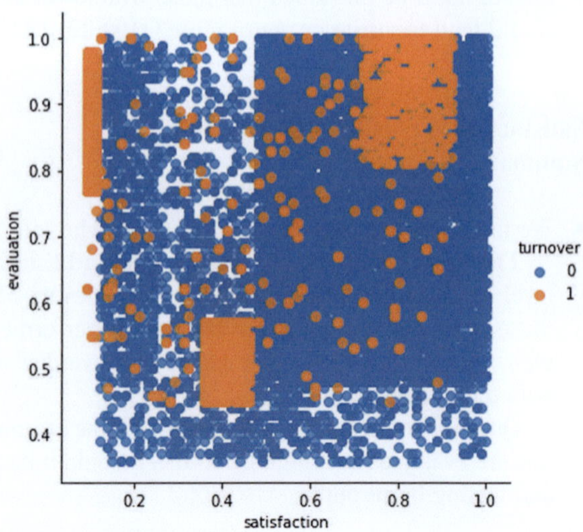

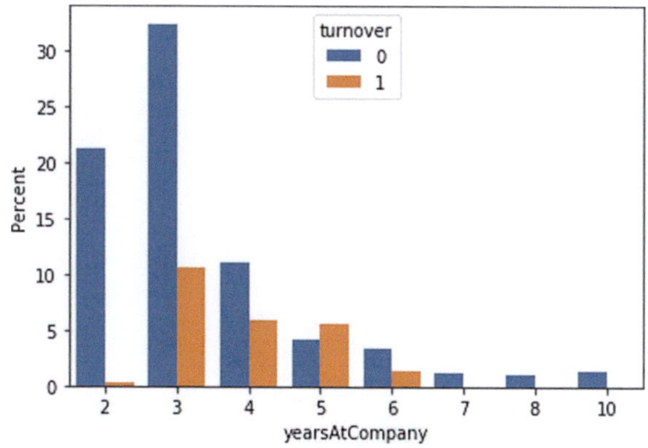




**Exhibit 12.25** Employee tenure versus turnover

## Stop and Think

- Why are those within the 3–5 year tenure range so vulnerable to attrition and churn?
- Do we know more about those who left in terms of their persona traits, demographics, etc.?
- Which categories of staff do they come under—part time or full time employees? (Exhibit 12.25).

## K-Means Clustering of Employee Turnover

**Cluster 1 (Blue):** Hard working and Sad Employees

**Cluster 2 (Red):** Low-performing and Sad Employees

**Cluster 3 (Green):** Hard working and Happy Employees.

**Clustering PROBLEM**

- How do we come to the conclusion that there are three clusters?
- Latent variables or aspects could be present could be present (Exhibit 12.26).

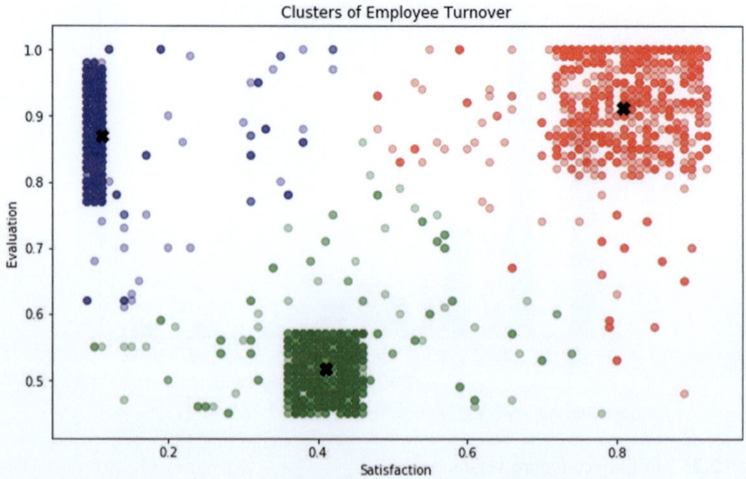




**Exhibit 12.26** Cluster analysis of employee turnover

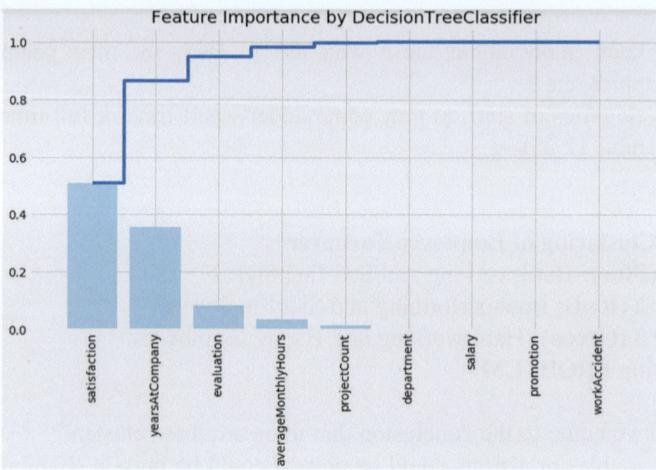




**Exhibit 12.27** Feature importance plots by decision tree classifier

## Summary

By using a decision tree classifier, it could rank the features used for the prediction. The top three features were employee satisfaction, tenure at company, and performance evaluation. This is helpful in creating your model for logistic regression because it will be more interpretable to understand what goes into the model when fewer features are utilized (Exhibit 12.27).

# People Analytics Industry Landscape—Has its Time Come? 13

## 13.1 Context

Analytics industry is driven more by "skill arbitrage" than "cost arbitrage" with access to skilled workforce and faster time to market being critical factors. The segment can be classified into:

- Market Research: Survey techniques, research design, collection of consumer data to analyse market opportunity for products and services. Determine pricing strategies and so on.
- Consumer Insights: Data modelling, insight generation to analyse how end consumers perceive products and services, also analyse the brand value and recall with a view to devising brand positioning strategies—"top of mind recall", etc.
- Financial Modelling: Credit scoring, risk modelling, financial projections, etc.
- Business Intelligence: Decision-making models to arrive at optimal business decisions around key business levers like revenue, cost, profitability, market share, etc.

In a nascent industry, timing is still good for niche start-ups to be relevant and successful.

People Analytics start-ups can play a pivotal role in enabling organizations towards meeting key challenges by managing human capital in a strategic manner, leveraging the workforce through well thought out people strategies and interventions to enhance productivity by setting new benchmarks, engaging critical talent with challenging jobs and ensuring the organization meets revenue and profitability targets.

HR in organizations needs to evolve overtime to reach its maximum potential. It should change its role from being operationally reactive to strategically proactive and equip itself to analyse the relationships between resourcing and headcount numbers and mix, rewards and benefits, persona traits and behaviours, capabilities

 
R. Ghatak, *People Analytics*, Management for Professionals,
https://doi.org/10.1007/978-981-19-3873-3_13

and competencies, organization structures and design, performance and potential, people cost and productivity along with other factors to enable companies to reach their potential in terms of ROI behind human resources. It needs to map out its role in the organization with the business strategy so as to have the right pool in proactively achieving the organization goals.

For many decades now, HR has been working hard to earn its place in the boardroom and transform itself to consistently deliver and prove its value to the business. When we examine the activities that HR has managed over the years—we see that activities like maintaining records; compliance to regulations and internal controls; assisting and implementing HR practices; developing HR systems have virtually shared the same proportion of time over decades. When HR leaders spend time serving as members of the management team; get involved with strategic HR planning, organizational design and strategic change—then we start to see a fundamental shift in the way HR is perceived.

Niche start-ups in the People Analytics space can enable HR functions to get started on this transformation journey. It will require top-level commitment and resource allocation towards investing in this area which undoubtedly will pay back several times over. Cutting-edge tools are getting built to enable HR to analyse and cull out critical insights from the massive repository of data now available.

## 13.2 Social Networks

The area where analytics is starting to get leveraged is "Employee & Candidate Experience"; around "People Promise" and the power of the "Employer Brand". Well-documented research has brought out that nearly 78% will tell their family and friends about a bad interviewing experience; 19% will post it on social media with 68% saying the interview experience impacts their decision to join the company. Talent is 4x times more likely to accept a job offer if constructive feedback is provided.

The high social acceptance and explosion of social media in India today is reflected in the 300 million plus active Facebook/meta user base. A large number of organizations are starting to leverage social media sites for engaging with employees. LinkedIn for instance has brought recruiters, companies and potential candidates on a single platform getting them to interact with one another. Sites like Glassdoor and AmbitionBox provide data on employee experience within companies across a host of parameters such as work environment, pay and benefits, facilities, culture and so on, enabling potential candidates make up their minds on which companies to apply to. For companies, these posts are a reflection of the employer brand and provides an opportunity for these companies to shore up their employee value proposition.

Social networks are increasingly being leveraged to drive communication, collaboration and knowledge sharing within organizations. It all began with bulletin boards, graduated to the intranet and now portals like Yammer are used to share ideas, recognize talent, chat with peers and co-workers across multiple locations, celebrate events and even post job openings. HR is now starting to make use of these tools to enhance employee experience and build a more open culture.

Social networking sites are also being monitored and tracked by third-party start-ups to pick up signals relating to churn and potential unrest among employees who may use these sites to apply for openings externally. Some claim that their analysis throws up predictive patterns relating to an employee continuing with or exiting the organization. There are others that leverage artificial intelligence and machine learning to deliver valuable insights to organizations with a view to enabling agile and optimized decision-making in real time.

## 13.3 Leveraging Artificial Intelligence

AI is dedicated to solving cognitive issues related to matters of human intelligence through agile learning, robotic process automation, cognitive reading and so on. We are also now starting to see *Machine Learning* and *Natural Language Processing* tools in HR, particularly around the use of text and word cloud analysis of unstructured data and qualitative feedback. Chatbot and other such applications are also being used to drive real-time engagement, enhance on-boarding experience and as querying solutions around policies and practices; a la-Alexa of the workplace.

## 13.4 Recruitment

With the talent and skills landscape in continuous motion and the massive number of candidates applying online for roles, recruiters certainly have their task cut out—finding the "right-fit". A wrong hiring decision, especially in mission-critical roles, can set back the organization a long way both in terms of financial impact and in terms of team morale. When so many recruitment and talent decisions are based on intuition and gut feel or corporate convention, hiring biases do still exist. This is an area where fortunately AI and ML tools are starting to play a role in creating impact by reducing bias in hiring decisions.

## 13.5 Augmented Writing

Augmented writing refers to text analysis which goes into coming up with impactful role descriptions and job postings, highlight critical success factors of the role or open position through usage of keywords that could attract potentially more "right-fit" candidates to apply as opposed to potentially "bad-fit" ones applying.

## 13.6 Sourcing

While sourcing from passive talent pools has got easier today due to virtual marketplaces like LinkedIn, it continues to be a challenge to find "right-fit" candidates due to the crowding of the talent market due to the multiplicity of recruiters chasing a limited talent pool. How can AI be leveraged to search for that elusive candidate? How can search engines be trawled to find that ideal match or fit as they surf through passive talent communities? How rapidly can the matches be established between job descriptions on the one hand, competencies on the other along with behavioural indicators to arrive at the near-perfect fit? How can dormant databases be activated to bring to life candidates that may have been under the radar and hidden from view of recruiters or search sites? How can social networks be activated to generate referrals on an ongoing basis? How can chatbots be used to connect with individuals and have exploratory conversations to run the first level shortlist as opposed to manual interfaces or nudge them to update their profiles or upgrade their skills required for the new roles coming up?

Through this triad of AI, social networks and machine learning, organizations, potential candidates and recruiters have all benefited as the sourcing process not only has got democratized but have placed available choices in front of all three; for candidates having access to a lot more data about the companies, they wish to apply to, especially data that would not have been easily accessible to them earlier (on the back of social media sites like Glassdoor and AmbitionBox); for companies, having access to passive talent pools and communities and dormant databases that would have been inaccessible earlier and for recruiters who can now reduce the cycle time around sourcing by leveraging these tools to find the "right-fit" candidates at the right time.

## 13.7 Assessment and Selection

With a view to hiring the "right-fit" candidate, companies are also now starting to experiment with game-based simulations to derive the perfect match between role-based competencies/company values and the candidate profile and skills/values as highlighted by how they score on the gamified simulation that is based on real-live business situational and value dilemmas. These simulations are also used to hire for critical roles in banks, treasury, finance, procurement or construction, etc., with a view to mitigating future fraud risk. These game-based assessments also ensure an enhanced candidate experience while significantly reducing the hire cycle time.

The key benefits of the new-age assessment tools that leverage AI and ML are that it significantly enhances the probability of a "right-fit" match along with reducing the cycle time while doing so. This option is ideal for high volume recruiting in distributed geographies such as sales, programmers, retail customer service, business process outsourcing associates and insurance. However, AI and gamification assessments have not gone through any rigorous empirical and statistical testing as the more traditional methods from an academic perspective. While they certainly enhance the candidate experience while also demonstrating some predictive capabilities, it is also critical to bolster the authenticity of such tools through collection of hard evidence, backed by rigorous testing.

## 13.8 Chatbots

Chatbot is a wonderfully engaging tool to connect with candidates with a view to staying in touch with them tight through both the hiring process and if hired, the pre-joining and then of course the on-boarding experience. The chatbot leverages its real-time and machine learning capability to enhance the employee experience by making the signature moments count. It enables management to collect rich feedback on an ongoing basis thereby red flagging talent risks to enable them to take proactive action. They can help enhance candidate experience on the one hand, reduce workloads of recruiters and HR teams on the other while helping organizations connect with passive talent pools and hitherto hidden talent.

## 13.9 Market Opportunity

However, despite the gains been made on the technology front with data science, artificial intelligence and machine learning based on natural language processing providing new ways of leveraging the power of data to provide insights to HR and business managers in real time, the market opportunity on People Analytics remains far from being addressed. There are no pure play People Analytics companies in India; the big consulting firms still are not able to address the opportunity as the industry landscape depicted below demonstrates (Exhibit 13.1).

Analytics is one of the fastest growing segments of the BPO/KPO industry.

**Exhibit 13.1** People Analytics industry landscape

## The Analytics Industry Opportunity

**Analytics is one of the fastest growing segments of BPO/ KPO Industry**

KPO is the fastest growing segment among BPO service offerings

| Service Line | FY12E revenue (US$ mn) | FY10 revenue (US$ mn) | CAGR |
|---|---|---|---|
| CIS | 6,676 | 5,370 | 11.5% |
| F&A | 3,560 | 2,721 | 14.4% |
| Knowledge Services | 2,779 | 2,000 | 17.9% |
| Vertical sp. BPO | 2,233 | 1,786 | 11.8% |
| HR Admin | 332 | 267 | 11.5% |
| Other Horizontal Services | 214 | 180 | 9.0% |
| Procurement | 101 | 77 | 14.5% |
| Total | 15,895 | 12,401 | 13.2% |

With Data Analytics and LPO being the emerging segments in KPO

| Segment | FY15E revenue (US$ mn) | FY10 revenue (US$ mn) | CAGR |
|---|---|---|---|
| Business research | 2,207 | 884 | 20.1% |
| Data Analytics | 1,152 | 374 | 25.2% |
| LPO | 1,300 | 356 | 29.5% |
| Data Management | 560 | 232 | 19.3% |
| Market Research | 280 | 138 | 15.3% |
| Other | 101 | 47 | 16.7% |
| Total | 5,600 | 2,031 | 22.5% |

Source: NASSCOM Strategic report 2012, NASSCOM CRISIL research report

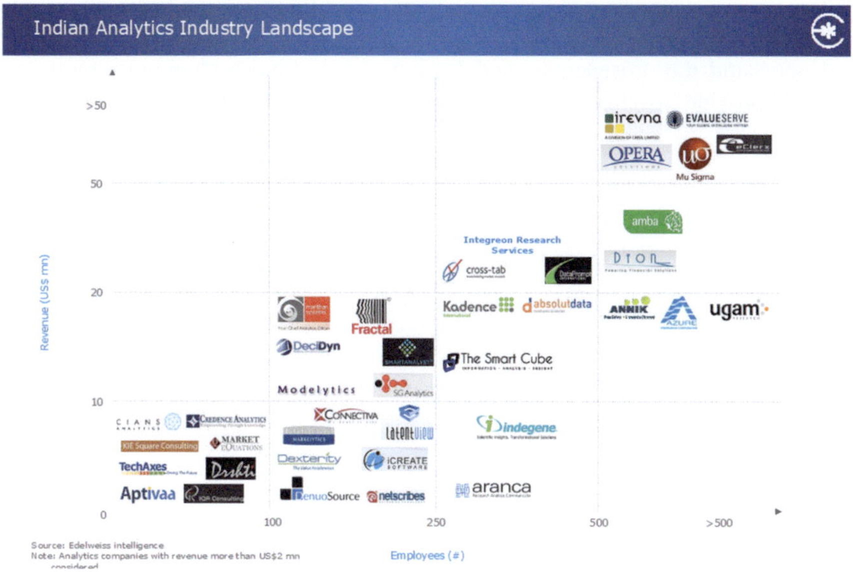


*Source: NASSCOM/CRISIL Report 2012*

**Exhibit 13.2** Analytics industry landscape in India: headcount versus revenue

See Exhibit 13.2.

Analytics is transformational by nature and radically alters the paradigm around decision-making in organizations. Mining massive repositories of data to generate evidence-based insights that enable organizations to run enterprises and manage talent and performance more effectively is becoming a core skill set and capability for the new HR professional.

This is where HR professionals need to think like a marketer—treat potential employees like potential consumers, seek to understand their motivations and behaviours, their life choices, spending patterns just as a marketer would of his consumer; their selection of roles, their preference for certain types of recognition or benefits; their desire for a specific rewards structure, etc. All of these analyses would be in conjunction with the following:

- Understand the demographics and profiles of potential candidates who you seek to attract into your organization.
- Understand the catchment areas on social media they traverse on—Instagram; Facebook/meta, LinkedIn, etc.
- Leverage those touchpoints to create a channel of communication; create stickiness
- Understand the power of your employer brand and be clear about the value proposition: what differentiates your proposition from competition.

- Benchmark your rewards structures with competition so you know where you stand.
- Understand the prospective candidates past behaviour and persona traits that could provide insights into whether the candidate will fit in with the company's values.

## 13.10 Current Adoption and Challenges

While People Analytics has drawn significant attention lately with the sheer range of possibilities it throws up for HR teams, the adoption of such tools and methods are still at a low level of maturity. There are reasons for this:

- Traditional Mindset

  Historically, the reliance has been more on gut, intuition, corporate belief systems and post facto reporting at the cost of statistical data evidence while taking people decisions. There is more understanding and awareness today that data-driven approaches and frameworks are more effective in providing solutions to organizational talent, performance and sustainability issues.
- Organization's Constraints around Data/Skills and Mindsets/Tools

  Most organizations struggle to set up and run analytics in-house. The lack of internal talent and knowledge of data science and statistical methods is a common bottleneck. Further, it requires investment in analytics tools and technologies requiring some capital investment which may deter some organizations. Lastly, lack of a unified data warehouse due to disparate HR systems might becomes a constraint in getting started.
- High Investment

  Going ahead with in-house capabilities and technology deployment will require initial investment in terms of people and capabilities, tools and systems. Given the scarcity of capabilities in this space, a number of organizations have resorted to setting up cross-functional teams to bring in quantitative and sharper data science skills supplementing it with core HR domain expertise.

## 13.11 People Analytics Third-Party Support Options

Given the fact that core People Analytics skill sets and capabilities are difficult to find in-house along with the tools and technologies required, organizations are turning to third-party product and service providers to help them get started.

By feeding off the advantages that both economies of scale and labour arbitrage would bring, the cost to implement analytics through third-party tie-ups is far more viable as opposed to the high investment required in-house, while putting a data warehouse together would require some initial investment the subsequent spends investments would be manageable since the outsourced vendor would bring in the analytics capabilities.

Moreover, the tools and technologies brought in by the vendor would be part of an overall service contract and come at a more reasonable cost as compared to buying it off the shelf in case of an in-house option. Further, the model could also work as a pay-per-use, subscription-based framework which would turn the whole thing into a variable OpEx investment as opposed to a capital investment/expenditure.

As a result, outsourcing of People Analytics is emerging as a viable option for companies who desire to get started without a large investment upfront.

## 13.12 Outsourcing of People Analytics

We typically see three approaches to vendor engagement as far as People Analytics is concerned:

1. Project-based People Analytics: This is a one-off requirement where the organization needs a solution to an immediate business problem within a fixed time-frame.
2. Outsourced Analytics:
   - Business-as-usual framework: This is about the buyer expecting the service provider to make incremental improvements through the use of analytics tools and frameworks while analytics may not be specifically mentioned in the contract.
   - Focused Analytics Delivery: In this case, the buyer is specifically engaging the service provider to deliver either an analytics product solution or services through problem solving projects.
3. Analytics-as-a-service: This is an ongoing engagement over an extended period, where analytics-related services are provided over a period of time
   - The buyer needs support at a point in time to meet a specific business need—This can arise either in cases of compensation restructuring or performance analytics post a performance cycle or culture diagnostic projects for instance as a pre-acquisition due diligence exercise, etc.
   - The other model is where the service provider is engaged for a more long-term approach to support in continuous improvement projects or creating predictive models or running diagnostic studies.

An example below is an extract from a sample contract regarding scope of an analytics service framework:

## 13.13 Illustration—Creation of Insight Dashboards

| | |
|---|---|
| Data quality | • Hierarchy—reporting; depth and span<br>• Dimensions—demographics<br>• Measures—compensation and salary ranges |
| HR operations | • Headcount trends—joiners and leavers (any time period)<br>• Headcount split by up to four variables—department; gender; performance/sales per employee; compa-ratio<br>• Absence trends—(any time period)<br>• Operating expenses roll-ups—actual versus budget |
| Talent acquisition- effectiveness and cost | • Current hiring status—open versus closed (roles, business unit, function, level/band, location, hiring/reporting manager, etc.)<br>• Time to fill status for all "critical vacancies"—recruiter wise<br>• Channel mix driving sourcing effectiveness<br>• Channel conversion rate (referral; media; portals, etc.)<br>• Early attrition trends—first 3 months<br>• Cost per hire: direct, indirect, total |
| Talent attrition and churn | • Voluntary, involuntary and total attrition<br>• Attrition as per channel mix (consultants, referral, media, direct portals, etc.)<br>• Attrition across tenure, roles, grade, function, location, business unit; performance, etc. |
| Talent succession, retention and career development | • Talent classification—nine box grid<br>• Succession pipeline<br>• Key talent retention trends |
| Performance management | • Sales target achievement %<br>• Performance distribution—org; team; individual<br>• Sales per employee distribution—org; team; individual |
| Rewards | • Variable/incentive distribution for employees/teams<br>• Variable pay efficacy scatterplot<br>• Salary cost roll-ups split by performance; sales per employee |
| Organization design | • Updated organization charts across business unit, function, location with reporting lines and summary cards<br>• Organization charts split by performance; sales per employee<br>• What-If modelling of organization structures<br>• Span of control status summary across role hierarchies split by performance; sales per employee; attrition and churn |

| | |
|---|---|
| Employee engagement | • Key engagement and sentiment themes<br>• Engagement/sentiment score split by performance; team sales; gender; tenure; role change and manager quality |

## 13.14 Illustration—Predictive Analytics Models

| Project type | Area of impact | Financial impact |
|---|---|---|
| Workforce planning | Capacity forecasting and resource planning | ROI on talent deployment optimization preventing overinvestment/underinvestment in talent impacting topline and bottom line |
| Compensation modelling | Budgeting; forecasting and rewards effectiveness vis-à-vis linkage to performance | ROI on rewards modelling; variable pay design efficacy and correlation to sales |
| Predict top and bottom performers | Raise bar on organization performance; save cost; multiply revenue | ROI on "lifetime value" of a top performing salesperson; reduced attrition of top performers; saving on salary of bottom performers; saving on cost of hiring, training a new hire, etc. |
| Predict attrition and churn | Who, when and why of attrition; bulge analysis; clustering | ROI on operating margin improvement; saving on cost of hiring, training a new hire |
| Predict future leader talent | Who are potential FL talent | ROI on investing behind "talent you punt on"; enhancing bench strength for key positions |
| Succession planning | Talent pipelining to build bench strength | ROI on internal versus external hire |
| Performance analysis | Performance distribution visualized across hierarchies and teams | ROI on organization performance and business results |
| Talent forecasting | What-If scenarios using FTEs in roles | ROI on optimization on talent mix and spend |
| Optimize roles and processes | Visualization of processes linked with roles using RACI; identify gaps in skills; roll-up of costs | ROI on process and cost optimization; cost to serve |
| Organization design | Restructuring through span of control analysis and modelling what-if scenarios | ROI on organization transformation |
| Service quality climate | Quality climate diagnostic | Predictors of service quality; ROI on customer service |

## 13.15 Summing-up

In an ever-changing business climate, it is critical more than ever before for Human Resources to be grounded to business strategy. With both knowledge repositories and capabilities in People Analytics increasing and with the start-up ecosystem coming up with innovative pay-per-use solutions, companies are feeling more confident about getting started on their analytics journey.

It is also heartening to see the range of tools and technologies that have emerged in this space around People Analytics enabling a much more sophisticated level of analysis and prediction that has the potential to game-change human capital management.

Over and above data management, visualizations and dashboards organizations are also attempting to harness the predictive capability of data science to provide them rapid insights and predictions about the future behaviour of their employees relating to retention, engagement, commitment, performance, diversity, inclusion and so on. In an age when technology is making rapid strides in every domain, it is heartening to experience this transformation in human resources led by people and workforce analytics that is putting HR leaders at the centre of organizational and business strategy. It is the inevitable data science solution that is starting to provide HR leaders with the data and insight validation for all people decisions hitherto taken based largely on gut and perception.

However, we need to be cautious in seeing technology as the saviour for HR teams looking to capitalize on big data. It is also about reimagining the function and changing the mindset to get more comfortable with data-driven approaches. This raises the question around how we are contributing towards building the capabilities of our HR future leaders to take advantage of the data revolution and not be left behind but rather to seize the moment and opportunity.

Large and big data tells a story but we need to listen! organizations are loaded with employee, HR, performance and personal data; not including social media and other external sources of people data. If cutting edge talent has to be attracted, retained and if performance has to be raised and sustained there is a critical need to embed people and talent analytics for addressing specific people and business problems. The application of talent analytics has also been deployed in professional sport as reflected in Michael Lewis's book "Moneyball". This has now been accepted in business. As a result, it is only a matter of time before we see people and talent analytics being deployed and leveraged extensively in organizations to deliver optimal value. While it has taken its time being understood, clearly its time has now come!

**There is reason for optimism. Over the last couple of years, there seems to be an upsurge in People Analytics adoption?**

First, cloud-based solutions are now being adopted with inbuilt security protocols, allowing organizations to view all their people data in an integrated manner. The "single source of truth" principle is starting to take root with many organizations going in for a single integrated HCM solution.

Second, we see a reorientation of capabilities around talent pools coming into the HR profession. More people with quantitative and analytical backgrounds are taking up HR roles and this is a welcome sign. companies are now looking at setting up cross-functional teams to run People Analytics—behavioural scientists, statisticians, and analysts from other domains into HR; for them analytics is a new exciting area. Data science as a career option has opened up avenues for those interested in taking up People Analytics as a career choice.

Third, People Analytics solutions and capabilities both in terms of products and in terms of services are now starting to be offered by vendors who have developed tools and technologies in this space. These are both plug and play and customizable solutions which can talk to multiple platforms and pull data into it from any kind of data warehouse.

Fourth, we also see people who were early adopters or evangelists of the domain being available now to consult with companies who are keen to adopt and embed People Analytics and a data science approach.

Finally, the clear business benefits are beginning to be seen by CEOs so they are pushing their HR teams to start building and deploying both the skill sets and the supporting tools and technologies. Organizations are now starting to invest behind in-house analytics capabilities as well as partnering with suitable vendors to get started on their journey.

# Case Studies—Summaries and Business Outcomes

| Sector | Area | Analytics challenge | Result |
|---|---|---|---|
| Business process outsourcing | Productivity | Productivity optimization of first line managers | • FLM utilization rate improves by 15%<br>• Headcount down 10%<br>• Operational metrics improve 20% |
| Real estate | Risk identification and mitigation | Key risks identification, prioritization and mitigation | • RAG status of key talent/org design/compliance risks<br>• Audit completion time reduced 75%<br>• Audit accuracy improves due to universal set analysis: 100% as opposed to sampling |
| Oil and gas | Performance management | Identification of individual and team performance | • Identification of hidden non-performers within large teams |
| Manufacturing | Culture building | Organization transformation through culture building | • Org. Health scores improve by 10%<br>• People Manager Scores on Manager Quality improve by 16%<br>• Talent Retention up 30% |
| Financial services call centre | Churn and attrition | Reduce early churn/attrition and improve exam pass rate of CSRs | • Exam pass % up by 11%<br>• Hiring cost reduced 40%<br>• CSR deployment time reduced by 50% |
| Financial services | Talent acquisition | Hiring the best sales persons | • Triggered introduction of a new screening process that saved the firm $4 million |



R. Ghatak, *People Analytics*, Management for Professionals,
https://doi.org/10.1007/978-981-19-3873-3

| Sector | Area | Analytics challenge | Result |
|---|---|---|---|
| Auto-component | Process mapping and redesign | Process mapping and transformation from AS-IS to TO-BE | • 34% savings within existing processes<br>• HR Team capability to redesign processes and make out a business case for change |
| Global services | Organization redesign | Redesign organization structure/span of control | • Delivery of better services at 20% lower cost<br>• Enhanced manpower productivity |
| Private insurance | Employee master data management | Rapid employee data cleansing and transformation | • Transformed dataset, thereby enhancing data integrity significantly<br>• Data analytics ready |
| Pharmaceutical | Salesforce performance | Salesforce performance measurement, tracking and analysis | • Dash-boarding capability with visual intelligence<br>• Team and Individual drill-downs with rapid insights |
| Global consumer goods | ETL of employee data across APAC for global HCM implementation | Fragmented employee data in multiple legacy systems; non-standard formats; riddled with errors; no single employee view | • ETL of @ 30,000 employee data as a first critical step towards global HCM<br>• Standardization of all employee data formats globally<br>• Data Accuracy enhanced |
| Pharmaceutical | SMAC implementation (social, mobile, analytics, cloud) | Distributed salesforce making it difficult to track PJP adherence, productive calls, etc. Lack of real-time information & analytics | • MR daily schedule time saving up to 20%<br>• Real-time access to all sales performance data (orders, incentives, etc.) enabling quick tactical decisions in the market to drive sales and distribution<br>• Productive call strike rate enhanced by 30% |
| Nylon fibre | Employee engagement | Sustained engagement for retention | • Engineer retention up 8% |
| Financial services | Talent acquisition | Hiring the best sales persons | • Triggered introduction of a new screening process that saved the firm $1 million |

| Sector | Area | Analytics challenge | Result |
|---|---|---|---|
| Auto-component | Process mapping and redesign | Process mapping and transformation from AS-IS to TO-BE | • 34% savings within existing processes<br>• HR Team capability to redesign processes and make out a business case for change |
| Consumer organization | Sales dashboards | Visualization of sales KPIs | • Embedded Sales KPI Dashboards |
| Fast moving consumer goods | Sales and business enhancement to take advantage of organized trade opportunity | Sales competencies forecasting for organized trade and sales organization restructuring | • Organized trade contribution to overall sales revenue up by 20%<br>• Organized trade salesforce productivity improves by 15%<br>• Salesforce Critical Talent Retention |

# Bibliography


Bassi. Toward a human capital measurement methodology.
Bassi, L., & McMurrer, D. (2007). *Maximizing your return on people.* Harvard Business Review.
Bersin, J., (2013). High-impact talent analytics: Building a world-class HR.
Boudreau, J., & Ramstad, P. (2007). *Beyond HR: The new science of human capital.* Harvard Business Press.
Cantrell, S., Benton, J., Laudal, T., & Thomas, R. Measuring the value of human capital investments. *Strategy and Leadership.*
Cascio, W., & Boudreau, J. (2008). *Investing in people: Financial impact of human resource initiatives.* FT Press.
Crestone, C. Cedar Crestone 2009–2010 HR Systems Survey.
Davenport, T., Harris, J., & Shapiro, J. (2010). *Competing on talent analytics.* Harvard Business Review.
Davenport, T., Morison, R., & Harris, J. (2010). *Analytics at work: Smarter decisions, better results.* Harvard Business Press.
Davenport et al., *Competing on talent analytics.*
Davenport et al. *Analytics at work.*
Dekas, K. (2011). *People Analytics: Using data to drive HR strategy and action.* https://www.youtube.com/watch?v=l6ISTjupi5g
Falletta, S. (2008). HR intelligence: Advancing people research and analytics. *IHRIM Journal, 12*(3).
Gates, S. (2008). Strategic human capital measures. *The Conference Board.*
Gibbons, J., & Woock, C. (2007). Evidence based human resources. *The Conference Board.*
Heskett, J., Jones, T., Loveman, G., & Sasser, E. (2008). Putting the service-profit chain to work.
IBM-Cognos. (2009). *Getting smart about your workforce.* IBM-Cognos.
Jac, F. E. (2010). *The new HR analytics: Predicting the economic value of your company's human capital investments.* American Management Association.
Johnson, G., Whittington, R., & Scholes, K. Fundamentals of strategy.
KPMG. Global M&A Survey Report 2005.
Lombardi, L. O., & White, D. *Intelligent human capital management.* Aberdeen Group.
Luketic, H. Human capital metrics trends 2008 survey report. *Research VOICE.*
NASSCOM Strategic Report. (2012). NASSCOM-CRISIL Research Report.
Pfeffer, J., & Sutton, R. (2006). *Hard facts profiting from evidence based management.* Harvard Business Press.
Raje, A. Paper on HR analytics.
Schneider, C. (2008). *The new human-capital metrics: A sophisticated crop of measurement tools could take the guesswork out of human-resources management.* CFO Magazine.
Whiteley, P. (2009). *Making it count: Human capital investments that deliver improved business performance.* Logica.





R. Ghatak, *People Analytics*, Management for Professionals,
https://doi.org/10.1007/978-981-19-3873-3

MIX
Papier aus verantwortungsvollen Quellen
Paper from responsible sources
FSC® C105338

If you have any concerns about our products,
you can contact us on
**ProductSafety@springernature.com**

In case Publisher is established outside the EU,
the EU authorized representative is:
**Springer Nature Customer Service Center GmbH**
**Europaplatz 3, 69115 Heidelberg, Germany**

Printed by Libri Plureos GmbH
in Hamburg, Germany